AP CHEMISTRY
ALL ACCESS™

Derrick C. Wood
AP Chemistry Teacher
Conestoga High School
Berwyn, Pennsylvania

Scott A. Best
Science Department Chairperson
AP Chemistry Teacher
Conestoga High School
Berwyn, Pennsylvania

Rita Gava
AP Chemistry Teacher
Albany High School
Albany, New York

Research & Education Association
Visit our website: www.rea.com/studycenter

Research & Education Association
61 Ethel Road West
Piscataway, New Jersey 08854
E-mail: info@rea.com

AP CHEMISTRY ALL ACCESS™

Library of Congress Control Number 2012931364

ISBN-13: 978-0-7386-1027-6
ISBN-10: 0-7386-1027-5

Contents

Chapter 9: Solutions 101

Chapter 10: Thermochemistry 113

Chapter 14: Nuclear Chemistry 159

Chapter 15: Descriptive and Organic Chemistry 165

Chapter 16: Laboratory Experiments 173

Practice Exam (also available online at *www.rea.com/studycenter*) ... 207

About Our Authors

Derrick C. Wood teaches AP Chemistry at Conestoga High School in Berwyn, Pennsylvania. He holds a bachelor's degree in Chemistry from Drew University, Madison, New Jersey, and, in 2007, he earned a Masters of Chemistry Education from the University of Pennsylvania. Mr. Wood will receive a Masters of Education with leadership emphasis from Cabrini College in May 2012.

Mr. Wood has given numerous presentations at both the National Science Teachers Association (NSTA) and the American Chemical Society's national conventions. He is the 2010 recipient of the Christopher Columbus Foundation Life Science Educator Award.

I wish to thank my wife, Anastasia, for all of her support and encouragement throughout this project. I would also like to thank my family and all of the teachers who have inspired my love for learning and science—I truly have been taught by the best!

Scott A. Best, Ph.D., is currently the Science Department Chair at Conestoga High School in Berwyn, Pennsylvania, where he teaches all levels of chemistry. He has taught AP Chemistry for twelve years. Dr. Best received his B.S. in Chemistry from Wheeling Jesuit University and his Ph.D. in Chemistry from Pennsylvania State University. He has published and presented multiple papers at American Chemical Society meetings.

Rita Gava received her Bachelor of Science degree in Science Education-Chemistry from Pennsylvania State University, and earned a Masters of Science degree in Science Education from the State University of New York, New Paltz. She has taught in both private and public high schools, as well as been adjunct faculty for both Duchess County Community College in Poughkeepsie, New York and Schenectady County Community College in Schenectady, New York. She holds certification in both AP Chemistry and IB Chemistry curriculums. Mrs. Gava is currently teaching for the Albany City School District at Albany High School, Albany, New York.

About Research & Education Association

Founded in 1959, Research & Education Association is dedicated to publishing the finest and most effective educational materials—including software, study guides, and test preps—for students in middle school, high school, college, graduate school, and beyond. Today, REA's wide-ranging catalog is a leading resource for teachers, students, and professionals.

Acknowledgments

In addition to our author, we would like to thank our technical reviewer, Steven R. Boone, a professor of inorganic chemistry and associate dean of the College of Arts, Humanities, and Social Sciences at the University of Central Missouri. During his 20-plus year career in higher education, Professor Boone has published 12 papers, one book, and given dozens of presentations in the areas of physical inorganic chemistry, chemical education, and environmental sustainability.

Also, we would like to thank Larry B. Kling, Vice President, Editorial, for supervising development; Pam Weston, Publisher, for setting the quality standards for production integrity and managing the publication to completion; John Paul Cording, Vice President, Technology, for coordinating the design and development of the REA Study Center; Diane Goldschmidt and Michael Reynolds, Managing Editors, for coordinating development of this edition; Claudia Petrilli, Graphic Designer, for interior book design; S4Carlisle Publishing Services for typesetting; and Weymouth Design and Christine Saul for cover design.

Welcome to REA's All Access for AP Chemistry

A new, more effective way to prepare for your AP exam.

There are many different ways to prepare for an AP exam. What's best for you depends on how much time you have to study and how comfortable you are with the subject matter. To score your highest, you need a system that can be customized to fit you: your schedule, your learning style, and your current level of knowledge.

This book, and the free online tools that come with it, will help you personalize your AP prep by testing your understanding, pinpointing your weaknesses, and delivering flashcard study materials unique to you.

Let's get started and see how this system works.

How to Use REA's AP All Access

The REA AP All Access system allows you to create a personalized study plan through three simple steps: targeted review of exam content, assessment of your knowledge, and focused study in the topics where you need the most help.

Here's how it works:

Review the Book	Study the topics tested on the AP exam and learn proven strategies that will help you tackle any question you may see on test day.
Test Yourself & Get Feedback	As you review the book, test yourself. Score reports from your free online tests and quizzes give you a fast way to pinpoint what you really know and what you should spend more time studying.
Improve Your Score	Armed with your score reports, you can personalize your study plan. Review the parts of the book where you are weakest, and use the REA Study Center to create your own unique e-flashcards, adding to the 100 free cards included with this book.

Finding Your Weaknesses: The REA Study Center

The best way to personalize your study plan and truly focus on your weaknesses is to get frequent feedback on what you know and what you don't. At the online REA Study Center, you can access three types of assessment: topic-level quizzes, mini-tests, and a full-length practice test. Each of these tools provides true-to-format questions and delivers a detailed score report that follows the topics set by the College Board.

Topic-Level Quizzes

Short, 15-minute online quizzes are available throughout the review and are designed to test your immediate grasp of the topics just covered.

Mini-Tests

Two online mini-tests cover what you've studied in each half of the book. These tests are like the actual AP exam, only shorter, and will help you evaluate your overall understanding of the subject.

Full-Length Practice Test

After you've finished reviewing the book, take our full-length exam to practice under test-day conditions. Available both in this book and online, this test gives you the most complete picture of your strengths and weaknesses. We strongly recommend that you take the online version of the exam for the added benefits of timed testing, automatic scoring, and a detailed score report.

Improving Your Score: e-Flashcards

Once you get your score report, you'll be able to see exactly which topics you need to review. Use this information to create your own flashcards for the areas where you are weak. And, because you will create these flashcards through the REA Study Center, you'll be able to access them from any computer or smartphone.

Not quite sure what to put on your flashcards? Start with the 100 free cards included when you buy this book.

After the Full-Length Practice Test: Crash Course

After finishing this book and taking our full-length practice exam, pick up REA's *Crash Course for AP Chemistry*. Use your most recent score reports to identify any areas where you are still weak, and turn to the *Crash Course* for a rapid review presented in a concise outline style.

REA's Suggested 8-Week AP Study Plan

Depending on how much time you have until test day, you can expand or condense our eight-week study plan as you see fit.

To score your highest, use our suggested study plan and customize it to fit your schedule, targeting the areas where you need the most review.

	Review 1-2 hours	Quiz 15 minutes	e-Flashcards Anytime, anywhere	Mini-Test 30 minutes	Full-Length Practice Test 2 hours
Week 1	Chapters 1-4	Quiz 1	Access your e-flashcards from your computer or smartphone whenever you have a few extra minutes to study. Start with the 100 free cards included when you buy this book. Personalize your prep by creating your own cards for topics where you need extra study.		
Week 2	Chapters 5-6	Quiz 2		
Week 3	Chapters 7-8	Quiz 3		
Week 4	Chapter 9	Quiz 4	Mini-Test 1 (The Mid-Term)	
Week 5	Chapters 10-11	Quiz 5		
Week 6	Chapters 12-13	Quiz 6		
Week 7	Chapters 14-15	Quiz 7		
Week 8	Chapter 16	Quiz 8	Mini-Test 2 (The Final)	Full-Length Practice Exam (Just like test day)

Need even more review? Pick up a copy of REA's *Crash Course for AP Chemistry,* a rapid review presented in a concise outline style. Get more information about the *Crash Course* series at the REA Study Center.

Test-Day Checklist

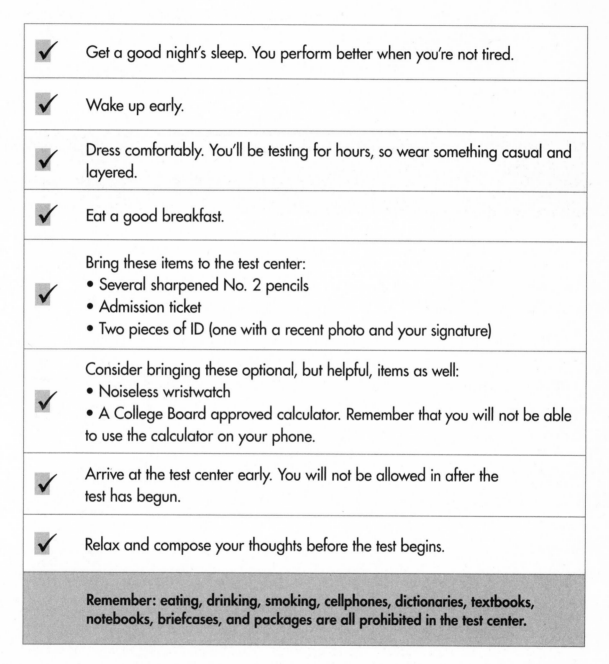

✔	Get a good night's sleep. You perform better when you're not tired.
✔	Wake up early.
✔	Dress comfortably. You'll be testing for hours, so wear something casual and layered.
✔	Eat a good breakfast.
✔	Bring these items to the test center: • Several sharpened No. 2 pencils • Admission ticket • Two pieces of ID (one with a recent photo and your signature)
✔	Consider bringing these optional, but helpful, items as well: • Noiseless wristwatch • A College Board approved calculator. Remember that you will not be able to use the calculator on your phone.
✔	Arrive at the test center early. You will not be allowed in after the test has begun.
✔	Relax and compose your thoughts before the test begins.

Remember: eating, drinking, smoking, cellphones, dictionaries, textbooks, notebooks, briefcases, and packages are all prohibited in the test center.

Strategies for the Exam

What Will I See on the AP Chemistry Exam?

One May morning, you stroll confidently into the testing center, where you're scheduled to take the AP Chemistry Exam. You know your stuff: you paid attention in class, followed your textbook, took plenty of notes, and reviewed your coursework by reading a special test prep guide. You can write out the products of chemical reactions, relate the structure of molecules to their function, and solve an equilibrium problem like the best of them. So, how will you show your knowledge on the test?

The Multiple-Choice Section

First off, you'll complete a lengthy multiple-choice section that tests your ability to not just remember facts about the major chemical concepts, but also to apply that knowledge to solve basic problems that may include calculations—without the use of a calculator. This section will require you to answer 75 multiple-choice questions in 90 minutes. The AP Chemistry Exam is quite broad in its scope. Following are the major topics including the approximate percentage of the topic found on the exam.

I. Structure of Matter (20%)

The major topics included are atomic theory and structure, chemical bonding, intermolecular forces, nuclear chemistry, and topics concerning the electron.

II. States of Matter (20%)

Gas laws and the kinetic molecular theory are covered extensively. Phase diagrams, solution chemistry, and colligative properties are other major topics in this area.

III. Reactions (35%–40%)

Reactions comprise a large percentage of the exam. The major topics included in this section are stoichiometry, acid–base chemistry, equilibrium, thermochemistry, electrochemistry, and chemical kinetics.

IV. Descriptive Chemistry (10%–15%)

This portion of the test includes chemical reactivity and predicting products of chemical reactions. You should know your solubility rules as well as the colors of various solutions. Periodic trends and basic organic chemistry nomenclature and reactions are included, as well.

V. Laboratory (5%–10%)

There are a number of required laboratory experiments for the AP Chemistry Exam and these are discussed in Chapter 16. Questions pertaining to chemistry labs are found on both the multiple-choice and free-response sections. Question types include lab safety as well as specific questions about a laboratory experience. The required laboratory question on the free-response section may or may not require you to use a calculator, depending on the lab scenario.

That's a lot of ideas to cover in just one test, and certainly 75 multiple-choice questions is a lot of items to respond to in a short period of time. But by *working quickly and methodically* you'll have plenty of time to address this section effectively. We'll look at this in greater depth later in this chapter.

The Free-Response Section

After time is called on the multiple-choice section, you'll get a short break before diving into the free-response section. There are two parts for the free-response section, for which you are given a periodic table as well as an equation sheet. For Part A, you are allowed to use a calculator and are given 55 minutes to complete the section. The first question for Part A is always based on chemical equilibrium. The laboratory question may appear in Part A as well and may be quantitative, or may be located in Part B and be qualitative. For Part B, you are given 40 minutes and you **may not use a calculator** for this section. Part B contains one problem in which you are required to write chemical formulas and predict products for a chemical reaction. Similar to the multiple-choice section, the free-response portion of the exam expects you to be able to *apply your own* *knowledge to analyze information,* in addition to being able to solve basic problems and perform calculations.

What's the Score?

Although the scoring process for the AP exam may seem quite complex, it boils down to two simple components: your multiple-choice score plus your free-response scores. The multiple-choice section accounts for 50% of your overall score; the free-response section accounts for the remaining 50% of your total score. Within the free-response section, questions 1–3 in Section A are weighted at 20% each. For Section B, the predicting products question is weighted at 10% and the remaining two qualitative questions are 15% each. Trained graders read students' written responses and assign points according to grading rubrics. The number of points you accrue out of the total possible will form your score on the free-response section.

The test maker awards AP scores on a scale of 1 to 5. Although individual colleges and universities determine what credit or advanced placement, if any, is awarded to students at each score level, these are the assessments typically associated with each numeric score:

5   Extremely well qualified

4   Well qualified

3   Qualified

2   Possibly qualified

1   No recommendation

Section I: Strategies for the Multiple-Choice Section of the Exam

In the first part of the exam, you are given 90 minutes to complete 75 multiple-choice questions. For this part of the exam, you are given a periodic table and you are not allowed to use a calculator. There are two different types of questions found on the multiple-choice section. The first type includes a list of five headings followed by a list of phrases. You are to match the heading to the phrase. Headings may be used more than once or not at all.

■ EXAMPLE: **Questions 1–3 refer to atoms of the following elements.**

a)   Sulfur

b)   Tellurium

c)   Oxygen

d)   Gallium

e)   Actinium

1.   Has the smallest atomic radius

2.   Contains electrons in f-orbitals

3.   Has the highest value for the first ionization energy

■ SOLUTION:

1.   C

2.   E

3.   C

The second type of question is a traditional multiple-choice question containing five choices. Pick the best answer for each question, bearing in mind that some questions may have more than one answer that may seem correct. You should underline the important facts of the question, because this will force you to read the question and to not assume what a question is asking. Initially try to answer the question without looking at the possible answers given. Secondly, since you can write on the exam, make it easier on yourself by crossing out any answers that you can immediately rule out. This will enhance your chances of a correct answer if you are not quite sure. Remember that you are not penalized for incorrect answers on the multiple-choice section and should answer all questions. There is a variety of these types of questions; following is a small sample to get you acquainted.

EXAMPLE: Which of the following species is NOT sp^2 hybridized?

   (A) BCl_3

   (B) NO_3^{-1}

   (C) CO_3^{-2}

   (D) NCl_3

   (E) SO_2

SOLUTION: Carefully read the question and underline the word NOT. Eliminate answers that are obviously wrong, then draw the Lewis structures for the remaining choices.

Answer: D

EXAMPLE: A power plant contains 100. grams of Po-210 to run one of its smaller reactors. The reactor becomes inefficient and the sample must be replaced when there is less than 25 grams of Po-210 remaining. If the half-life of Po-210 is 140 days, how long will the reactor run before the sample should be replaced?

   (A) 70 days

   (B) 280 days

   (C) 140 days

   (D) 420 days

   (E) 35 days

SOLUTION: Write down the starting amount, followed by the amount after each half-life. Then multiply the half-life by the number of decays that occurred.

$$100 \text{ g} \rightarrow 50 \text{ g} \rightarrow 25 \text{ g} \quad 2 \times 140 \text{ days} = 280 \text{ days}$$

Answer: B

It is easier to quickly write down the amounts rather than try to use the first-order integrated rate equation to solve for the mass amount. Always take the easiest route to solving a problem.

EXAMPLE: A certain chemical reaction has a negative ΔH at 300 K. Which of the following must be true?

I. The reaction rate is fast at 300 K.

II. The reaction is exothermic.

III. The reaction will occur spontaneously at 300 K.

(A) I only

(B) II only

(C) I and II only

(D) II and III only

(E) I, I, and III

SOLUTION: This type of question requires you to examine the three possible statements given to you prior to determining the correct answer. Once you figure out which statements are correct, choose the correct multiple-choice answer.

Answer: B

There are some equations you should know without the aid of the equation sheet. $\Delta G = \Delta H - T\Delta S$ is one of these equations. Remember, you are not given an equation sheet for the multiple-choice section of the exam! Statement one is eliminated because thermodynamics has nothing to do with kinetics. ΔG indicates whether a reaction is spontaneous or nonspontaneous, and the sign of ΔG cannot be determined from the information given, so statement III can be eliminated. A negative ΔH indicates that the reaction is exothermic, so only statement II is true.

EXAMPLE:

$$4 NH_{3 (g)} + 3 O_{2 (g)} \rightarrow 2 N_{2 (g)} + 6 H_2O_{(g)}$$

According to the preceding equation, how many grams of oxygen gas (atomic mass of oxygen = 16 g/mol) are needed to produce 4.0 moles of water?

(A) 16 g

(B) 32 g

(C) 64 g

(D) 72 g

(E) 96 g

SOLUTION:
For this question, you must be able to quickly compute some basic mathematical computations. Remember, you do not have a calculator for the multiple-choice section of the exam.

$$g\ O_2 = \frac{4.0\ mol\ H_2O}{1} \times \frac{3\ mol\ O_2}{6\ mol\ H_2O} \times \frac{32\ g\ O_2}{1\ mol\ O_2} = 64\ g\ O_2$$

Answer: C

To simplify, (4) × (1/2) = 2. You are left with 2 × 32 = 64 grams. Look for these types of simplifications when completing mathematical computations.

■ EXAMPLE:

$$Cr_2O_7^{-2} + H_2SO_3 + H^+ \rightarrow Cr^{+3} + SO_4^{-2} + H_2O$$

When the equation for the preceding redox reaction is balanced and all of the coefficients are reduced to lowest whole-number terms, the coefficient for SO_4^{-2} is:

(A)   2

(B)   3

(C)   4

(D)   6

(E)   8

■ SOLUTION:

Identify the chemical equation as a redox equation and balance it without looking at the answers. When balancing a redox equation, rewrite the equation without the H^+ and H_2O, because it will be much easier to balance. The half-reaction method discussed in Chapter 3 is an efficient method for balancing redox reactions.

Answer: B

If you are not able to balance the equation quickly, skip it and come back to it when you have finished the remainder of the multiple-choice questions. The time it takes you to balance a chemical equation may cost you since you could have answered a number of other questions in the same amount of time it took you to balance the chemical reaction.

Tips for the Multiple-Choice Section

- Spend a maximum of 1 minute on each question. This should give you approximately 15 minutes of time at the end of the exam to go back over the exam and address questions that you may have skipped over.

- You are not supposed to get every question correct. If you cannot answer a question, don't get stressed. Simply move on to the next question that you can answer correctly.

- Questions at the end of the test are no more difficult than those at the beginning.

- Answer all questions! You are not penalized for wrong answers, so make an educated guess for all questions.

- Eliminate obviously wrong answers and put a line through them to not waste time looking at these choices over and over. This will also help in deducing the correct answer.

- Underline important terms in each question. This will help you answer the question you are being asked.

- Practice estimating mathematical computations including logarithms (suggestions for estimating logarithms are provided in the next section).

- Initially try to predict the answer without looking at the choices provided.

- If you skip a question, be sure to skip the same answer on the bubble sheet.

- Don't be afraid to write on the test.

- Place a pencil in the margin of the page with the periodic table so you can quickly turn to the page—time is of the essence.

- Make sure to completely erase all stray marks and answers that you may have changed.

- Don't overthink a question—more often than not your first intuition will be the correct answer.

Section II: The Free-Response Section

There are two parts to the free-response section, for which you are given a periodic table, a table of reduction potentials, as well as an equation sheet. You are allowed 55 minutes to complete Part A and 40 minutes to complete Part B. Remember, for Part A of the free-response section, you are allowed to use a calculator. Each of the different types of questions will be addressed in the next section.

Part A

There are three questions associated with Part A each having multiple parts. Each question is weighted 20% toward the total free-response score.

Problem 1

The first problem in the free-response section is always an equilibrium question. There is a variety of equilibrium questions to be familiar with:

- Equilibrium reaction based on the concentrations of reactants and products

- Equilibrium reaction based on the pressures of gaseous reactants and products

- Weak acid problem

- Weak base problem

- Hydrolysis of ionic salts

- Equilibrium of a buffer system

- Titrations involving weak acids and bases

- Slightly soluble salts (solubility products)

The problem will contain multiple questions concerning equilibrium and will generally lead you through the problem step by step. Be sure to show all work in order to gain as many points as possible, since the average score is usually 4.5 out of a possible 9 points. Show any equation that you will use—especially the equilibrium expression, since points are often awarded for doing this. Pay close attention to units and significant figures because a point will be deducted per problem for each infraction.

Many times you will be required to use an answer from the previous problem to answer subsequent questions. Don't worry if you have a wrong answer, because the AP Reader will usually not penalize you throughout the rest of the problem. You will only lose the point for the wrong answer once. If you have no idea how to answer a problem but you know you must use the answer of that question, simply state that you are using a number of your choosing to work the new computation (pick the number 1 since it will simplify calculations). This way, you will lose a minimal amount of points. Any point you can gain toward your final score is extremely important!

Problems 2 and 3

These questions are also weighted at 20% of the free-response score and will also require the use of a calculator. Typical topics include kinetics, thermodynamics, electrochemistry, gas laws, and any other type of question requiring computation. Most often the topics will be mixed together, which ensures that you are able to interrelate the topics in chemistry. For example, you might be required to use a gas law to determine the molar mass of a gas and then determine the molecular formula of the gas from an empirical formula computation.

One of these two questions may also be the laboratory-based question. A laboratory scenario is given where you will have to manipulate data or interpret graphs. Further study of laboratory-based questions is described later in this review book in Chapter 16. As with problem 1, remember to write equations and show all work to gain as many points as possible. Don't forget your significant figures and units.

Part B

You will still have the equation sheet but will not have a calculator for this part of the exam. You will have 40 minutes to complete this portion of the exam.

Problem 4

The first question of Part B of the free-response section is predicting products and is worth 10% of the free-response section. There are three reactions to predict worth 5 points each, and every reaction will have products (you will never write "no reaction"). Each of the reactions must be written as a net ionic equation and must also be balanced. The final part of each equation is a question about the reaction. You do not have to list the phases of the reactants and products. The scoring rubric for this problem is as follows:

1 point for correctly writing the reactants

2 points for correctly predicting the products

1 point for correctly balancing the reaction

1 point for correctly answering a question pertaining to the chemical reaction

EXAMPLE: Methane is burned in air. How many liters of oxygen gas are required to react with 2.0 moles of methane at STP?

SOLUTION:

$$CH_4 + 2\,O_2 \rightarrow CO_2 + 2\,H_2O$$

Based on the reaction, 2 moles of methane will react with 4 moles of oxygen gas. At STP, 1 mole gas = 22.4 L and therefore 89.6 L of O_2 is necessary.

Know your solubility rules and nomenclature for this section. If you happen to forget the oxidation state of a metal ion, refer to the table of reduction potentials. If you do not know the products for a reaction, make sure to write down the reactants to gain at least 1 point.

Problems 5 and 6

Questions 5 and 6 are each weighted 15% toward the total free-response score. These questions are qualitative and will require you to write specific responses. Your answers should be concise yet specific enough to answer the question that is being asked. The answers may be written in paragraph form, but you may also use dashes or bullets to express your thoughts. When appropriate, drawings, examples, and mathematical equations may be used as part of the responses.

There are topics for which you should be an expert. These questions include the following topics: molecular structures and bonding, intermolecular forces, periodic trends, and the concept of shielding. If a question pertaining to a laboratory was not asked in Part A, it will be asked in this section.

Some More Advice

- Read through the entire question before beginning to answer any parts. Later questions may provide hints to earlier parts of the question.

- Stay on topic, be concise, and answer the question being asked! Addressing the question fully is the single most important way to earn points on the exam.

- When writing explanations, be careful to use the terms *atom, molecule, compound, ion,* and *formula unit* correctly. These are all different terms that cannot be used interchangeably!

- Be neat! An AP Reader will not spend time guessing what you intended your answer to be. Remember, a happy grader is a forgiving grader!

- Always write down the equation for all problems.

- Include units with all answers, excluding equilibrium constants.

- Make sure to use the correct number of significant figures.

- Make sure you do not spend too much time on any one problem. You must maximize your points.

- The equilibrium question will generally take more time than the remaining two questions in Part A.

- Leave a few minutes to review your work and check to make sure you have not made any simple errors.

- Do not worry if you cannot answer a question. You are not supposed to get every question correct. Shoot for at least 80% and you are well on your way to a 5 on the exam.

Two Final Words: Don't Panic!

The two sections of the exam are designed to test your overall knowledge of chemistry. You have prepared well for the exam by completing numerous practice problems, reviewing chemistry concepts, and taking multiple practice tests. Do not try to cram the night before for the test. Get a restful night of sleep before the exam so that you will be alert and ready to demonstrate your knowledge! You are not supposed to get a perfect score. The exam is scaled, so do the best you can by maximizing the amount of points earned for each section.

AP Chemistry Exam Essentials

In addition to the myriad of topics and test strategies necessary to earn a 5 on the AP Chemistry Exam, there are some essential terms and skills that you should master. This includes the concepts of nomenclature, estimation of calculations, and significant figures.

Nomenclature

Naming is our chemistry language. You must be an expert with naming, because one small error with a name or formula can translate into a number of issues in a problem; writing reactions, balancing equations, and performing stoichiometry calculations are almost impossible to solve if the formulas are incorrect.

Naming Inorganic Compounds

Inorganic compounds are easy to identify because they contain a metal cation and a nonmetallic anion. The metal cation is named first and takes the name of the element. Cations capable of multiple oxidation states should have the oxidation state listed with a

Roman numeral in parentheses. You should be familiar with elements that have multiple oxidation states with some common metal cations listed in the following table.

Metal	Possible Oxidation States
Sn	Sn^{+2} and Sn^{+4}
Pb	Pb^{+2} and Pb^{+4}
Hg	Hg_2^{+2} and Hg^{+2}
Cu	Cu^{+1} and Cu^{+2}
Fe	Fe^{+2} and Fe^{+3}

Monoatomic anions take the name of the element, but end with the suffix – *ide*. As an example, NaCl is named as sodium chloride. Polyatomic ions are ions that exist when multiple atoms are bonded covalently but have a net charge. There is a large number of polyatomic ions that you should have committed to memory. A list of the most common ions is shown in the following table.

Common Cations and Anions

Acetate	CH_3COO^{-1}	Hypochlorite	ClO^{-1}
Ammonium	NH_4^{+1}	Iodide	I^{-1}
Bicarbonate (Hydrogen Carbonate)	HCO_3^{-1}	Nitride	N^{-3}
Bisulfate (Hydrogen Sulfate)	HSO_4^{-1}	Nitrate	NO_3^{-1}
Bromide	Br^{-1}	Nitrite	NO_2^{-1}
Carbonate	CO_3^{-2}	Oxalate	$C_2O_4^{-2}$
Chlorate	ClO_3^{-1}	Oxide	O^{-2}
Chloride	Cl^{-1}	Permanganate	MnO_4^{-1}
Chlorite	ClO_2^{-1}	Peroxide	O_2^{-2}

(continued)

Chromate	CrO_4^{-2}	Phosphate	PO_4^{-3}
Cyanate	OCN^{-1}	Phosphite	PO_3^{-3}
Cyanide	CN^{-1}	Sulfate	SO_4^{-2}
Dichromate	$Cr_2O_7^{-2}$	Sulfide	S^{-2}
Fluoride	F^{-1}	Sulfite	SO_3^{-2}
Hydronium	H_3O^{+1}	Tartrate	$C_4H_4O_6^{-2}$
Hydroxide	OH^{-1}	Thiocyanate	SCN^{-1}
Hydride	H^{-1}	Thiosulfate	$S_2O_3^{-2}$

Naming Covalent Compounds

Covalent compounds, also known as *molecules*, consist of two or more nonmetal elements bonded together to form a neutral compound. When naming covalent compounds, prefixes are used to illustrate how many of each atom is present. The first element is named as the name of the atom. The second element is named using the element's name plus the suffix –ide. As mentioned previously, prefixes are used to illustrate how many of each atom type is present. The exception to not using a prefix occurs when there is only one of the first atom in the molecule.

Prefixes and Number of Atoms for Covalent Compounds

Prefix	Number of Atoms	Prefix	Number of Atoms
mono-	1	hexa-	6
di-	2	hepta-	7
tri-	3	octa-	8
tetra-	4	nona-	9
penta-	5	deca-	10

Estimating Logarithms and Other Mathematical Computations

The multiple-choice section of the AP Chemistry Exam does not allow for the use of a calculator and you must be able to compute answers using mental math. Multiple-choice questions on the exam that require you to calculate the correct answer will involve computations that involve basic calculations. The following are some tips:

- Round numbers to the nearest 10. This will allow easy computations and although not exact, will enable you to determine the best answer.

- Write out all steps of the problem before doing any computations. Remember that you can write on the exam! Often, you will be able to cancel out factors in the problem and minimize the number of computations.

- Put units with all numbers to avoid errors.

In addition, you must be able to estimate logarithms. This may seem like a daunting task but it is actually a fairly easy computation. This type of calculation often is found when calculating pH and pOH, or possibly pK_a and pK_b. The first step in estimating a logarithm is to write the number in scientific notation. This will enable you to determine the range within which the number resides. Following is an example of estimating a logarithm.

EXAMPLE: What is the pH of a 3.5×10^{-4} M HCl solution?

SOLUTION: The concentration falls in between 1.0×10^{-4} and 1.0×10^{-3}

Concentration [H$^+$]	Approximate pH
1.0×10^{-3}	3.00
7.5×10^{-4}	3.15
5.0×10^{-4}	3.30
2.5×10^{-4}	3.60
1.0×10^{-4}	4.00

You need to know the pH of 5.0×10^{-4} M is 3.30. Take half of .30 to get the pH for 7.5×10^{-4} M and double the 0.30 to get the pH for 2.5×10^{-4} M. You can simply estimate the pH based on the table. 3.5×10^{-4} M would have an approximate pH = 3.40.

Significant Figures

Chemistry is an empirical science that was developed through experiments largely over the past 200 years. Experiments require measurements, and every measurement has a degree of uncertainty—or error—associated with it. So we utilize significant figures ("sig figs") to express the appropriate amount of precision with measurement. There are some basic rules for determining the number of significant figures in a particular measurement:

- All nonzero digits are significant (e.g., 2.16 has 3 sig figs).

- Zeros that fall between other numbers are significant (e.g., 7.0257 has 5 sig figs).

- For numbers less than 1, the zeros following the decimal place up to the first nonzero number are not significant (they would disappear in scientific notation) (e.g., 0.00611 has 3 sig figs).

- If the zero is given after the decimal place, it is significant (e.g., 6.200 has 4 sig figs).

- For numbers that do not have a decimal place, the final zeros at the end of the number are not significant (e.g., 224000 has 3 sig figs).

- A final zero can be considered significant if a decimal place is placed at the end (e.g., 90800. has 5 sig figs).

When performing calculations with significant figures, the rules vary depending on whether you are multiplying/dividing or adding/subtracting.

- For multiplication/division, the final answer should only have as many sig figs as the original number that had the least number of significant figures (e.g., $7.24 \times 8.1602 = \mathbf{59.1}$).

- When adding/subtracting, the number of significant figures depends upon the last common decimal place between the numbers. First, determine the number of decimal places in each number to be added or subtracted. Then, calculate the actual "theoretical" answer. Finally, round the final number to the last common decimal place. Note that the number of significant figures in the final answer may be more or less than the original numbers (e.g., $5.20 + 11.263 = \mathbf{16.46}$).

Stoichiometry & Chemical Equations

Chemical Equations

- Chemical equations are prescribed recipes that chemists use to represent the ingredients and the end product(s) for chemical reactions.

- Equations also indicate the amounts and states of matter of the species involved in a reaction.

- It is always necessary to balance chemical equations; otherwise, the reaction would violate the **law of conservation of mass.**

- Equations are balanced by adding coefficients in front of the atoms or compounds. You may only change the number of each species that you have on the reactant or products side of an equation. Never change the formula of the compound!

In order to efficiently balance equations:

1. Write out the correct formulas for the reactants and products.

2. Balance atoms other than oxygen and hydrogen first.

3. Try to balance polyatomic ions as a unit.

4. Balance oxygen and hydrogen after most of the other atoms are balanced.

5. If there are any single atoms or diatomic molecules like O_2 in the equation, save them for last.

6. Avoid fractions as coefficients!

7. Redox reactions must be balanced for both atoms and charge. See the next section on "Balancing Redox Reactions."

■ EXAMPLE: Aqueous solutions of ammonium phosphate and calcium chloride react to form solid calcium phosphate and a solution of ammonium chloride.

■ SOLUTION: See the following steps for the explanation; changes for each step are underlined and in bold.

Step 1: $(NH_4)_3PO_{4(aq)} + CaCl_{2(aq)} \rightarrow Ca_3(PO_4)_{2(s)} + NH_4Cl_{(aq)}$

Step 2: $(NH_4)_3PO_{4(aq)} + \underline{\mathbf{3}}\,CaCl_{2(aq)} \rightarrow Ca_3(PO_4)_{2(s)} + NH_4Cl_{(aq)}$

Step 3: $\underline{\mathbf{2}}\,(NH_4)_3PO_{4(aq)} + 3\,CaCl_{2(aq)} \rightarrow Ca_3(PO_4)_{2(s)} + \underline{\mathbf{6}}\,NH_4Cl_{(aq)}$

Double check to make sure everything is balanced, such as the chlorine atoms. Otherwise, this equation is balanced.

TEST TIP

If you are having trouble balancing an equation, check to make sure that the formulas are correct. Writing the incorrect formula from the name is a common error that has severe and enduring consequences on AP Chemistry problems.

Balancing Redox Reactions

Balancing oxidation–reduction reactions requires balancing both mass and charge. Not only must the same number of each kind of atom exist on both sides of the equation, but also the number of electrons lost in oxidation must equal the number of electrons gained during reduction. Balancing redox reactions is NOT the result of trial and error, but rather meticulously going through a series of proven steps:

1. Write all reactants and products except H^+, OH^-, and H_2O in the form of <u>separate oxidation and reduction half-reactions</u>. The half-reactions should showcase the species that are changing in charge between reactants and products. Ignore any other molecules or ions given such as H^+, OH^-, H_2O, or other spectator ions.

2. Balance all atoms except for H and O for each half-reaction.

3. If the number of oxygen atoms differs between the left and right sides of the equation, add H_2O to the side that needs more oxygen atoms.

4. Balance the number of hydrogen atoms for each half-reaction by adding H^+.

5. Calculate the total charge on the left and right sides of each half-reaction. Balance the charge using electrons. The oxidation half-reaction will have electrons on the right. The reduction will have electrons on the left. You need both in order to have a redox reaction!

6. Multiply each half-reaction by a small integer in order to make the number of electrons lost in one half-reaction equal to the number of electrons gained in the other.

7. Add the equations for the half-reactions together, canceling the electrons and excess H_2O and H^+.

8. **IF DONE IN BASIC SOLUTION:** Balancing is done the same way as for the acidic solution (discussed earlier). Then add OH^- ions to **both** sides of the final equation to convert all of the H^+ into H_2O molecules. Cancel any newly formed H_2O molecules, if necessary.

DIDYOUKNOW?

Stomach acid is composed mostly of 0.10 M hydrochloric acid (HCl). Coincidentally, this is the same concentration of the same acid that is used in most lab experiments and chemistry problems.

EXAMPLE: Balance the following reaction that was performed in basic solution:

$$Cr_2O_7{}^{2-} + H_2SO_3 \rightarrow Cr^{3+} + SO_4{}^{2-}$$

SOLUTION: See the following steps for the explanation; changes for each step are underlined and in bold.

Step 1: $Cr_2O_7{}^{2-} \rightarrow Cr^{3+}$

$H_2SO_3 \rightarrow SO_4{}^{2-}$

Step 2: $Cr_2O_7{}^{2-} \rightarrow \underline{\mathbf{2}}\ Cr^{3+}$

$H_2SO_3 \rightarrow SO_4{}^{2-}$

Step 3: $Cr_2O_7^{2-} \rightarrow 2\,Cr^{3+} + \mathbf{7\,H_2O}$

$\mathbf{H_2O} + H_2SO_3 \rightarrow SO_4^{2-}$

Step 4: $\mathbf{14\,H^+} + Cr_2O_7^{2-} \rightarrow 2\,Cr^{3+} + 7\,H_2O$

$H_2O + H_2SO_3 \rightarrow SO_4^{2-} + \mathbf{4\,H^+}$

Step 5: $+12 = +6$

$\mathbf{6\,e^-} + 14\,H^+ + Cr_2O_7^{2-} \rightarrow 2\,Cr^{3+} + 7\,H_2O$

$0 = +2$

$H_2O + H_2SO_3 \rightarrow SO_4^{2-} + 4\,H^+ + \mathbf{2e^-}$

Step 6: $6\,e^- + 14\,H^+ + Cr_2O_7^{2-} \rightarrow 2\,Cr^{3+} + 7\,H_2O$

$\mathbf{3}\,H_2O + \mathbf{3}\,H_2SO_3 \rightarrow \mathbf{3}\,SO_4^{2-} + \mathbf{12}\,H^+ + \mathbf{6}\,e^-$

Step 7: $6\,e^- + 14\,H^+ + Cr_2O_7^{2-} + 3\,H_2O + 3\,H_2SO_3$
$\rightarrow 2\,Cr^{3+} + 7\,H_2O + 3\,SO_4^{2-} + 12\,H^+ + 6\,e^-$

$\mathbf{2\,H^+ + Cr_2O_7^{2-} + 3\,H_2SO_3 \rightarrow 2\,Cr^{3+} + 4\,H_2O}$
$\mathbf{+\,3\,SO_4^{2-}}$

Step 8: $\mathbf{2\,OH^-} + 2\,H^+ + Cr_2O_7^{2-} + 3\,H_2SO_3 \rightarrow 2\,Cr^{3+}$
$+\,4\,H_2O + 3\,SO_4^{2-} + \mathbf{2\,OH^-}$

$\mathbf{2\,H_2O} + Cr_2O_7^{2-} + 3\,H_2SO_3 \rightarrow 2\,Cr^{3+} + 4\,H_2O$
$+\,3\,SO_4^{2-} + 2\,OH^-$

FINAL ANSWER: $Cr_2O_7^{2-} + 3\,H_2SO_3 \rightarrow 2\,Cr^{3+}$
$\mathbf{+\,2\,H_2O + 3\,SO_4^{2-} + 2\,OH^-}$

Remember: You can always check your answer when balancing a redox reaction. First, verify that the number of each of the atoms is the same on both sides, then verify that the charges are equivalent.

DIDYOUKNOW?

Apples turn brown if you take a bite out of them and allow them to be exposed to the air due to a redox reaction. Tyrosinase is an enzyme found in many fruits that oxidizes to form the brown color. This redox reaction can be inhibited by adding an acid such as lemon juice.

Factor-Label Method & Conversions

- Scientists use dimensional analysis, also known as the *factor-label method* or simply *unit conversion*, to solve quantitative problems.

- The factor-label method is based upon the algebraic premise that $\frac{x}{x} = 1$; that is—if there is a unit in the numerator it can be canceled out by the same unit in the denominator.

- Conversion factors are ratios that allow you to convert from one unit to another unit. For example, if there are 60 seconds in 1 minute, you can write that as either of the following: $\frac{1\ min}{60\ s}$ or $\frac{60\ s}{1\ min}$.

- The key to the whole method is setting the problems up so that the units cancel one another out.

$$\frac{number\ with\ \cancel{original\ unit}}{1} \times \left(\frac{new\ unit}{\cancel{original\ unit}} \right) = new\ number\ with\ new\ unit$$

The Mole

- A **mole** is a unit that allows you to make accurate comparisons of number for atoms and compounds: 1 mole = 6.022×10^{23} particles (atoms, molecules, ions, or formula units).

- Every atom on the periodic table has a different mass, so if you have 10 g of oxygen and 10 g of carbon, you have different numbers of atoms of each.

- The sum of the atomic masses for all of the atoms in a compound is the **molar mass (M)**, which has the unit of grams per mole of substance (g/mol).

- Based on the ideal gas law, **1 mol** of any gas at standard temperature and pressure (STP = 1 atm, 273 K) is **22.4 L**.

- In a balanced chemical equation, the coefficients will represent the mole relationship between the reactants and products.

EXAMPLE 1: How many chloride ions are in 0.20 moles of calcium chloride?

SOLUTION 1: $\#ions\ Cl^- = \dfrac{0.20\ mol\ CaCl_2}{1} \times \dfrac{6.022 \times 10^{23}\ formula\ units\ CaCl_2}{1\ mol\ CaCl_2}$

$\times \dfrac{2\ ions\ Cl^-}{1\ formula\ unit\ CaCl_2} = \mathbf{2.4 \times 10^{23}\ ions\ Cl^-}$

EXAMPLE 2: What is the mass of 2.24 moles of ammonium carbonate?

SOLUTION 2: $molar\ mass\ (NH_4)_2CO_3 = 2(14.00) + 8(1.0079) + 1(12.011)$
$+ 3(16.00) = 96.07\ g/mol$

$\#g\ (NH_4)_2CO_3 = \dfrac{2.24\ \cancel{mol\ (NH_4)_2CO_3}}{1} \times \dfrac{96.07\ g\ (NH_4)_2CO_3}{1\ \cancel{mol\ (NH_4)_2CO_3}}$

$= \mathbf{215\ g\ (NH_4)_2CO_3}$

TEST TIP

Molar masses should never limit the significant figures in a problem. Making sure that you have at least 4 sig figs should set you up well for the vast majority of problems.

EXAMPLE 3: Air is composed of approximately 1.0% argon gas. How many liters of argon are in a 58-g sample of air at STP?

SOLUTION 3: g Ar in air = 1.0% (58 g) = 0.58 g

$\#L\ Ar = \dfrac{0.58\ \cancel{g\ Ar}}{1} \times \dfrac{1\ \cancel{mol\ Ar}}{39.948\ \cancel{g\ Ar}} \times \dfrac{22.4\ L\ Ar}{1\ \cancel{mol\ Ar}} = \mathbf{0.33\ L\ Ar}$

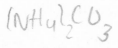

Solutions

Most chemical reactions seen on the AP Chemistry exam involve aqueous solutions. The most typical unit of concentration for solutions is molarity, which is the number of moles of solute per liter of solution.

$$M = \frac{mol \ solute}{L \ solution}$$

As a result, molarity can be used as a conversion factor in solution stoichiometry problems to convert between moles of a solute and liters of solution and vice versa.

EXAMPLE: How many grams of sugar $(C_{12}H_{22}O_{11})$ can be crystallized from 250 mL of a 0.11 molar solution?

SOLUTION: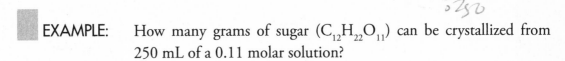

$$\# g \ C_{12}H_{22}O_{11} = \frac{250 \ \cancel{mL \ soln}}{1} \times \frac{1 \ \cancel{L}}{1,000 \ \cancel{mL}}$$

$$\times \frac{0.11 \ \cancel{mol \ C_{12}H_{22}O_{11}}}{1 \ \cancel{L \ soln}} \times \frac{342.17 \ g \ C_{12}H_{22}O_{11}}{1 \ \cancel{mol \ C_{12}H_{22}O_{11}}} = 9.4 \ g \ C_{12}H_{22}O_{11}$$

TEST TIP

If you are unsure of what to convert to in a particular problem, try converting to a central unit such as the mole.

Stoichiometry Problems

Stoichiometry allows chemists to make comparisons and convert between the species involved in a chemical reaction. The coefficients in a balanced chemical equation define the mole ratio between all of the reactants and products, and are the centerpiece of a stoichiometry problem. In general, stoichiometry problems can be solved using the following steps:

1. Write out the balanced chemical equation.

2. Identify the unit and compound that the problem is asking you to find.

3. Convert the given compound into moles (this may take multiple steps).

4. KEY STEP: Convert moles of the given compound into moles of the desired compound using the coefficients in the balanced chemical equation.

5. Convert the number of moles of the desired compound into the units required in the problem.

EXAMPLE: How many grams of oxygen are necessary to react with 0.724 g of natural gas (methane)?

SOLUTION: $CH_{4(g)} + 2 O_{2(g)} \rightarrow CO_{2(g)} + 2 H_2O_{(g)}$

$$\# g\ O_2 = \frac{0.724\ \cancel{g\ CH_4}}{1} \times \frac{1\ \cancel{mol\ CH_4}}{16.043\ \cancel{g\ CH_4}} \times \frac{2\ \cancel{mol\ O_2}}{1\ \cancel{mol\ CH_4}} \times \frac{32.00\ g\ O_2}{1\ \cancel{mol\ O_2}}$$

$$= \textbf{2.89 g } O_2$$

Limiting Reactants

- Rarely are chemical reactions performed where perfect mole ratios of the reactants are put together to form a defined amount of product. Instead, most reactions have something called a *limiting reactant* (limiting reagent).

- Limiting reactant problems require you to first figure out which reactant is limiting by performing a stoichiometry problem for *each* of the reactants.

- The limiting reactant is the reactant that produces the *least amount of product*.

- It would be unusual on the AP Chemistry exam for the problem to indicate that it was a limiting reagent problem. Limiting reagent problems will give the amounts for each of the reactants either directly as masses or through a small calculation such as PV=nRT.

- The steps for solving a limiting reagent problem are as follows:

1. Choose one product.

2. Figure out how many moles of that product will be formed based on the amounts of each reactant. This will require two separate stoichiometry problems.

3. Whichever reactant gave the smaller amount of product is the limiting reagent.

4. Convert to grams as required by the problem.

[handwritten: Pb(NO3)₂ + K·I → P K₂]

EXAMPLE: A student mixed 150.0 mL solutions of 0.25 M lead (II) nitrate and 0.10 M potassium iodide to form a yellow precipitate. What mass of precipitate is formed?

[handwritten: ^mol, 250 mL, = 0.150 L]

SOLUTION:

1. Write out the balanced chemical equation and correctly identify which of the products is the precipitate, which is based on solubility rules.

$$Pb(NO_3)_{2\ (aq)} + 2\ KI_{(aq)} \rightarrow PbI_{2\ (s)} + 2\ KNO_{3\ (aq)}$$

2. Choose one of the products. It is best to choose PbI_2 because the problem is focused on this particular product, though either product will work.

3. Convert the amounts of each reactant into moles of PbI_2.

$$\#\ mol\ PbI_2 = \frac{150.0\ mL\ Pb(NO_3)_2}{1} \times \frac{1\ L}{1{,}000\ mL} \times \frac{0.25\ mol\ Pb(NO_3)_2}{1\ L\ Pb(NO_3)_2}$$

$$\times \frac{1\ mol\ PbI_2}{1\ mol\ Pb(NO_3)_2} = \mathbf{0.038\ mol\ PbI_2}$$

$$\#\ mol\ PbI_2 = \frac{150.0\ mL\ KI}{1} \times \frac{1\ L}{1{,}000\ mL} \times \frac{0.10\ mol\ KI}{1\ L\ KI} \times \frac{1\ mol\ PbI_2}{2\ mol\ KI}$$

[handwritten: .724 g × 1 mol / 16 MB (4)]

$$= \mathbf{0.0075\ mol\ PbI_2}$$

**KI is the limiting reagent

4. Convert the smallest amount of product to grams as requested by the problem.

$$\#\ g\ PbI_2 = \frac{0.0075\ mol\ PbI_2}{1} \times \frac{461.02\ g\ PbI_2}{1\ mol\ PbI_2} = \mathbf{3.5\ g\ PbI_2}$$

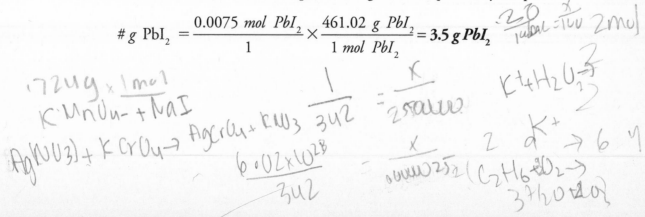

Empirical Formulas and Percent Composition

The percent composition is the ratio of the mass of an element in a compound compared to the total mass of the compound.

$$\text{mass } \% = \frac{mass\ element}{mass\ compound} \times 100$$

The most valuable piece of information that can be obtained from the percent composition is the empirical formula. The empirical formula showcases the simplest ratio of elements in a compound, which may or may not be the same as the molecular formula. To determine the empirical formula:

1. Assume that there are 100 g of the compound, which allows you to convert the percent of each element to a mass (for example, 72.4% = 72.4 g).

2. Convert the masses of each element to moles.

3. Divide the moles of each element by the smallest number of moles calculated in Step 2.

4. If the moles of each of the elements are not whole numbers, multiply by the smallest integer that will make them all integers.

5. The moles of each of the elements represent the simplest ratio between the elements, which is the empirical formula.

6. If you need to find the molecular formula of the compound, divide the molar mass of the compound over the mass of the empirical formula. This will reveal the integer that links the empirical formula to the molecular formula.

$$integer = \frac{molar\ mass}{empirical\ mass}$$

83.6   C
16.4   H

■ EXAMPLE: A molecular substance is 83.6% carbon and the remaining portion is hydrogen. Determine its molecular formula if the molar mass is about 172 g/mol.

■ SOLUTION:

$$\# \ mol \ C = \frac{83.6 \ g \ C}{1} \times \frac{1 \ mol \ C}{12.011 \ g \ C} = \frac{6.96 \ mol}{6.96} = 1 \times 3 = 3 \ mol \ C$$

$$\# \ mol \ H = \frac{16.4 \ g \ H}{1} \times \frac{1 \ mol \ H}{1.0079 \ g \ H} = \frac{16.3 \ mol}{6.96} = 2.33 \times 3 = 7 \ mol \ H$$

empirical formula: C_3H_7

empirical mass = $3(12.011) + 7(1.0079) = 43.088$ g/mol

$$\frac{\textbf{molar mass}}{\textbf{empirical mass}} = \text{integer} \qquad \frac{172 \ g \ / \ mol}{43.088 \ g \ / \ mol} = 4(C_3H_7) = \textbf{molecular formula} = \textbf{C}_{12}\textbf{H}_{28}$$

TEST TIP

Empirical formula problems can be combined with almost every other type of problem in chemistry, so make sure you are really proficient at solving them!

Chemical Reactions

Predicting Products of Chemical Reactions

On the AP Chemistry exam, a section is devoted to predicting the products of chemical reactions. It is essential that you are able to write the formulas of compounds, predict the products based on the given reactants, and balance the chemical equation. The reaction must be written as a net ionic equation, so make sure that you know your solubility rules. You will not have to list the states of matter of the reactants or the products present in the reaction.

Solubility Rules

In order to predict whether a precipitate will form, you will need to know solubility rules. Below is a general list of solubility rules, but realize that there may be exceptions.

- All nitrate salts are soluble.

- All ammonium salts are soluble.

- All lithium, sodium, potassium, and rubidium (Group IA) metal salts are soluble.

- All acetates are generally soluble.

- All chlorides, bromides, and iodides are soluble except for those bonded with silver, mercury (I), and lead.

- All salts of chlorates and chlorites are generally soluble.

- All sulfates are soluble except for $BaSO_4$, Ag_2SO_4, Hg_2SO_4, $PbSO_4$, $SrSO_4$, and $CaSO_4$.

- All hydroxides are insoluble except for the strong bases.

- All carbonates are insoluble except for salts of NH_4^+, Li^+, Na^+, K^+, and Rb^+.

- All sulfides are insoluble except for salts of NH_4^+, Li^+, Na^+, K^+, and Rb^+.

Precipitation Reactions

Double replacement (ionic) reactions are the most common type of precipitation reactions. Double replacements are easily identifiable because they have two ionic compounds (four ions) given as reactants. The net ionic equation is a summary of the most important parts of the chemical reaction, showing which reactants come together to form the products. Remember, net ionic equations do not include any spectator ions, which are the ions present before and after the reaction occurs that are not involved with reaction. Only write and balance those ions that react to form an insoluble compound.

EXAMPLE: Solutions of silver nitrate and potassium iodide are mixed.

SOLUTION: This is a double-replacement reaction. $K^+_{(aq)}$ and $NO_3^-{}_{(aq)}$ are not included in the net ionic equation because they are spectator ions. Spectator ions are the ions of a soluble ionic salt in a reaction.

$$Ag^+ + I^- \rightarrow AgI$$

TEST TIP

There are three equations for which you must predict products on the AP Chemistry exam. All reactions form a product when writing the net ionic equation.

Gas-Forming Reactions

One driving force in a chemical reaction is the formation of a gas. Pay particular attention if any of the following species are produced in a chemical reaction. If they are formed, write the products of their decomposition.

$$H_2CO_{3(aq)} \rightarrow CO_{2(g)} + H_2O_{(\ell)}$$
$$NH_4OH_{(aq)} \rightarrow NH_{3(g)} + H_2O_{(\ell)}$$
$$H_2SO_{3(aq)} \rightarrow SO_{2(g)} + H_2O_{(\ell)}$$
$$H_2S_{(aq)} \rightarrow H_2S_{(g)}$$

Oxidation–Reduction Reactions

In an oxidation-reduction reaction, one element increases in oxidation state (oxidized), while a second element is reduced in oxidation state (reduction). This type of reaction was discussed in Chapter 3. There are numerous reactions that involve changes in oxidation state, including single-replacement, decomposition, combustion, and synthesis reactions.

$AgNO_3 + KI$

Synthesis

Combines the two reactants, usually in their elemental states, to form a new compound having new oxidation states.

■ EXAMPLE: Magnesium metal is burned in air.

■ SOLUTION: $2\,Mg + O_2 \rightarrow 2\,MgO$

Combustion Reactions

An organic molecule is burned in the presence of oxygen gas to form carbon dioxide and water.

■ EXAMPLE: Butane gas ignites in the presence of oxygen gas.

■ SOLUTION: $2\,C_4H_{10} + 13\,O_2 \rightarrow 8\,CO_2 + 10\,H_2O$

Decomposition Reactions

Decomposition reactions always contain one reactant that breaks apart into two or more different products.

■ EXAMPLE: Hydrogen peroxide solution is exposed to bright light.

■ SOLUTION: $2\,H_2O_2 \rightarrow 2\,H_2O + O_2$

Single-Replacement Reactions

Single-replacement reactions contain a neutral species such as a metal or diatomic molecule that is reacted with an ionic compound.

EXAMPLE: Copper metal is placed in a solution of silver nitrate.

SOLUTION: $Cu + 2\,Ag^+ \rightarrow Cu^{+2} + 2\,Ag$

Another Single Replacement: Solid Metal Placed into an Acidic Solution

The metal is oxidized and hydrogen gas is formed.

EXAMPLE: Magnesium metal is placed into a solution of hydrochloric acid.

SOLUTION: $Mg + 2\,H^+ \rightarrow Mg^{+2} + H_2$

Metal Oxide + Water

When a metal oxide is added to water, it will always produce a base via a synthesis reaction.

EXAMPLE: Solid sodium oxide is added to water.

SOLUTION: $Na_2O + H_2O \rightarrow 2\,Na^+ + 2\,OH^-$

Nonmetal Oxide + Water

When a nonmetal oxide is added to water, it will always produce an acid via a synthesis reaction.

EXAMPLE: Sulfur dioxide gas is bubbled into water.

SOLUTION: $SO_2 + H_2O \rightarrow H_2SO_3$

DIDYOU**KNOW?**

Sulfur trioxide (SO_3) is a gas molecule that is trapped inside the membrane of onions. When the onions are chopped up, the gas is released and it combines with water on the surface of the eyes via a synthesis reaction to form H_2SO_4 (sulfuric acid). This strong acid is diluted and removed from the eye by forming tears—explaining why people cry when they cut up onions.

Acid–Base Chemistry

The chemistry of acids and bases is quite extensive. For the AP Chemistry exam, you should be able to identify acids and bases and recognize their reactivities. There are three different definitions for acids and bases: **Arrenhius**, **Brønsted-Lowry**, and **Lewis Theory**.

- **Hydronium ions** (H_3O^+) are essentially H^+ ions that are attached to water molecules; they are one and the same, though H^+ ions do not technically exist by themselves in solution.

- Arrenhius theory describes an acid as any substance that produces H_3O^+ in aqueous solution. A base is any substance that generates OH^- in aqueous solution.

- Brønsted-Lowry theory is slightly less specific. An acid is defined as any substance that can donate a proton (H^+) and a base as any substance that will accept a proton.

- Lewis theory provides the most general definition of an acid and a base and is based on electrons. An acid is defined as a substance that can accept a pair of electrons, while a base is an electron pair donor.

- The strength of an acid or base is dictated by the concentration of either $[H_3O^+]$ or $[OH^-]$ in solution.

- There are six strong acids that dissociate completely in solution: HCl, HBr, HI, HNO_3, H_2SO_4, and $HClO_4$.

- Strong bases also dissociate completely and consist of the group I and group II metal hydroxides, excluding Be and Mg (which are not soluble enough to act as strong bases).

DIDYOU**KNOW?**

In areas where there are high levels of acid rain, marble buildings and statues are slowly eroded away. The tiny holes or "pits" are caused by the acid–base reaction between the acid rain and the calcium carbonate, which forms carbon dioxide and water.

Autoionization of Water

Water molecules can react with themselves in a process called **autoionization,** where two water molecules react to form a hydronium ion and hydroxide ion.

$$2 \, H_2O \leftrightarrow H_3O^+ + OH^-$$

$$K_w = [H_3O^+][OH^-] = 1.0 \times 10^{-14}$$

- For a neutral solution, $[H_3O^+] = [OH^-] = 1.0 \times 10^{-7}$ M.

- A solution is acidic if the $[H_3O^+] > [OH^-]$ in aqueous solution.

- A solution is basic if the $[H_3O^+] < [OH^-]$ in aqueous solution.

- More detail on the equilibria of acids and bases can be found in Chapter 12, Equilibrium.

Calculation of the Acidity or Basicity of a Solution

The pH scale is used to make it easier to determine the acidity or basicity of a substance when dissolved in aqueous solution. It is merely a more convenient method for indicating the acidity rather than reporting $[H_3O^+]$ directly, since the "molar concentration of hydronium ions" would not be easily interpreted by those who are not chemists. The pH is calculated using the following equation:

$$pH = -\log[H_3O^+]$$

EXAMPLE: What is the pH of 0.0010 M HCl?

SOLUTION: $pH = -\log[0.0010] = 3.00$

TEST TIP

Watch significant figures when using logarithms. The number before the decimal is *never* significant when performing logarithmic calculations.

The pOH is computed for a solution using the following equation:

$$pOH = -\log[OH^-]$$

The relationship between pH and pOH is $pH + pOH = 14$.

TEST TIP

Make sure to read the question carefully to determine if you are asked to calculate pH or pOH.

Estimating Logs

Remember that you will not have a calculator for the multiple-choice section of the AP Chemistry exam, but you will be required to estimate logarithms. This is not as difficult as you may think. In order to accomplish the estimation, you need to know the approximate values for the logs of three values: 2.5, 5.0, and 7.5 × 10^(power), which give decimal places of 0.6, 0.3, and 0.15 with respect to the power of 10 used.

[H₃O⁺]	pH
1.0×10^{-3}	3.00
2.5×10^{-3}	2.60
5.0×10^{-3}	2.30
7.5×10^{-3}	2.15
1.0×10^{-2}	2.00

1. Write the concentration in scientific notation.

2. Compare the value to those in the table by determining where the concentration falls in relation to the concentrations in the table.

3. Make an estimation based on extrapolating from the known pH values.

Acid–Base Reactions

Remember that most acid–base reactions simply involve the donation of a proton (H^+) from one reactant to another (Brønsted acid–base reaction).

A Strong Acid Neutralizes a Strong Base, Producing a Salt and Water

The net ionic reaction for this type of acid–base neutralization is always the same. You should know the strong acids and strong bases.

- **Strong Acids**: HBr, HCl, HI, HNO_3, H_2SO_4, and $HClO_4$

- **Strong Bases**: Group I and group II metal hydroxides, except $Be(OH)_2$ and $Mg(OH)_2$

EXAMPLE: A solution of hydrochloric acid is added to a solution of sodium hydroxide.

SOLUTION: When a strong acid and strong base react, the salt will always be soluble and will not be included in the net ionic equation.

$$H^+ + OH^- \rightarrow H_2O$$

A Strong Acid Neutralizes a Weak Base

A proton from the strong acid combines with the weak base to form the conjugate acid of the weak base. Weak bases include ammonia and organic amines.

EXAMPLE: A solution of hydrochloric acid is added to a solution of ammonia.

SOLUTION: $H^+ + NH_3 \rightarrow NH_4^+$

A Strong Base Reacts with a Weak Acid

A proton from the weak acid combines with the hydroxide ion of the strong base to form the conjugate base of the weak acid and water.

EXAMPLE: Solutions of sodium hydroxide and acetic acid are mixed.

SOLUTION: $CH_3COOH + OH^- \rightarrow CH_3COO^- + H_2O$

TEST TIP

Always separate strong acids and bases into their individual ions when writing net ionic equations. If a weak acid or base is present, *do not* separate them into individual ions.

Lewis Acid–Base Reactions

Watch for Lewis acid–base reactions, in which the Lewis acid accepts a shared pair of electrons from the base, which acts as an electron pair donor. Reactions that form metal complexes are Lewis acid–base reactions.

EXAMPLE: Solutions of boron trifluoride and ammonia are mixed.

SOLUTION: Ammonia acts as the Lewis base and boron trifluoride acts as the Lewis acid.

$$BF_3 + NH_3 \rightarrow BF_3NH_3$$

TEST TIP

Boron-containing compounds will act as Lewis acids.

Amphoterism

A compound that can act as both an acid and a base is said to be **amphoteric.** If the substance is able to both donate and accept a proton (H^+), it is said to be **amphiprotic.**

Metal Complexes

A **metal complex** is a metal that is bonded to a group of ions or surrounding molecules. Metal complexes may or may not have a charge and can often be found in the predicting products section of the test.

EXAMPLE: A solution of silver nitrate is added to excess hydrochloric acid.

SOLUTION: $Ag^+ + 2\,Cl^- \rightarrow AgCl_2^{-1}$

TEST TIP

When you see the term *excess* in the problem, it usually indicates that a metal complex will be produced.

Time for a quiz
- Review strategies in Chapter 2
- Take Quiz 1 at the REA Study Center
  (www.rea.com/studycenter)

Atomic Theory and the Periodic Table

Development of Atomic Theory

Around 400 BCE, the Greek philosopher Democritus theorized that everything is comprised of indivisible particles, or "atomos." For the next 2,200 years, there was no substantive change in how people viewed matter. However, beginning with John Dalton in the early 1800s, atomic theory evolved with sweeping changes. It is important to remember that no one has actually "seen" an atom, so scientists must utilize the data collected from a myriad of experiments to guide their theories.

Dalton

John Dalton was the pioneer of modern atomic theory. Dalton proposed that all matter is composed of subunits called **atoms**, which were essentially solid spheres. There are different types of atoms, called **elements**. Elements combined together in definite whole-number ratios to form **compounds**. Dalton also used his mass experiments as a basis for the idea that atoms are never created or destroyed during chemical reactions—they are merely rearranged to form new compounds.

Thompson

J. J. Thompson performed research with cathode ray tubes where he observed the deflection of particles inside the tube. Thompson concluded that atoms are composed of positive and negatively charged particles. He developed the "plum pudding" model of the atom (see Figure 5.1), where **electrons** were arbitrarily spread throughout an atom that was uniformly composed of positive charges.

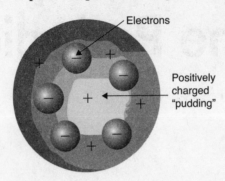

Figure 5.1. Thompson Model of the Atom

Millikan

Robert Millikan performed research on the electron. He is best known for his oil-drop experiment where he calculated the charge of an electron based upon a mass-to-charge ratio.

Rutherford

Ernest Rutherford was a contemporary of J. J. Thompson. Rutherford is known for his gold foil experiment where positively charged alpha particles were fired at a thin sheet of gold foil. Rutherford measured the resulting scatter patterns of the alpha particles after they were fired into the foil. He found that most of the alpha particles moved right through the foil, or were deflected slightly. However, some alpha particles were deflected at large angles, as though they had collided with a heavier, charged object and bounced back. Rutherford concluded that atoms are mostly empty space, but they contain a massive, positively charged center (nucleus). This directly countered Thompson's "plum pudding" model.

Planck

Max Planck determined that electromagnetic energy is quantized, or composed of discrete bundles of energy.

Bohr

Niels Bohr applied the idea of quantized energy to show that electrons exist around the nucleus at a fixed radius. Electrons with higher potential energy exist farther from the nucleus. Bohr's model (see Figure 5.2) eloquently described the absorption and emission of photons by atoms, linking energy changes to electron transitions. However, the Bohr model is only accurate for the one electron system of hydrogen.

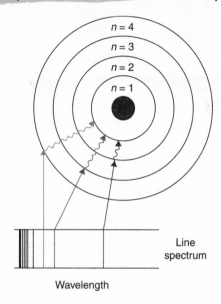

Figure 5.2. Bohr's Model

de Broglie

Louis de Broglie identified the wave characteristics of matter by combining Einstein's relationship between mass and energy ($E = mc^2$) and the relationship between velocity and the wavelength of light ($E = hv$). This means that all particles have a wavelength, though it may be so small that it could never be measured (it also gives new meaning to the phrase "We're on the same wavelength."). The de Broglie equation represents the relationship between the wave and particle nature of the electron.

$$\lambda = \frac{h}{mv}$$

λ = wavelength

h = Planck's constant

m = mass of an electron

v = velocity of an electron

Heisenberg

Werner Heisenberg formulated the uncertainty principle, which stated that it is impossible to simultaneously know both the position and the momentum of an electron. As a result, we need to utilize a wave model rather than a particle model to understand the behavior of electrons.

Schrödinger

Erwin Schrödinger described electrons using a wave model. The wavefunction describes the probability of where an electron might exist. The regions of high probability are called **orbitals**, which is the area in space where an electron is likely to exist. When the solutions to Schrödinger's equation are graphed, this gives rise to the *s*, *p*, *d*, and *f* orbitals used to denote electron configurations described later in this chapter. However, the derivation of the wavefunctions themselves is beyond the scope of an AP Chemistry course.

Atomic Number, Mass Number, Isotopes, and Atomic Mass

Atomic Number

The atomic number (Z) is the number of protons located in the nucleus of an atom. For a neutral atom, the atomic number is also the number of electrons surrounding the nucleus. For example, a carbon atom has an atomic number of 6. Therefore, a neutral atom would have 6 protons in its nucleus and a total of 6 electrons around the nucleus.

Mass Number

The mass of an atom consists of the cumulative mass of all the particles in the atom, which includes protons, neutrons, and electrons. The mass of electrons is insignificant when compared to protons or neutrons. Therefore, the mass number (A) is calculated by summing up the masses of the protons and neutrons found in the nucleus. For example, the following table illustrates the numbers of protons, neutrons, and electrons for a helium atom having a mass number of 4 atomic mass units.

Atom	# Protons	# Neutrons	# Electrons	Mass Number
Helium	2	2	2	4

Isotopes

Atoms that have the same number of protons but differing numbers of neutrons are called **isotopes** (same atomic number but different mass numbers). Isotopes have similar chemical properties and characteristics, but some isotopes have a greater natural abundance than others. The exact percentages of each isotope of an atom can be determined through an analytical technique known as *mass spectrometry*. For example, carbon-12 and carbon-14 are isotopes.

Atom	# Protons	# Neutrons	# Electrons	Mass Number
Carbon-12	6	6	6	12
Carbon-14	6	8	6	14

An isotope's atomic number, mass number, and charge can be depicted using the following element notation.

$$\text{mass number}: A \atop \text{atomic number}: Z} X^{\text{charge}}$$

where X represents any element on the periodic table

Atomic Mass

In nature, elements naturally exist as a combination of the isotopes. The atomic mass of an element is defined as the weighted average of the individual isotopes for that atom. This number is also known as the **molar mass** of the element, or the mass in grams of 1 mole of atoms. On the periodic table, the atomic mass of the element is given in addition to the atomic number. Remember, the atomic mass is used to compute the moles of an atom or molecule.

 **EXAMPLE:**   Naturally occurring lead (Pb) exists as a combination of four isotopes, Pb-204, Pb-206, Pb-207, and Pb-208. Given the natural abundance of each isotope, calculate the average atomic mass of lead.

Pb-204 1.42%   Pb-207 22.10%

Pb-206 24.10%   Pb-208 52.40%

SOLUTION: Multiply the decimal equivalent (percent divided by 100) of each isotope by the mass of each isotope. Take the sum of each isotope's contribution to compute the average atomic mass.

$$(0.0142)(204) + (0.241)(206) + (0.221)(207) + (0.524)(208) = 207 \text{ g/mol}$$

Electrons

Electrons reside in regions outside of the nucleus known as **atomic orbitals**. These atomic orbitals can have a variety of shapes and represent the most probable region where an electron can be located. Electrons found in the outermost shells are known as **valence electrons** while electrons found closer to the nucleus are **core electrons**.

TEST TIP

An understanding of valence electrons and core electrons are essential in describing trends in the periodic table.

Electrons in Atoms

You may be wondering why so much attention is given to electrons. It is because that is where all of the most important chemistry resides! Thus, if you have an understanding of the electrons you will understand how chemistry, and indeed the world, works. There are different ways to model the location of electrons in atoms: electron configurations, orbital notation, and quantum numbers.

Electron Configurations

The electron configuration of an atom assigns the location of electrons with respect to the energy level and type of orbital in which the electron resides. The electron configuration is written with a number corresponding to the energy level (principal quantum number) and a letter (s, p, d, or f) that depicts the sublevel where the electron resides. The sublevels can be broken into groups within the periodic table called **blocks**. This is illustrated Figure 5.3. A superscript is used after the letter to signify the number of electrons in that sublevel.

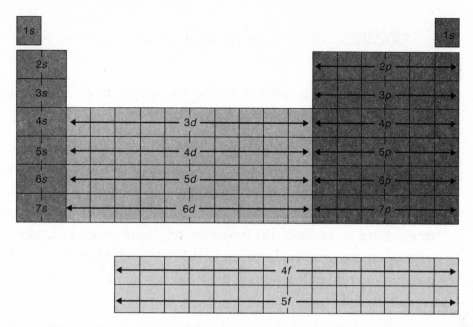

Figure 5.3. Periodic Table Illustrating the Electron Configuration of Atoms

The maximum number of electrons in a sublevel is based upon the type of sublevel as illustrated in the following table and Figure 5.4.

Sublevel	Number of Orbitals in Sublevel	Number of Electrons in Sublevel
s	1	2
p	3	6
d	5	10
f	7	14

Figure 5.4. Sublevels and the Maximum Number of Electrons

It is easiest to write electron configurations utilizing the periodic table. The energy level of the periodic table corresponds to the period (or row) where the atom is located within the table, and the sublevel is determined based on the major *s, p, d,* and *f* blocks seen in the Figure 5.3.

EXAMPLE: Write the electron configuration for fluorine.

SOLUTION: You must show the location of all electrons. Fluorine contains 9 electrons and the configuration is $1s^2 2s^2 2p^5$.

Aufbau Principle

The electrons are distributed in a specific order from lowest energy to highest energy, which is called the **Aufbau principle**. The order in which the electrons fill the atomic orbitals on the periodic table can be likened to how you read a book—left to right, top to bottom. The lowest-energy electrons are located in the first row and increase in energy as you proceed to the right and down the periodic table. Remember that you cannot begin to fill higher-energy sublevels until the previous sublevel is completely full.

Make sure to note that for the d-block elements (transition metals), you must subtract one from the row in which the element resides (the 3d group of elements are located in the 4th period). The f-block consist of the lanthanide and actinide series and you must subtract two from the row in which it resides (the 4f group of elements are located in the 6th period).

Exceptions for Electron Configurations

There are a number of exceptions to the rules in the preceding section, especially with respect to the electron configurations of transition metals.

- In general, half-filled and completely filled orbitals are especially stable. Most exceptions fall into one of these categories.

- A half-filled s and d orbital is lower in energy than an $s^2 d^4$ electron configuration—which will become $s^1 d^5$. This would apply to elements such as Cr and Mo.

- A completely full d-sublevel will be lower in energy than a configuration of $s^2 d^9$—which will simply become $s^1 d^{10}$. This would apply to elements such as Cu and Ag.

Orbital Notation

The orbital notation for an atom is very similar to the electron configuration, except it provides the exact location of the electrons in each orbital. According to the Pauli exclusion principle, an orbital can hold a maximum of 2 electrons, each of which must have opposite spins. These spins can be represented using arrows: An arrow pointing upward represents 1 electron while an arrow pointing downward represents the other electron in an orbital.

EXAMPLE: Write the orbital notation for fluorine.

SOLUTION:

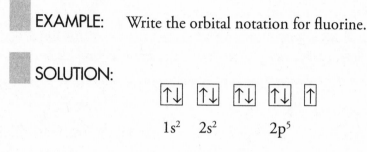

$1s^2$ $2s^2$ $2p^5$

Hund's Rule

Remember that when putting electrons into a sublevel with multiple orbitals, a single electron having the same spin is placed in each orbital first before pairing them with an electron having the opposite spin. This is known as **Hund's rule of multiplicity** and is illustrated with nitrogen's orbital notation where each 2p orbital has only 1 electron of the same spin.

Nitrogen: ⬆⬇ ⬆⬇ ⬆ ⬆ ⬆

$1s^2$ $2s^2$ $2p^3$

Shorthand (Noble Gas/Core) Configurations

Electron configurations for atoms having a large atomic number can become cumbersome. Therefore, a shorthand notation may be utilized. As an example, look at the following electron configuration of chlorine:

Chlorine: $1s^2\ 2s^2\ 2p^6\ 3s^2\ 3p^5$

When writing the shorthand notation, the noble gas that immediately precedes that element is utilized as the core electrons, indicated as a noble gas surrounded by brackets. In this case, the noble gas is neon and you can replace the $1s^2\ 2s^2\ 2p^6$ portion of the configuration with [Ne]. Thus, the shorthand electron configuration would be: [Ne] $3s^2\ 3p^5$.

Quantum Numbers

Quantum numbers are essentially addresses for electrons. Each electron in an atom can be uniquely described with a set of four quantum numbers that are described in the following section. It should be noted that no two electrons can have the same set of four quantum numbers, which is again described by the Pauli exclusion principle.

Principal Quantum Number: n

The **principal quantum number** indicates the energy of the electron, which is the distance the electron is located from the nucleus and the energy shell in which the electron is located. This quantum number is easily determined as it relates to the period (row) on the periodic table where the atom resides. The values for the principal quantum number are integers that range from 1–7. Electrons having higher values of n are located further from the nucleus and have higher potential energy.

Angular Momentum Quantum Number: ℓ

The **angular momentum quantum number** corresponds to the subshell the electron occupies and can have values ranging from 0 to $(n-1)$. The value of ℓ describes the shape of an electron's orbital with the sublevel. Essentially, this number tells you the type of orbital as follows:

- if $\ell = 0$, s-type orbital
- if $\ell = 1$, p-type orbital
- if $\ell = 2$, d-type orbital
- if $\ell = 3$, f-type orbital

Magnetic Quantum Number: m_ℓ

The **magnetic quantum number** represents the orbital position/orientation as well as the number of atomic orbitals in a particular sublevel. The values of m_ℓ are integers that range from $-\ell \ldots 0 \ldots +\ell$ for all possible values of n.

When $\ell = 0$, $m_\ell = 0$ (there is one value, representing one possible s orbital)

When $\ell = 1$, $m_\ell = -1, 0, 1$ (there are three possible p orbitals)

When $\ell = 2$, $m_\ell = -2, -1, 0, 1, 2$ (there are five possible d orbitals)

When $\ell = 3$, $m_\ell = -3, -2, -1, 0, 1, 2, 3$ (there are seven possible f orbitals)

Magnetic Spin Quantum Number: m_s

Each orbital can contain a maximum of 2 electrons having opposite spin. In order to distinguish between the 2 electrons, 1 electron is given a spin value of $+1/2$ while the second electron is given a spin of $-1/2$. The possible values for quantum numbers are given in the following table.

Possible values for quantum numbers

n	ℓ	m_ℓ	m_s
1	0	0	$\pm 1/2$
2	0	0	$\pm 1/2$
2	1	$-1, 0, +1$	$\pm 1/2$
3	0	0	$\pm 1/2$
3	1	$-1, 0, +1$	$\pm 1/2$
3	2	$-2, -1, 0, +1, +2$	$\pm 1/2$

EXAMPLE: List the four quantum numbers for the highest energy electrons of oxygen.

SOLUTION: The electron configuration of oxygen is $1s^2\ 2s^2\ 2p^4$. The $2p^4$ electrons have the highest energy.

n	ℓ	m_ℓ	m_s
2	1	-1	$+1/2$
2	1	0	$+1/2$
2	1	$+1$	$+1/2$
2	1	-1	$-1/2$

Based on Hund's rule of multiplicity, each p orbital gets a single electron before a second electron is added to an already occupied orbital.

TEST TIP

It is important to understand how quantum numbers, electron configurations, and the periodic table are interrelated, because this is a core component of many explanations you may be required to give.

Paramagnetism and Diamagnetism

Diamagnetic elements have paired electrons in every orbital. These elements are not affected by an external magnetic field. In contrast, **paramagnetic** elements have an unpaired electron in at least one atomic orbital. The unpaired electron creates a magnetic field within the atom that responds to an external magnetic field. Although oxygen molecules are commonly drawn with a double bond, experimental evidence indicates that oxygen is paramagnetic—thus giving rise to the theory that oxygen is actual a di-radical compound.

Electrons and Energy

Each electron within an atom is attracted to the positively charged nucleus. As the electrons move further away from the nucleus, the potential energy associated with this attraction increases according to Coulomb's law. The electrons can only exist at certain energy levels and thus are quantized. For example, think of electrons as steps on a staircase. Electrons cannot exist halfway between steps but only at specific intervals, each with a specific energy. For the hydrogen atom, the energy of a shell can be computed using the equation:

$$E_n = \frac{-2.178 \times 10^{-18} \; Joule}{n^2}$$

Electrons will usually exist in the lowest possible energy states, known as the *ground state*. An electron can be promoted to an excited state by adding either heat or electromagnetic radiation. The amount of radiation needed to excite the electron is directly related to the differences between energy levels in the atom. Following excitation, electrons will fall back to their ground state and in the process release a specific amount of energy referred to as a **quantum**. Following is the relationship between the amount of energy either absorbed or emitted between energy levels.

$$c = \lambda v \text{ and } E = hv$$

c = speed of light (3.0×10^8 m s^{-1})

λ = wavelength of the electromagnetic radiation

v = frequency of the electromagnetic radiation

h = Planck's constant (6.63×10^{-34} J s)

E = energy

Because the energy levels are specific to a single atom, the wavelength of electromagnetic radiation needed to excite an electron (absorption spectra) or emitted from an atom in its excited state as it falls back to its ground state (emission spectrum) is unique. These spectra can be used to identify elements—and is the reason that early scientists knew that the sun contained hydrogen and helium.

DIDYOUKNOW?

Most of us enjoy fireworks with their bright and colorful displays. The colors that you see are directly related to electrons giving off energy as they fall from an excited energy state to their ground state. Different colors correspond to different atoms.

EXAMPLE: What are the frequency and the energy of electromagnetic radiation having a wavelength of 500 nm?

SOLUTION:

Frequency:

3.0×10^8 m/s $= (5.00 \times 10^{-7}$ m$)(v)$

$v = 6.0 \times 10^{14}$ s^{-1}

Energy:

$E = (6.63 \times 10^{-34}$ J s $)(6.00 \times 10^{14}$ s$^{-1})$

$E = 3.9 \times 10^{-19}$ J

Relationships in the Periodic Table

Atomic Radii

The atomic radii of atoms increase when moving from right to left across the periodic table. The atomic radius also increases as you move down the periodic table. Cations have smaller radii than their corresponding neutral atoms. This is due to a greater effective nuclear charge (greater number of protons in the nucleus compared to electrons) and thus the positively charged nucleus pulls the valence electrons closer. Anions have larger radii than their corresponding neutral atoms. This can be attributed to the addition of valence electrons and their repulsion, thus increasing the atomic radius.

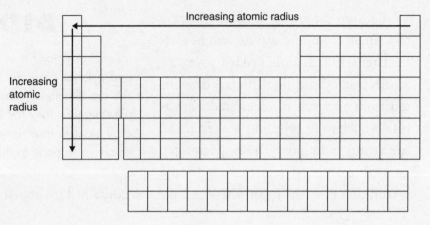

Figure 5.5.

TEST TIP

For the AP Chemistry exam, be able to describe why the trends in the atomic radius exist.

Ionization Energy

The ionization energy is the energy required to remove an electron from an atom, resulting in the formation of a cation. The ionization energy decreases when moving from right to left across the periodic table. It also decreases when moving down a group within the periodic table. It should be noted that more than 1 electron may be removed to form ions of greater charge, but the energy required to remove successive electrons will increase exponentially. Cations that have electron configurations containing filled octets are extremely stable and require an enormous amount of energy to remove an electron.

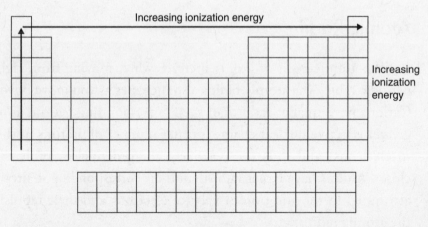

Figure 5.6.

Electron Affinity

Electron affinity is the ability of an atom to gain electrons in order to form anions. Nonmetal atoms have a much higher electron affinity, because metals will not form anions. The electron affinity increases moving from left to right across the periodic table (see Figure 5.7). It also increases when moving up a group within the periodic table.

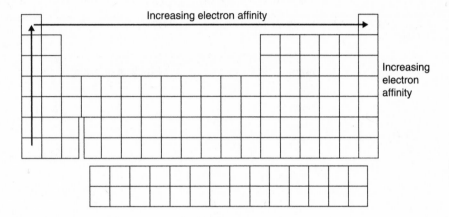

Figure 5.7.

TEST TIP

An explanation of most of these trends on the periodic table can be linked to the concept of the atomic radius.

Electronegativity

Electronegativity is the ability of an atom to attract electron density to it when forming a covalent bond. The electronegativity of an atom exhibits the same trend as electron affinity in the periodic table. You should know the values from Pauling's scale of electronegativity for all nonmetallic atoms. This will enable you to determine if the covalent bond is polar or if a molecule is polar. The chart below shows the electronegativity values for the most common nonmetals.

Atom	Electronegativity
Fluorine	4.0
Oxygen	3.5
Nitrogen	3.0
Chlorine	3.0
Bromine	2.8
Carbon	2.5
Sulfur	2.5
Iodine	2.5
Phosphorus	2.1
Hydrogen	2.1

Chemical Bonding

Intramolecular Forces: Bonds Between Atoms

Bonds are the forces of attraction that hold atoms together. There are many types of bonding including ionic, metallic, and covalent bonds. You can figure out the difference between the bonding types if you look at what role the **valence electrons** are playing in the chemical bond—because bonding is all about the valence electrons. Many of the electrons in an atom have no impact on bonding because they are located close to the nucleus, and thus are called **core electrons**. In general, the valence electrons are the outermost s-shell and p-shell electrons in an electron configuration. For transition metals, the outermost d-shell electrons will also play a role. Elements will typically form bonds in order to have eight electrons in the valence shell, which is called the **octet rule**. The vast majority of chemical bonds that occur obey the octet rule, although a significant number of exceptions to the octet rule exist, which will be covered later in this chapter.

Ionic Bonds

- **Ionic bonding** is a bond between a cation and an anion held together by electrostatic attractions. Coulomb's law dictates that oppositely charged particles are attracted to one another, and this is the fundamental principle behind ionic bonding.

- In an ionic bond, an electron is removed from the least electronegative atom to form a positively charged ion (cation). This electron is then transferred to a more electronegative atom to form a negatively charged ion (anion).

$$Na\cdot + \ddot{:}\overset{..}{\underset{..}{Cl}}: \longrightarrow [Na]^+ \ [:\overset{..}{\underset{..}{Cl}}:]^-$$

- Ionic bonds form in order to fulfill the octet rule for the elements involved with the bond. The metal loses electrons to have a filled shell. The nonmetal gains electrons to have a filled shell.

- Ionic bonds usually occur between a metal and a nonmetal that have a difference in electronegativity greater than or equal to 1.7. This number is only given as a reference point, because experimental data indicates that there are compounds with a greater difference that seem to have covalent bonding, and compounds with a smaller difference that demonstrate properties of ionic bonds.

- The strength of attraction in an ionic bond is directly proportional to the charges and inversely proportional to the square of the distance between the two charges (Coulomb's law). Thus, a compound composed of a cation with a +2 charge attracted to an anion with a −2 charge would have a stronger attraction than a compound formed with +1 and −1 charges. The size of the ions will also play a role in the attraction because the distance of separation will change depending on the ionic radius.

- Although it may seem straightforward and simple, ionic bonds are the strongest bonds that are observed in the chemical realm.

Covalent Bonds

- In **covalent bonds**, electrons are shared between two atoms to simultaneously fulfill the octets for both atoms.

- A covalent bond will typically occur between nonmetal elements that have a difference in electronegativity between 0 and 1.7.

- Single bonds occur when two electrons are shared between two atoms—each atom donating one of its electrons to form the bond. The covalent bond occurs when the orbitals of the two elements overlap with one another along the same axis, which is called a **sigma bond** (σ).

$$\text{H–H}$$

- Double bonds involve the sharing of four electrons between two atoms. The first covalent bond between the elements is a sigma bond. However, the second bond that is made is a **pi bond** (π), which involves the overlap of unhybridized p-orbitals.

$$\ddot{\text{O}}=\ddot{\text{O}}$$

- Triple bonds share six electrons between two atoms and occur in a similar fashion as double bonds. The first bond is a sigma bond, and the remaining two bonds are pi bonds.

$$:N \equiv N:$$

- **Nonpolar covalent bonds** occur when there is a small, almost negligible difference in the **electronegativity** values between two elements. If the difference is less than or equal to 0.4, the electrons being shared in the bond are being shared equally (for the most part).

$$:\ddot{F} - \ddot{F}:$$

$$\begin{array}{c} H \\ | \\ H \diagup \overset{|}{C} \diagdown H \\ | \\ H \end{array}$$

- **Polar covalent bonds** are formed when the electronegativity difference between the elements in a bond are between 0.4 and 1.7. A polar covalent bond has weakly ionic properties or partial charges. The partial charges are represented by the lower-case Greek symbol delta (δ). The element that has the greater electronegativity will be slightly negative (δ^-) and the other element will be slightly positive (δ^+).

$$\overset{\delta^+ \quad \delta^-}{H - \ddot{C}l:}$$

- **Dipoles** are molecules that contain polar covalent bonds that are not completely canceled out by other polar bonds. The polar bonds add together like vectors to create a total dipole moment on the molecule, which results in the molecule having separate centers of positive and negative charge.

$$\begin{array}{c} \delta^- \\ :O: \\ \diagup \quad \diagdown \\ \delta H_+ \quad\quad H_+\delta \end{array}$$

Network Covalent Bonding

- Network covalent crystals are groups of nonmetal atoms held together by covalent bonds.

- The bonding in a network covalent solid is extensive, and repeats throughout the crystalline structure.

- Network covalent crystals tend to have very high melting and boiling points, and a large amount of energy is needed to break apart the crystal.

- The most common example of a network covalent solid is a diamond, which is a network covalent crystal of sp^3 hybridized carbon atoms bonding to one another over and over again. (See Figure 6.1.)

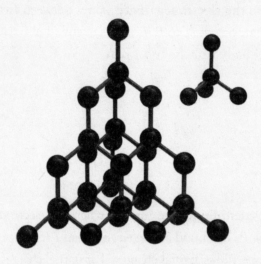

iStockphoto/Thinkstock

Figure 6.1. Structure of a Diamond

TEST TIP

Network covalent solids are usually the same type of atom bonded over and over again. Look for chemical formulas such as S_8 or C_{60} or common names such as diamond or graphite.

Metallic Bonds

- Metals compose the majority of elements on the periodic table, and all elements to the left of the metalloids on the periodic table (except hydrogen) are metals.

- Metallic bonding can be thought of as cations surrounded by a sea of electrons. The metal atoms share their valence electrons in this electron sea and they move freely between the outer energy levels of the different atoms.

DID YOU KNOW?

Graphite conducts electricity because the sp^2 hybridized orbitals allow for one double bond per carbon atom. This double bond is delocalized and moves freely throughout the structure, thus conducting electricity. In addition, the planar sheets of graphite move easily past one another, which makes it a good lubricant.

- The valence electrons of metals are delocalized, which means that they are not held to a particular location and are shared between multiple atoms/bonds.

- Delocalized electrons give metals many of their physical properties such as luster, electrical conductivity, and thermal conductivity because they are easy to promote to an excited state and are relatively mobile.

- Metals are malleable (can be hammered into a sheet) and ductile (can be drawn into wire).

Continuum of Bonding

Bonding is rarely straightforward and should be thought of as a continuum rather than definitive types. This is especially true for covalent bonds, which many times demonstrate properties and characteristics similar to ionic bonds. By holding this type of mindset, you will not get nearly as frustrated by the anomalies that occur with bonding, such as with compounds like H-F that have a difference in electronegativity greater than 1.7, but are best considered covalent compounds.

Lewis Structures

Lewis structures are diagrams that show how the atoms in a molecule are connected together. Bonds are symbolized using sticks/lines that represent the two electrons shared between the two atoms. Here are some steps for drawing Lewis structures:

1. Count up the number of valence electrons that are in the molecule or ion.

   - The number of valence electrons for each element corresponds to the major group number on the periodic table (for example, carbon is in Group IV so it has four electrons).

   - For a neutral molecule, you just add up the electrons.

   - If there is an anion, you must add the electrons for each element and then add on the negative charge (for example, NO_3^{-1} has $23 + 1 = 24$ valence electrons).

   - For cations, you must subtract the charge from the total number of electrons (for example, NH_4^{+1} has $9 - 1 = 8$ valence electrons).

2. Choose a central atom to bond with the other elements.

    *   This is usually the atom with the lowest electron affinity.

    *   Halogens are usually terminal atoms for neutral molecules, which mean that they only make one bond.

3. Draw a preliminary or skeleton structure that connects the atoms together with single bonds.

    *   Each line represents two electrons shared between the elements.

    *   Count up how many electrons are being used for these bonds and subtract this from the total number of valence electrons available for bonding.

4. Place the remaining electrons around the other to fulfill the octet rule.

    *   Hydrogen only needs two electrons (duet rule).

    *   The Lewis structure may have no more and no less electrons than the total number of valence electrons.

5. If there is an issue with the number of electrons:

    *   Double and/or triple bonds allow you to provide two atoms with an octet in an efficient manner. If there does not seem to be enough electrons available to provide each element with an octet, make multiple bonds.

    *   Extra pairs of electrons can be placed on the central atom if the element resides in Period 3 or below on the periodic table.

EXAMPLE: Draw the Lewis structure for the nitrate ion.

SOLUTION: See the following steps for the explanation.

Step 1: NO_3^{-1}

$5 + 3(6) + 1 = 24$ valence electrons

Step 2:   Nitrogen is the central atom.

Step 3: A total of six electrons are being used in this structure, leaving 18 electrons to fulfill the octets of the remaining elements.

Step 4: The 18 electrons are placed around the oxygen atoms to fulfill their octets, although the nitrogen does not have eight electrons surrounding it.

Step 5: One of the lone pairs on the oxygen atom was shifted to form a double bond between nitrogen and oxygen, thus fulfilling the octets of both elements without adding any additional electrons. Remember, you can have no more and no less electrons in your Lewis structure than the total number of valence electrons.

Resonance

Resonance structures are alternative Lewis structures that result from the shifting of electrons in a structure. Resonance is an attempt to model how electrons can be delocalized. Resonance is not merely a rotation of the molecule, but rather the actual movement of electrons. For example, the nitrate ion would have three resonance structures as seen in the following diagram:

Although there are two single bonds and one double bond in all three resonance structures, experimental evidence indicates that all of the nitrogen–oxygen bonds are equivalent and have bond strength and length between single and double bonds.

Exceptions to the Octet Rule

Atoms form covalent bonds in order to complete their valence shells. For most atoms, this will require a total of eight valence electrons. However, there are some atoms that defy the octet rule with fewer or a greater number of electrons, termed **reduced octets** and **expanded octets**. Table 6.1 shows some common exceptions to the octet rule.

Table 6.1.   Common Exceptions to the Octet Rule

Reduced Octet		Expanded Octet	
Element	# of electrons	Element	# of electrons
H	2	P	10
Be	4	S	12
B	6	Cl	10, 12
		Xe	10, 12

TEST TIP

Reduced octets only occur for elements in the first two periods of the periodic table, whereas expanded octets can only occur for elements in Period 3 or below due to the presence of empty d-orbitals.

Formal Charge and Electroneutrality

Despite hard work and persistence, some Lewis structures may not seem to make sense to you. Atoms like nitrogen make four bonds instead of three, as in the case with the nitrate ion; and chlorine, which usually makes one bond, will bond with fluorine to form ClF_5 with five bonds and a lone pair on the central atom. How and why does this occur? Formal charge and electroneutrality is the answer to most of the questions that arise with Lewis structures. **Formal charge** is a calculation of the charge on a given atom in a structure based on the number of valence electrons it normally has compared to how many are incorporated in the Lewis structure. The following equation can be used to calculate the formal charge on an atom:

$$formal\ charge = group\ \# - \left[lone\ pair\ electrons + \frac{1}{2}\ bonding\ electrons \right]$$

As you can see, once you know how to calculate the formal charge on all of the atoms in a Lewis structure, you can figure out where the negative charge resides on an ion such as nitrate and also ascertain why nitrogen is making four bonds in that structure. More importantly though, you can use the concept of electroneutrality to determine what is the best, and thereby most probable, Lewis structure. There are a few keys to electroneutrality:

1. The electrons in a molecule are distributed so that formal charge is minimal.

2. The most probable Lewis structure is the one with the minimal formal charge.

3. Negative formal charge should reside on the most electronegative element.

4. A formal charge greater than $+2$ and less than -2 is not likely for most molecules.

EXAMPLE: Determine the most probable Lewis structure for OCN^{-1}.

SOLUTION: Using the concept of resonance, there are three possible structures for OCN^{-1}.

$$:O{\equiv}C{-}\ddot{N}: \longleftrightarrow \ddot{O}{=}C{=}\ddot{N} \longleftrightarrow :\ddot{O}{-}C{\equiv}N:$$

The formal charge should be calculated for each element in all of the resonance structures.

$$\overset{+1\ \ \ 0\ \ -2}{:O{\equiv}C{-}\ddot{N}:} \longleftrightarrow \overset{0\ \ \ 0\ \ -1}{\ddot{O}{=}C{=}\ddot{N}} \longleftrightarrow \overset{-1\ \ \ 0\ \ \ 0}{:\ddot{O}{-}C{\equiv}N:}$$

The third Lewis structure is the most probable one because it minimizes formal charge and places the negative charge on the most electronegative element: oxygen.

$$\overset{-1\ \ \ 0\ \ \ 0}{:\ddot{O}{-}C{\equiv}N:}$$

TEST TIP

Use the concept of formal charge to determine where the unpaired electrons are placed in free radical compounds.

Hybridization, VSEPR, and Bond Geometry

- **Hybridization** refers to the process by which atomic orbitals are combined together to create new, hybrid orbitals to undergo bonding.

- Without hybridization, bonds would only occur at 90° and 180° bond angles—which experimental evidence refutes.

- The hybridization model also helps explain the difference in bond strength between sigma and pi bonds and correctly predicts the geometry of molecules.

- **VSEPR theory**, or *valence shell electron-pair repulsion theory*, dictates that electron pairs will repel each other, thus creating a molecular geometry. The key to VSEPR theory is to situate the electron pairs as far away as possible from one another.

- Lone pair electrons cause more repulsion than bonding pairs in the VSEPR model, and thus occupy more space in the resulting geometry.

- The notation used to describe the various geometries is called *A-X-E notation*, where *A* is the central atom, *X* is terminal atoms, and *E* is the lone pair electrons on the central atom. The A-X-E notation will depend on how many atoms are bonded and how many long pair electrons are on the central atom. Table 6.2 shows the various geometries, hybridization, bond angles, and corresponding A-X-E notation.

Table 6.2. Summary: Hybridization and Geometry

Bonds	# Lone Pairs	A-X-E Notation	Geometry	Hybridization	Bond Angle(s)	Example
2	0	AX_2	Linear	sp	180°	BeF_2 :F̈—Be—F̈:
3	0	AX_3	Trigonal planar	sp^2	120°	BF_3
2	1	AX_2E_1	Bent	sp^2	<120°	SO_2
4	0	AX_4	Tetrahedral	sp^3	109.5°	CH_4

(continued)

Table 6.2. (*continued*)

Bonds	# Lone Pairs	A-X-E Notation	Geometry	Hybridization	Bond Angle(s)	Example
3	1	AX_3E_1	Pyramidal	sp^3	90° to <109.5°	NH_3
2	2	AX_2E_2	Bent	sp^3	90° to <109.5°	H_2O
5	0	AX_5	Trigonal bipyramidal	sp^3d	90°, 120°, 180°	PCl_5
4	1	AX_4E_1	See-saw	sp^3d	90°, <120°, 180°	SF_4
3	2	AX_3E_2	T-shaped	sp^3d	90°, 180°	ClF_3
2	3	AX_2E_3	Linear	sp^3d	180°	XeF_2
6	0	AX_6	Octahedral	sp^3d^2	90°, 180°	SF_6
5	1	AX_5E_1	Square pyramidal	sp^3d^2	90°, 180°	IF_5
4	2	AX_4E_2	Square planar	sp^3d^2	90°, 180°	XeF_4

TEST TIP

You should know the names, bond angles, hybridization, and how to draw all of these geometries for the AP Chemistry exam.

Isomers

- Isomers are molecules that have the same chemical formula, but different Lewis structures.

- To form an isomer, there needs to be a different physical arrangement of the atoms. Rotations or flips of the molecular structures are not isomers; the atoms must be connected together in new ways.

- Isomers will have different physical and chemical properties, which will depend on how the atoms are arranged and the resulting intermolecular forces that exist.

EXAMPLE: Draw all of the isomers for C_3H_8O.

SOLUTION: There are three different Lewis structures that have the formula C_3H_8O: n-propanol, isopropyl alcohol, and ethyl-methyl ether.

```
  H   H   H          H   H   H          H       H   H
  |   |   |          |   |   |          |       |   |
H-C - C - C - OH   H - C - C - C - H   H - C - O - C - C - H
  |   |   |          |   |   |          |       |   |
  H   H   H          H   OH  H          H       H   H
```

Intermolecular Forces: Attractions Between Molecules

The bonds that hold atoms together such as covalent and ionic bonds are classified as intramolecular forces—the strongest types of forces that are observed. However, there are also attractions that occur between molecules, which are called **intermolecular forces**. Although the force of attraction is significantly weaker, intermolecular forces play a large role in determining the properties of molecules. There are three types of intermolecular forces: van der Waals/dispersion, dipole–dipole, and hydrogen bonds. See Figure 6.2.

STRONGEST FORCES OF ATTRACTION

Intramolecular forces
{
Ionic bonds
Metallic bonds
Network covalent
Covalent

Intermolecular forces
{
Hydrogen bonding
Dipole – dipole
van der Waals (London Dispersion)

WEAKEST FORCES OF ATTRACTION

Figure 6.2. Summary of Strength of Attraction

van der Waals Forces

- van der Waals forces are also called *London dispersion* or simply *dispersion forces*.

- Van der Waals forces are caused by the formation of an instantaneous dipole that induces and is attracted to neighboring dipoles.

- The strength of van der Waals forces is proportional to the number of electrons in the molecule.

- van der Waals forces are generally the weakest of all of the intermolecular forces, and only become apparent if there are many electrons or if the molecules come very close together.

- van der Waals forces occur in all molecules but are more pronounced in non-polar molecules.

Dipole–Dipole Forces

- **Dipole–dipole** forces result from the attraction between permanent dipoles (polar molecules).

- The partially charged ends of polar molecules line up so that the electrostatic attractions are maximized and repulsions are minimized.

- Dipole–dipole attractions are generally much stronger than van der Waals forces.

- Dipole–dipole forces induce dispersion forces, enhancing those intermolecular attractions.

Hydrogen Bonding

- **Hydrogen bonding** occurs when a hydrogen atom is covalently bonded to either a fluorine, oxygen, or nitrogen (FON) atom and is simultaneously attracted to a neighboring nonmetal atom.

- Hydrogen bonding is an extreme case of a dipole–dipole intermolecular force.

- Hydrogen bonding is the strongest of all the intermolecular forces.

- This explains the many unusual properties of water such as why ice floats, why snowflakes have six sides, and why a meniscus is formed in a graduated cylinder filled with water.

Structure and Physical Properties

- **Physical properties are related to the forces between atoms and molecules.** Stronger attractions mean that there is more resistance to change phase. Hardness, melting point, and boiling point are all measures of the strength of the intramolecular and intermolecular forces holding the substance together. Stronger attractions also result in lower vapor pressures.

- **Ionic crystals** have the strongest attractions that are observed. Despite the simplicity of the electrostatic attraction between cations and anions, they constitute the strongest of all of the forces holding atoms together. They tend to have high melting and boiling points, and are poor conductors in the solid phase (because the electrons are in fixed positions). However, when ionic crystals are in the aqueous phase, they are good conductors because the cations and anions that comprise the crystal are mobile.

- **Metallic bonds** are also quite simplistic, but nonetheless extremely strong. This gives rise to the fact that almost all metals are solids at room temperature. When metals are mixed to form **alloys**, the physical properties are different from the metals that comprise the mixture and depend on the percent composition of the elements in the mixture. Steel is a good example of an alloy.

- **Network covalent crystals** have extremely strong attractive forces holding them together. They have high melting and boiling points. Substances such as diamond and graphite should come to mind.

- **Polar molecules** have intermolecular attractions that are weaker than ionic, metallic, and network covalent forces, but are much stronger than nonpolar molecules. The melting and boiling points of polar compounds depend on the strength of the dipole moment of the two compounds. The larger dipole moment, the greater the intermolecular attraction and the higher the melting and boiling points. Molecules that exhibit hydrogen bonding will also gain an attraction edge over those that merely have dipole–dipole attractions.

- **Nonpolar molecules** only have the weakest of intermolecular forces to rely upon for attraction: van der Waals interactions. Consequently, these compounds are typically soft crystals, liquids, or gases, are easily deformed, and vaporize easily. They have much lower melting and boiling points than polar compounds of similar molar mass. Nonpolar molecules are poor conductors and tend to be more volatile because of their high vapor pressures.

DIDYOUKNOW?

A thin stream of water can be bent if a static charge is brought nearby, which proves that water molecules are polar. This is an experiment you can do at home to prove to yourself (and others) that VSEPR theory predicts the correct molecular geometry for water. Blow up a balloon and rub it on your hair to build up a charge. Then bring the balloon near an extremely thin stream of water at the sink. The stream of water will bend toward the balloon—proving that water has a polar, bent structure as opposed to a nonpolar, linear structure.

TEST TIP

Properties of molecules are dictated by structure. Therefore, if there are any questions on the AP Chemistry exam that discuss properties, you should give careful thought and consideration to the intramolecular and intermolecular forces that give rise to those properties.

Time for a quiz
- Review strategies in Chapter 2
- Take Quiz 2 at the REA Study Center

(www.rea.com/studycenter)

Gases

Pressure

Pressure is defined by the force a gas exerts on a given surface area. Atmospheric pressure is caused by the weight of all of the molecules in the atmosphere and is typically measured by using a mercury barometer. There are a number of different units for measuring the pressure for a gas which includes the SI unit, the **pascal** (Pa). The more commonly used units that are utilized for calculations and measurement of pressure are the **atmosphere** (atm), **mmHg**, and the **torr**. You should be able to convert between each unit.

$$\textbf{1 atm} = \textbf{760 mmHg} = \textbf{760 torr} = \textbf{101.3 kPa}$$

Enclosed gas pressures can be measured using an open-ended manometer as seen in Figure 7.1. The pressure of the gas is measured by measuring the difference between the height of mercury, as illustrated.

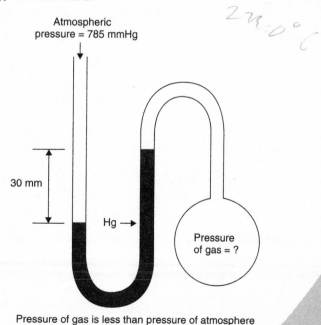

Atmospheric pressure = 785 mmHg

30 mm

Hg →

Pressure of gas = ?

Pressure of gas is less than pressure of atmosphere
(level is 30 mm higher on the side connected to gas)

P-gas =785 mmHg - 30 mmHg = 755 mmHg

Figure 7.1. Measuring Pressures with a Manometer

Standard Temperature and Pressure (STP)

When working with gases, chemists use a set of standard measurements called STP (**standard temperature and pressure**) to make comparisons with their measurements.

At STP:

- Temperature (T) = 0°C or 273 Kelvin

- Pressure (P) = 1 atmosphere or 760 mmHg

- 1 mole of any gas = 22.4 L at STP

Gas Laws

Gases exhibit properties that are easily measured and manipulated by chemists: temperature, pressure, volume, and amounts (moles). Before early scientists had definitive proof about the chemical makeup of gases they were able to discover fundamental relationships or gas laws. There are five basic gas laws: Boyle's law, Charles' law, Gay-Lussac's law, combined gas law, and the ideal gas law.

Boyle's Law

Boyle's law states that pressure and volume are inversely related when the temperature and number of moles are kept constant.

$$P_1V_1 = P_2V_2$$

EXAMPLE: A 4.0-L elastic weather balloon travels from sea level, at 1.0 atm pressure, to a higher altitude, where the pressure is 0.20 atm. What is the new volume of the balloon?

SOLUTION: $P_1 = 1.0$ atm $\qquad P_2 = 0.20$ atm

$V_1 = 4.0$ L $\qquad V_2 = ?$

$$(1.0 \text{ atm})(4.0 \text{ L}) = (0.20 \text{ atm}) V_2$$

$$V_2 = 20. \text{ L } \textbf{(Watch sig figs!)}$$

Charles' Law

Charles' law states that volume is directly related to the absolute temperature (Kelvin) when the pressure and moles are kept constant.

$$\frac{V_1}{T_1} = \frac{V_2}{T_2}$$

$PV = nRT$

> ### DIDYOUKNOW?
> Cake mixes include high-altitude baking instructions to account for the lower pressures experienced at high altitudes. Otherwise, the cake would rise *too* much in the oven, which would inhibit the structural integrity of the cake when it cools—and it would become flat as a pancake!

TEST TIP

Make sure for all gas law calculations that the temperature is in Kelvin. This is a common and costly mistake.

EXAMPLE: A gas occupies 2.0 L at 27°C. What is the volume of the gas at −73°C, assuming that the pressure is held constant?

SOLUTION: $T_1 = 27°C + 273 = 300. \text{ K}$ $T_2 = −73°C + 273 = 200. \text{ K}$

$V_1 = 2.0 \text{ L}$ $V_2 = ?$

$$\frac{(2.0\ L)}{300.K} = \frac{V_2}{200.K}$$

$$V_2 = 1.3 \text{ L}$$

Gay-Lussac's Law

Gay-Lussac's law states that pressure is directly related to the absolute temperature (Kelvin) when the volume and moles are kept constant.

$$\frac{P_1}{T_1} = \frac{P_2}{T_2}$$

■ **EXAMPLE:** A gas in a rigid container exerts 6.0 atm at 300. K. What is the pressure that the gas exerts at 500. K?

■ **SOLUTION:**

T_1 = 300. K T_2 = 500. K

P_1 = 6.0 atm P_2 = ?

$$\frac{(6.0 \ atm)}{300.K} = \frac{P_2}{500.K}$$

V_2 = 10. atm

Combined Gas Law

The combined gas law unifies all the variables in Boyle's, Charles', and Gay-Lussac's laws into one equation. This equation is used when comparing two different conditions of a gas. The equation is:

$$\frac{P_1 V_1}{T_1} = \frac{P_2 V_2}{T_2}$$

In this equation, V is the volume, P is the pressure, and T is the absolute temperature of the gas for two different conditions represented by the two sets of subscripts. In solving these types of gas law problems, it is helpful to initially list the variables and then substitute into the combined gas law equation.

■ **EXAMPLE:** A sample of neon gas was collected at 35.0°C in a 25.0-mL container with a pressure of 1.80 atmospheres. What would be the final pressure of the gas if the temperature was raised to 50.0°C and the volume of the container was doubled?

■ **SOLUTION:**

P_1 = 1.80 atm P_2 = ?

V_1 = 25.0 mL V_2 = 50.0 mL

T_1 = 35.0°C + 273 = 308 K T_2 = 50.0°C + 273 = 323 K

$$\frac{(1.80 \ atm)(25.0 \ mL)}{308 \ K} = \frac{P_2(50.0 \ mL)}{323 \ K}$$

P_2 = 0.944 atm

Dalton's Law of Partial Pressures

Dalton's law of partial pressures states that if there is more than one gas in a container, the individual pressures of each of those gases will add up to give the total pressure inside the container.

$$P_{Total} = P_1 + P_2 + P_3 + etc. \ldots$$

EXAMPLE: What is the total pressure inside a container that contains He at a pressure of 0.45 atm and Ar at a pressure of 0.75 atm?

SOLUTION: $P_{Total} = P_{He} + P_{Ar}$

$$P_{Total} = 0.45 \text{ atm} + 0.75 \text{ atm} = 1.20 \text{ atm}$$

The partial pressure of an individual gas in a sample of many gases can be determined from the total pressure of the gases in a container. This is accomplished using the mole fraction of the gas and multiplying it by the total pressure.

$$P_A = P_{Total} \times X_A, \text{ where } X_A = \frac{moles\ A}{total\ moles}$$

Ideal Gas Law

The ideal gas law enables chemists to calculate either the pressure, volume, temperature, or number of moles of a gas for a given set of conditions. All gases follow the ideal gas law under all conditions except instances of high pressure or low temperature where intermolecular forces and gas volume discrepancies arise. The ideal gas law constant, R, represents the value that links together pressure (atm), volume (L), temperature (K), and moles of any gas and has a value of 0.0821 L atm mol^{-1} K^{-1} when completing any problems dealing with gases.

$$PV = nRT$$

In this equation, P is the pressure of the gas, V is the volume of the gas, n is the number of moles of gas, and T represents the temperature of the gas in Kelvin. Remember to include the units with all quantities in these types of problems.

TEST TIP

Use the correct value of R based on the equation and units you are trying to cancel out. If it is a pressure-based calculation, use 0.0821 L atm mol^{-1} K^{-1}. If the calculation involves energy, use 8.31 J mol^{-1} K^{-1}.

EXAMPLE: What would be the number of moles of chlorine gas present if the gas fills a 75.0-mL flask having a pressure of 755 mmHg and a temperature of 100.0°C?

SOLUTION: $P = \dfrac{755 \, mmHg}{760 \, mmHg} = 0.993$ atm   T = 100.0°C + 273 = 373 K

V = 0.0750 L $R = 0.0821 \dfrac{L \, atm}{mol \, K}$

$(0.993 \text{ atm}) (0.0750 \text{ L}) = n \left(0.0821 \dfrac{L \, atm}{mol \, K} \right) (373 \text{ K})$

n = 0.00243 moles

Often, the ideal gas law is used to calculate the molar mass of an unknown gas:

$$PV = \frac{m}{M} RT$$

In this equation, m is the mass of the gas and M is the molar mass of the gas.

EXAMPLE: A sample of propane gas having a mass of 10.7 g is placed in a 2.0-L container. The pressure and temperature were measured to be 3.0 atm and 300. K, respectively. What is the molar mass of propane?

SOLUTION: P = 3.0 atm   T = 300. K   m = 10.7 g

V = 2.0 L $R = 0.0821 \dfrac{L \, atm}{mol \, K}$

$(3.0 \, atm) (2.0 \, L) = \dfrac{10.7 \, g}{MM} \left(0.0821 \dfrac{L \, atm}{mol \, K} \right) (300.K)$

M = 44 g/mol

TEST TIP

It is easy to combine gas law questions that involve molar mass calculations with other types of problems such as empirical formulas.

The ideal gas law is often used to calculate the density of a gas. Due to the low density of gases, the density is calculated in g/L rather than g/mL.

$$D = \frac{m}{V} = \frac{P(M)}{RT}$$

EXAMPLE: What is the density of propane gas (C_3H_8) if the pressure of the gas was measured to be 3.5 atm at 285 K?

SOLUTION: P = 3.5 atm   T = 285. K

M = 44.0 g/mol $R = 0.0821 \dfrac{L\,atm}{mol\,K}$

$$D = \frac{(3.5\ atm)(44.0\ g/mol)}{\left(0.0821\ \dfrac{L\ atm}{mol\ K}\right)(285\ K)}$$

D = 6.6 g/L

TEST TIP

Multiple-choice questions will often utilize STP in stoichiometry types of questions. Remember that under STP conditions, 1 mole of any gas occupies 22.4 L.

Kinetic Molecular Theory

Kinetic molecular theory describes the motion of molecules, which consist of translational, vibrational, and rotational motion for molecules in the gas phase. It is essential to understand the following ideas:

- Gases are mostly empty space with the distance between the particles being much larger than the particles themselves.

- Gases are in constant, rapid, random, straight-line motion.

- The molecules collide with one another in perfectly elastic collisions (no net loss in energy).

- The average kinetic energy of all the molecules of gas is directly proportional to the absolute temperature of the gas.

- All molecules of a gas at the same temperature have the same kinetic energy.

The kinetic energy of a single molecule is defined through the equation KE = ½ mv^2, where m is the mass of a molecule (kg) and v is velocity (m/s). In any sample of gas, different molecules will have different velocities. However, the average kinetic energy of a sample of gas molecules depends on the Kelvin temperature; higher temperatures will result in higher average kinetic energies. The relationship between mass, average speed, and temperature is defined by Maxwell's equation:

$$u_{rms} = \sqrt{\frac{3RT}{M}}$$

Realize that there are no pressures or volumes associated with this equation, so $R = 8.31$ J mol^{-1} K^{-1}, and that the Molar Mass (**M**) is in kg/mol in order to cancel out the units of Joules. Also, the kinetic energy per mole of molecules can be derived through the substitution of Maxwell's equation into the original equation:

$$KE \text{ per mole} = \frac{3}{2}RT$$

One final piece that you should recall is the Maxwell-Boltzman distribution (see Figure 7.2), which is a distribution of speeds of molecules at different temperatures. In general, the higher the temperature, the faster molecules will move.

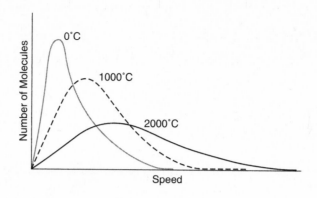

Figure 7.2.   Maxwell-Boltzman Distribution

EXAMPLE: Nitrogen comprises 78% of the air you are breathing. How fast are the molecules of nitrogen running into the sides of your body at room temperature (25°C)?

SOLUTION:

$$u_{rms} = \sqrt{\frac{3RT}{M}} = \sqrt{\frac{3(8.31 \text{ J/mol K})(298 \text{ K})}{2 \times 0.014007 \frac{kg}{mol}}} = 515 \text{ m/s (or 1,150 mi/hr!)}$$

Again, make sure the appropriate value of R is used and that the molar mass is in kg mol⁻¹. You're lucky that nitrogen molecules have a miniscule mass and thus minimal momentum, otherwise they would knock you off your chair!

Diffusion & Effusion

Diffusion is the mixing of gases due to molecular motion. When someone sprays perfume on the other side of the room, it only takes a few brief moments before the aromatic gas molecules travel to the other side of the room (see the previous example). In contrast, **effusion** is the process by which a gas escapes from a tiny hole from an area of higher pressure to a lower one (such as a pinhole in a balloon). The rate of effusion of a gas is inversely proportional to the square root of its molar mass, according to Graham's law:

$$\frac{r_1}{r_2} = \sqrt{\frac{M_2}{M_1}} \qquad r = \text{rate of effusion} \quad M = \text{molar mass}$$

EXAMPLE: A balloon is filled with air (a mixture of oxygen and nitrogen) and a small pinhole causes the balloon to leak. Conceptually, which gas escapes faster? How much faster?

SOLUTION: Nitrogen weighs less than oxygen, so it should move faster.

$$\frac{rate\ N_2}{rate\ O_2} = \sqrt{\frac{M_{O_2}}{M_{N_2}}} = \sqrt{\frac{(2 \times 16.00)}{(2 \times 14.007)}} = 1.069$$

Nitrogen gas moves 1.069 times faster than oxygen gas.

Avogadro's Hypothesis

Amadeo Avogadro is memorable to chemistry students for his work with the mole concept and the number named in his honor. However, few students recognize that the origin of the mole concept began with Avogadro's research on gases. Avogadro developed a hypothesis that equal volumes of gases at the same temperature and pressure have the same number of molecules. Granted, every gas will have a different mass but the volumes will be identical under the same conditions of temperature and pressure. At STP, 1 mole of any gas will occupy 22.4 L.

Real Gases: Deviations From Ideal Behavior

There is no such thing as an "ideal gas." As it turns out, under typical room conditions (or those accessible by most chemists), the ideal gas laws are obeyed. However, the assumptions of kinetic molecular theory cause deviations under extreme conditions of temperature and pressure. There are two reasons for this: (1) gases actually have a volume, and (2) gases are attracted to one another. A 1-L container of gas does not mean gas molecules have 1 L to move around—but rather slightly less, because the molecules themselves take up space. In addition, there will always be intermolecular attractions between gases.

Real gases deviate from ideal behavior under two main conditions: low temperature and high pressure. At low temperatures, the molecules are moving slowly; at high pressures, they are forced close together. The van der Waals Equation corrects for the deviations caused by real gases:

$$\left(P + \frac{n^2 a}{V^2}\right)(V - nb) = nRT$$

P = pressure of the gas (atm)

V = volume of the gas (L)

n = moles of gas (mol)

R = gas law constant; 0.0821 L atm mol^{-1} K^{-1}

T = absolute temperature (K)

a = constant that corrects for intermolecular attractions (unique for each gas)

b = constant that corrects for the volume occupied by the gas particles (unique for each gas)

TEST TIP

Remember to include units in all calculations—especially for the ideal gas law constant—so that you won't make the mistake of using wrong units!

Time for a quiz

- Review strategies in Chapter 2
- Take Quiz 3 at the REA Study Center
  (www.rea.com/studycenter)

Solids & Liquids

Relationship to Bonding

The properties of substances are directly impacted by their bonding forces, both intramolecular and intermolecular. This is an important point to consider as you investigate the states of matter. Greater amounts of attraction mean more resistance to change from the current state of matter. Also, if the particles in a substance are extremely attracted to one another, they will be more likely to be found in the solid or liquid state than in the gaseous state.

Phase Diagrams

- A **phase diagram** shows the states of matter (solid, liquid, gas) at a particular temperature and pressure.

- The lines on the diagram represent the boundaries between phases. Movement across the lines represents a phase change.

> ### DIDYOUKNOW?
>
> Phase diagrams are used daily by artists who cast statues in bronze foundries. In order to get the bronze to solidify and exhibit the ideal properties, artists use complex phase diagrams that show where certain weight percentages of copper and tin will undergo phase changes—thereby informing them how much heat to apply when casting.

- At low temperatures and high pressures, most substances are solids (pressure forces particles together, particles have very little movement).

- At high temperatures and low pressures, most substances are gases (particles have high kinetic energy and little restriction of movement).

- The **critical point** is the highest point on the liquid–gas boundary, above which the phases are indistinguishable from one another and have the properties of a supercritical fluid.

- The **triple point** is the temperature and pressure at which a substance exists in all three phases simultaneously in equilibrium with one another.

- The slope of the boundary lines is an indicator of the density of a substance. A positive slope indicates that the state of matter further to the right has a lower density than the substance to the left.

- The **vapor pressure curve** defines the boundary between the liquid and gas phases on the phase diagram. The vapor pressure curve indicates the pressure exerted by a vapor at a given temperature, as shown in Figure 8.1.

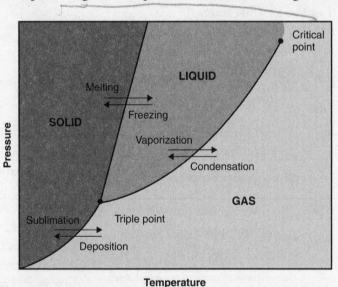

Figure 8.1.   Phase Diagram

TEST TIP

Most phase diagrams that you may encounter on the AP Chemistry exam look similar to the preceding diagram. However, note that the phase diagram for water will have a negative slope for the solid-liquid boundary due to the lower density of ice compared to liquid water.

Phase Changes

- Phase changes are caused by changes in temperature or pressure.

- The solid state is least energetic, exhibits only vibrational motion, and the particles are closest together. See Figure 8.2.

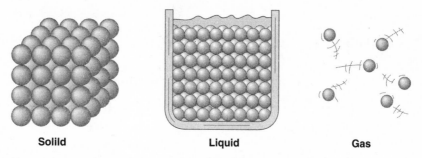

Solid   **Liquid**   **Gas**

Source: Dorling Kindersley RF/Thinkstock

Figure 8.2.   Proximity of Particles in Different Phases

- The liquid state exhibits higher energy than solids, exhibit vibrational and translational motion, and the particles are spread further apart. See Figure 8.2.

- Gases have the greatest amount of kinetic energy compared to other states, have translational, vibrational, and rotational motion, and contain particles whose distance between the particles is much larger than the particles themselves. See Figure 8.2.

- Phase changes involve a change in enthalpy (ΔH) that is unique for each substance and each transformation. A positive enthalpy ($\Delta H > 0$) means that energy must be put into the system, whereas a negative enthalpy ($\Delta H < 0$) means that energy must be released or removed from the system. See Table 8.1.

Table 8.1.   Energy Involved with Phase Changes

Phase Change	States Involved	Enthalpy Change
Melting	Solid to liquid	$\Delta H > 0$
Freezing	Liquid to solid	$\Delta H < 0$
Vaporization	Liquid to gas	$\Delta H > 0$
Condensation	Gas to liquid	$\Delta H < 0$
Sublimation	Solid to gas	$\Delta H > 0$
Deposition	Gas to solid	$\Delta H < 0$

TEST TIP

When providing explanations involving states of matter, frame your answer from a kinetic molecular standpoint: How fast are the molecules moving, what kind of motion do they have, and how close are the particles to one another?

Heating and Cooling Curves

- A **heating curve** is a graph that shows what happens to a substance when heat is added at a constant rate. A heating curve will have an overall positive slope. See Figure 8.3.

- The plateaus (flat areas) on a heating curve indicate the temperatures at which a phase change is occurring.

- The sloped areas indicate where a substance is changing temperature when energy is placed into the system.

- To calculate the amount of heat required for a phase change (plateau of temperature), use the following equation: $q = n\Delta H$, where q is heat, n is the number of moles, and ΔH is the enthalpy of vaporization or fusion (ΔH_{vap} is used for liquid–gas phase changes, ΔH_{fus} is used for solid–liquid phase changes).

- To calculate the amount of heat required to raise the temperature of a substance, use the equation: $q = mc\Delta T$, where q is heat, m is the mass, c is the **specific heat** of the substance, and ΔT is the change in temperature of the substance for a particular region on the curve. Note that the specific heat of a substance will be different for each state of matter.

- The total amount of energy required to heat a substance from one temperature to another is a summation of the energies required for phase change(s) and heating the material at each individual state. This energy will always be positive because the system is absorbing energy.

- A **cooling curve** is the opposite of a heating curve. The negative slope of the graph indicates that energy is being removed from the system. All of the energies for cooling the substance in each state as well as the phase change(s) will be negative. See Figure 8.3.

- More information and calculations can be found in Chapter 10: Thermochemistry.

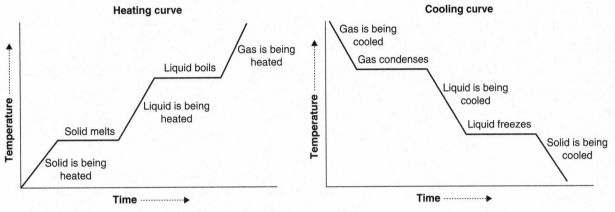

Figure 8.3. **Heating and Cooling Curves**

EXAMPLE: Calculate the total amount of heat needed to raise 20.0 g of ice at $-10°C$ to steam at $115°C$.

Given:

Specific heat of ice $= c_{ice} = 2.1$ J/g°C

Specific heat of liquid water $= c = 4.2$ J/g°C

Specific heat of steam $= c_{steam} = 1.8$ J/g°C

$\Delta H_{fus\ water} = 6.0$ kJ/mol

$\Delta H_{vap\ water} = 40.7$ kJ/mol

SOLUTION: The answer equals the sum of the heats of the following processes.

Heat needed to raise ice to melting point:

$$q = mc\Delta T = (20.0\,g)\left(2.1\frac{J}{g°C}\right)(0°C - (-10°C)) = 420\ J = \mathbf{0.42\ kJ}$$

Heat needed to melt ice:

$$q = nH_{fus} = \left(\frac{20.0\text{g}}{18.02 \frac{g}{mol}} \right) \left(6.0 \frac{kJ}{mol} \right) = \textbf{6.7 } \textbf{\textit{kJ}}$$

Heat needed to raise water to the boiling point:

$$q = mc\ \text{T} = (20.0\text{g}) \left(4.2 \frac{J}{g°C} \right) (100°C - 0°C) = 8400\ J\ = \textbf{8.4 } \textbf{\textit{kJ}}$$

Heat needed to vaporize (boil) water:

$$q = nH_{vap} = \left(\frac{20.0\text{g}}{18.02 \frac{g}{mol}} \right) \left(40.7 \frac{kJ}{mol} \right) = \textbf{45.2 } \textbf{\textit{kJ}}$$

Heat needed to raise steam to the final temperature:

$$q = mc\Delta T = (20.0\text{g}) \left(1.8 \frac{J}{g°C} \right) (115°C - 100°C) = 540\ J = \textbf{0.54 } \textbf{\textit{kJ}}$$

Total heat needed:

$$0.42 \text{ kJ} + 6.7 \text{ kJ} + 8.4 \text{ kJ} + 45.2 \text{ kJ} + 0.54 \text{ kJ} = 61.3 \text{ kJ}$$

61.3 kJ are required to raise 20.0 g of ice at −10°C to steam at 115°C.

TEST TIP

Be careful with problems that involve heating or cooling a substance from one temperature to another, because many students just solve it as one q = mcΔT equation as opposed to the multiple steps (up to five) that are required due to a substance changing state.

Boiling and Freezing Points

- The **normal melting point** is the temperature that corresponds to the solid–liquid equilibrium at 1.0 atm of pressure.

- The **normal boiling point** is the temperature that corresponds to the liquid–gas equilibrium at 1.0 atm of pressure.

- The same type of methodology for finding the normal boiling point applies to phase diagrams and vapor pressure diagrams. See Figure 8.4. The only difference is that a vapor pressure diagram does not have any information about solids.

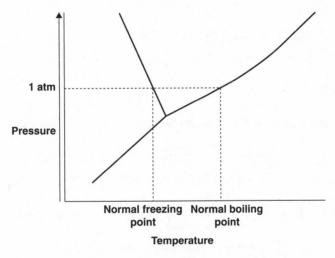

Figure 8.4.   Boiling and Freezing Points on a Phase Diagram

TEST TIP

Watch for the word "normal," because it refers specifically to 1 atm of pressure!

Properties of Liquids

- Liquids are composed of molecules that are in constant translational and vibrational motion, rolling around one another like marbles in a glass.

- Liquids have a definite volume, but they take the shape of their container.

- Attractive forces hold molecules close together in a liquid, so pressure has little effect on the volume of a liquid. Liquids are generally not compressible.

- Changes in temperature cause only small changes in volume.

- Liquids diffuse more slowly than gases. Diffusion increases as temperature increases.

- **Surface tension** is the inward force of a liquid toward itself due to intermolecular attractions. Surface tension decreases as temperature increases.

Properties of Solids

- The attractive forces between atoms, molecules, or ions in a solid are relatively strong. The particles are held in a fixed positions relative to one another.

- Solids are in constant vibrational motion.

- Solids have a definitive shape and volume and are generally not compressible.

- Crystalline solids have sharp melting points and are composed of repeating structural units bounded by a specific geometric pattern called *unit cells*.

- The following are different configurations of atoms in crystals:

  - Simple cubic unit cells have one atom at each of the corners of the cube. One-eighth of each of the eight atoms is inside the cube, so a simple cubic contains a total of one atom per unit cell.

  - A body-centered crystal is a simple cubic unit cell, with one additional atom in the center of the cube. There are a total of two atoms per unit cell.

  - A face-centered crystal is a simple cubic unit cell, with one additional atom shared between two unit cells on each face of the cube. There are a total of three atoms per unit cell.

  - Amorphous solids do not exhibit specific geometries and do not have sharp melting points. Glass is an amorphous solid.

— **Lattice energy** refers to the attractive forces that hold a crystal lattice together. In general, stronger electrostatic attractions will result in higher lattice energies.

— The attractive forces for ions $+2/-2$ ions will be larger than $+1/-1$ ions.

— Crystals with higher lattice energies will have correspondingly higher melting points.

TEST TIP

Keep in mind that phases and phase changes have everything to do with bonding, so that should weigh heavily into explanations of why a substance exhibits particular properties.

Solutions

The Solution Process

- A **solution** is composed of a **solute** and a **solvent**, and by definition is homogeneous.

- The solute is what is being dissolved, while the solvent does the dissolving. The solvent is present in the larger amount.

- **Solvation** describes the process of making a solution. Solutions form when there are intermolecular attractions between the solute and the solvent.

- The attraction between solute and solvent must be greater than the force that holds the solute together in order for the solute to dissolve. If the solute particles are extremely attracted to one another, they will not dissolve.

- **Hydration** describes the solvation process when water is the solvent.

- A **tincture** is a solution in which alcohol is the solvent.

- **Miscible** solutions are formed when two liquids are completely soluble in one another.

- In general, compounds with similar intermolecular forces dissolve in one another. This concept is referred to as "like dissolves like."

  — Nonpolar solutes dissolve in nonpolar solvents.

  — Polar and ionic solutes dissolve in polar solvents.

DIDYOUKNOW?

Although most everyday solutions are aqueous solutions, hand sanitizer is a tincture that contains approximately 60% ethanol by mass, along with water, fragrances, and other components such as moisturizers.

— Polar solutes in a nonpolar solvent are **immiscible**, meaning they do not mix.

— Nonpolar solutes in a polar solvent are also immiscible.

- Soluble ionic compounds dissociate into individual cations and anions when dissolved in solution. Consequently, these solutions are called **electrolytes** because the charged ions can carry electric charge in solution.

Factors Affecting Solubility

One of the major characteristics of a solution is that the amount of a solute dissolved in the solvent can be varied. The solubility of a solute is dependent upon three factors: concentration, temperature, and pressure.

Concentration

- Solubility is a measure of how much solute is dissolved in the solvent at a particular temperature and pressure.

- A dilute solution has a small amount of solute dissolved, whereas a concentrated solution has a large amount of solute dissolved in the solvent.

- A **saturated solution** occurs when the maximum amount of solute is dissolved in the solvent at a given temperature and pressure. No additional solute can be dissolved in a saturated solution because the solid solute is in equilibrium with dissolved solute.

- An **unsaturated solution** has less solute dissolved than is possible at a given temperature and pressure.

- **Supersaturated solutions** have solute dissolved past the normal point of saturation, which makes them extremely unstable. They are formed by heating a solution to increase solubility, saturating the solution, and then gently cooling the solution.

Temperature

- In general, as the temperature increases, the solubility of a solid in a liquid solution increases. This only applies for solids that require energy to dissolve (endothermic)—although most solids fall into this category.

- If a solid gives off energy when it is dissolved in solution (exothermic), increasing the temperature of the solution will decrease solubility.

- For gases dissolved in liquids, the solubility decreases with increasing temperature.

Pressure

- **Henry's law** describes the solubility of gases in liquids and states that the amount of gas that can dissolve in a liquid is directly proportional to the partial pressure of the gas above the liquid.

- Henry's law is most accurately obeyed for gases that do not dissociate or react with the liquid.

- Pressure does not appreciably affect the solubility of liquid or solid solutes dissolved in liquids.

TEST TIP

On a solubility curve, the line represents the saturation point at various temperatures. The area above the curve is indicative of a supersaturated solution, whereas below the curve is unsaturated.

Units of Concentration

There are many units that chemists use to express the concentration of a solution. Each unit has its cost and benefits. Some units are dependent upon the temperature of a solution, while others are independent of temperature. It is your job to be a "unit translator," because it is an essential skill to convert between the various units. The most important part to watch with the different units is the use of the terms *solute*, *solvent*, and *solution*. If you know what these terms are and what they represent, you will be well on your way to converting between the different units. The most common units of concentration are molarity, molality, mass percent, and mole fraction.

Molarity

Molarity (*M*) describes concentration as the moles of solute per liter of solution. It is the most common unit used by chemists to express concentration due to the ease of measuring out a given volume of solution and knowing how many moles of the solute is available to react. However, because the volume of a solution is dependent upon the temperature, the concentration of a solution will vary slightly based on the temperature conditions. Chemists also use brackets to express molar concentration, so $[MgCl_2]$ would specifically mean the molar concentration of an $MgCl_2$ solution. Also, when a solute dissolves in solution, you can easily determine the molar concentrations of the dissolved species based on simple stoichiometry.

$$molarity = M = \frac{moles\ solute}{L\ solution}$$

EXAMPLE: What are the concentrations of the ions present in a 1.5 molar $MgCl_2$ solution?

SOLUTION: The balanced dissolution equation is:

$$MgCl_{2\ (aq)} \rightarrow Mg^{+2}_{\ (aq)} + 2\ Cl^{-1}_{\ (aq)}$$

The mole ratio is 1:1:2, and thus:

$$[MgCl_2] = 1.5\ M$$

$$[Mg^{+2}] = 1.5\ M$$

$$[Cl^{-1}] = 3.0\ M$$

Molality

There is only one letter of difference between molarity and molality, but they differ from one another in a number of ways. Molality (m) describes concentration as the moles of solute per kilograms of the solvent. Molal concentrations are independent of temperature because molality is essentially a ratio of masses of the solute and the solvent.

$$molality = m = \frac{moles\ solute}{kg\ solvent}$$

TEST TIP

Molarity and molality can be converted between one another if the density of the solution is known.

Mass Percent

Mass percent is calculated as a typical percentage ratio: it is the mass of the solute divided by the mass of the solution. Like molality, mass percentage concentrations are temperature independent and for this reason are used quite a bit in the field of medicine.

$$mass\ percent = \frac{mass\ solute}{mass\ solution} \times 100$$

Mole Fraction

Mole fraction (X) is a ratio of the moles of the solute compared to the total number of moles of all of the components in the solution. Mole fractions are typically used when working with vapor pressure lowering explained by Raoult's law.

$$mole\ fraction = X_A = \frac{moles\ A}{total\ moles}$$

Colligative Properties

- **Colligative properties** are physical properties of solutions that depend on the concentration of a solution.

- The amount of change in the physical property is directly proportional to the moles of solute that are dissolved.

- The van 't Hoff factor takes into account dissociation that may occur when a solute dissolves.

  — When one mole of dissolved solute creates one mole of particles in solution (molecules/nonelectrolytes), the van 't Hoff factor would be 1.0.

  — When one mole of dissolved solute creates two moles of particles (ions/electrolytes), such as in the case of NaCl, the van 't Hoff factor would be 2.0.

  — For a compound such as $AlCl_3$, the van 't Hoff factor would be 4.0.

  — The van 't Hoff factor is often determined experimentally because 100% dissociation is quite rare due to ion-paring effects, so decimal values are common.

— Depending on the solute, the concentration of the ions may be double, triple, or more than the concentration of the solute itself—which has a direct impact on the properties.

- Molality and other temperature-independent units are used for colligative property calculations because the temperature changes during the process.

- There are four main colligative properties: freezing point depression, boiling point elevation, osmotic pressure, and vapor pressure lowering.

- Colligative properties are often used in determining the molar masses of unknown solutes.

Freezing Point Depression

Freezing point depression describes the phenomenon that when a solute is added to a solution, the freezing point decreases compared to the pure solvent. This is why salt is put on roads and sidewalks after a snowstorm. By adding solute (salt) to the solvent on the road (snow), the freezing point of the resulting solution decreases—and thus the snow melts.

DIDYOUKNOW?

Calcium chloride is the preferred salt of choice for melting ice on sidewalks. Calcium ions do not corrode or interfere with concrete, which already has a significant amount of calcium carbonate present in the solid mixture. Calcium chloride also gives off heat when it dissolves, making it especially appropriate for melting ice.

FREEZING POINT DEPRESSION

$$\Delta T = k_f mi$$

ΔT = change in solvent freezing point, °C

k_f = molal freezing point constant of the solvent, °C/m

m = molality of solute, mol/kg

i = van 't Hoff factor of solute

Boiling Point Elevation

Boiling point elevation occurs when a solute is added to a solution, and the boiling point increases compared to the pure solvent. This is why "antifreeze" is added to car radiators in climates where there is no snow: the ethylene glycol antifreeze not only lowers the freezing point so the radiator does not crack, but it also raises the boiling point of the solution so that the water does not vaporize away when it comes into contact with the hot engine.

BOILING POINT ELEVATION

$$\Delta T = k_b m i$$

ΔT = change in solvent boiling point, °C

k_f = molal boiling point constant of the solvent, °C/m

m = molality of solute, mol/kg

i = van 't Hoff factor of solute

TEST TIP

Boiling point elevation and freezing point depression are the most common colligative properties, so be prepared to explain these phenomena from an intermolecular forces and solutions standpoint.

Osmotic Pressure

The process of osmosis describes the movement of a pure solvent through a semipermeable membrane. The solvent particles migrate through the membrane from an area of high concentration to one of low concentration. **Osmotic pressure** is the pressure required to stop the flow of solvent particles across the membrane. The osmotic pressure will be greater for solutions of a higher concentration.

OSMOTIC PRESSURE

$$\pi = MRT$$

π = osmotic pressure, atm

M = molarity of solution, mol/L

R = ideal gas constant, 0.082 L atm / K mol

T = temperature, K

Vapor Pressure Lowering: Raoult's Law

When a solute is added to a solvent, there are intermolecular attractions formed between the solute and the solvent. Consequently, the greater attractions hinder solvent particles from escaping into the gas phase, thus lowering the vapor pressure and consequently raising the boiling point. The vapor pressure of the solution will always be lower than the vapor pressure of the pure solvent. Raoult's law describes how the vapor pressure curve of a solvent is depressed when a solute dissolves in the solvent.

RAOULT'S LAW

$$P = XP°$$

P = vapor pressure of solution, atm

P° = vapor pressure of pure solvent, atm

X = mole fraction of solvent

TEST TIP

When performing a Raoult's law calculation, be careful to calculate the mole fraction of the *solvent*—not the solute, as is typically done with solution concentration. It should be calculated as moles of solvent divided by the total number of moles of solute and solvent particles.

Nonideal Solutions

- Ideal solutions follow Raoult's law. The vapor pressure of a solution is directly proportional to the mole fraction of the solvent in the solution.

- Nonideal solutions have a vapor pressure that is different from that predicted by Raoult's law.

- Negative deviations from Raoult's law occur when there is a stronger solute–solvent attraction, such as hydrogen bonding, that prevents solvent molecules from escaping into the vapor phase—thus making the vapor pressure lower than expected. A negative deviation also occurs when the enthalpy of solvation, or energy required to form the solution, is large and exothermic.

- Positive deviations from Raoult's law occur when both the solute and solvent are very volatile, with weaker than expected intermolecular forces—thus making the vapor pressure higher than expected. A positive deviation also occurs when the enthalpy of solvation is large and endothermic.

TEST TIP

You should have a qualitative understanding of why deviations occur for nonideal solutions, but will never need to perform calculations to justify your answer.

Beer-Lambert Law (Beer's Law)

- Beer's law describes the factors that impact the absorption of light, A.

$$A = abc$$

- There are three variables that affect absorbance, including:

  — Molar absorptivity (a): Different compounds absorb light differently.

  — Path length (b): The further light must travel through a sample, the more light will be absorbed.

  — Concentration (c): The higher the concentration of a sample, the more light will be absorbed.

- The most common usage of Beer's law is to relate the concentration of a solution to the absorbance of light, which is a linear relationship.

Time for a quiz
- Review strategies in Chapter 2
- Take Quiz 4 at the REA Study Center
  (www.rea.com/studycenter)

Take Mini-Test 1
on Chapters 3–9
Go to the REA Study Center
(www.rea.com/studycenter)

Thermochemistry

Energy

Thermochemistry gives consideration to the fact that energy changes occur during chemical reactions. **Energy** (E) is defined as the ability do work (w) on a system. From a chemistry perspective, **kinetic energy** comes in the form of translational, vibrational, and rotational motion of molecules, whereas potential energy arises from chemical bonds and electrostatic interactions. Energy cannot be measured directly and is monitored through changes (ΔE).

First Law of Thermodynamics

The **first law of thermodynamics** is commonly called the law of conservation of energy: "energy cannot be created or destroyed." Energy can only be converted from one form into another during chemical reactions, and therefore the energy of the universe is constant. Energy transfers occur between the system (the reaction we are studying) and the surroundings (everything else in the universe).

Heat, Temperature, and Enthalpy

In the realm of thermochemistry, there are three frequently used terms that are distinctly different from one another: temperature, heat, and enthalpy. **Temperature** (T) is a measure of the average kinetic energy of molecules, which means that at higher temperatures molecules are moving faster. On the other hand, **heat** (q) measures the total kinetic energy of all of the particles in a sample. We use temperature as a means to monitor heat transfers. Heat transfers are kinetic energy transfers that go from a hotter object to a cooler object until both objects are at the same temperature. According to the first law of thermodynamics, heat lost by a hotter object is gained by a colder object. In contrast, **enthalpy** (H) refers to the energy released or absorbed by a chemical reaction.

Unless there is pressure–volume (PΔV) work performed by the system, changes in enthalpy (ΔH) are essentially the same as the heat exchanged during a reaction. ΔH is the difference between the enthalpy of the products and the enthalpy of the reactants.

Exothermic processes describe a heat transfer from the system into the surroundings. Heat is given off during an exothermic reaction (ΔH < 0) and the products of the reaction have less enthalpy than the reactants. **Endothermic** processes undergo a transfer of energy from the surroundings into the system. Heat is absorbed during an endothermic reaction (ΔH > 0), because energy must be put into the reaction to move it from reactants to products. The products of the reaction have more enthalpy than the reactants. Energy diagrams for exothermic and endothermic reactions can be found in Chapter 11, Kinetics.

Heat Capacity, Specific Heat, and Units

Heat capacity is a measure of how much an object changes temperature when a given amount of heat is absorbed. For example, when a metal pan is placed on a stovetop it only takes a few moments for the pan to get really hot. This is because metals have a low heat capacity. The units for heat capacity are in J/°C (J/K) as determined by the equation:

$$C_p = \frac{\Delta H}{\Delta T}$$

C_p = molar heat capacity at constant pressure

ΔH = heat added

ΔT = change in temperature; $T_{final} - T_{initial}$

Specific heat (c) is related to heat capacity because it defines the quantity of heat required to raise 1 gram of substance by 1°C (or 1 Kelvin). The energy unit of the calorie was originally defined in the early 1800s from the specific heat of water, which is the amount of energy required to raise 1 gram of water by 1°C. Of course, calories are not the same as Calories. The "food calorie" is sometimes written with the capital "C" and is actually kilocalories. Since then, scientists have embraced the SI unit of the Joule for measuring heat. As a result, a number of thermochemical calculations involve the specific heat of water, which is 4.18 J/g°C. If the mass (m), specific heat (c), and change in temperature (ΔT) is known for a process, the quantity of heat evolved or absorbed can be calculated using the following equation:

$$q = mc\Delta T$$

Calorimetry

Calorimetry is a laboratory technique used to measure heat exchanges. Based on the first law of thermodynamics, the heat given off by one substance will be absorbed by the other, which will most likely be water. The most common type of calorimeter is a coffee cup calorimeter, which uses the mass, specific heat of water, 4.18 J/g°C, and the temperature change of the water to easily calculate the quantity of heat absorbed or evolved using the formula: $q = mc\Delta T$. There is an assumption that all of the heat from a reaction is transferred to the water in the calorimeter. This amount of heat can then be used to calculate things such as the ΔH of a reaction or the specific heat of a metal. Bomb calorimeters operate on a similar principle, although other materials in addition to the water absorb the heat from the reaction. For bomb calorimeters, the total amount of heat is the sum of the energy change for the water ($q = mc\Delta T$) and the energy absorbed by the calorimeter based on its heat capacity ($q = C\Delta T$).

> ## DIDYOUKNOW?
>
> Popcorn can be classified as a hydrate, which is a substance that contains water molecules. The electromagnetic radiation produced by a microwave is at a wavelength that causes water molecules to vibrate quickly, and if given enough energy, convert the liquid water into gaseous steam. When the pressure of the water vapor builds up to a high enough level, the popcorn explodes and releases the water, leaving a fluffy popcorn kernel.

EXAMPLE: In a coffee-cup calorimeter, 100.0 mL of 1.0 M NaOH and 100.0 mL of 1.0 M HCl are mixed. Both solutions were originally at 24.6°C. After the reaction, the temperature rises to 31.3°C. What is the enthalpy change for the neutralization of HCl by NaOH? Assume the specific heats of the solutions are 4.2 J/g°C and the densities are 1.00 g/mL.

SOLUTION:

$$HCl + NaOH \rightarrow H_2O + NaCl \quad \Delta H = ?$$

$$q_{cal} = -q_{rxn}$$

Calorimeter:

The mass of the solution in the calorimeter is the sum of the solutions that were mixed together.

$$q_{cal} = (200.0 \text{ g})(4.2 \text{ J/g°C})(31.3°C - 24.6°C) = +5,600 \text{ J}$$

Reaction:

The amount of energy absorbed by the solution in the calorimeter was released by the reaction.

$$q_{rxn} = -5,600 \text{ J}$$

This energy represents the amount of heat given off for the quantity of reactants put into the calorimeter. In order to figure out the enthalpy (ΔH) for the reaction, it will be necessary to find out the amount of energy per mole of the reactants. Because both reactants are in perfect stoichiometry, you can calculate the moles of either reactant.

$$\# mol = \frac{100.0 \ mL}{1} \times \frac{1 \ L}{1,000 \ mL} \times \frac{1.0 \ mol}{1 \ L} = 0.10 \ mol$$

$$\Delta H = \frac{-5,600 \ J}{0.10 \ mol} = -56,000 \ J = -56 \ kJ/mol$$

For a problem involving a bomb calorimeter, a similar setup of the problem is completed except that you must consider the heat gained by the bomb calorimeter.

$$q_{cal} = q_{water} + q_{bomb} \text{ and } q_{cal} = -q_{rxn}$$

TEST TIP

The ΔH for a reaction is directly related to the stoichiometry of a reaction. That is why you will see a unit of kJ when written along with a reaction, but a unit of kJ/mol when trying to calculate the enthalpy based on one reactant.

State Functions

Just like there are many different roads you can take between Philadelphia and Washington, D.C., there are sometimes many different pathways by which a chemical reaction can go. State functions are properties of a system that depend only on the initial and final states, and therefore it does not matter how a reaction goes from the initial state to the final state. The mechanism of getting from one state to another is represented by the kinetics of a reaction as seen in Chapter 11, Kinetics. Most thermochemical quantities are state functions including: enthalpy (H), entropy (S), Gibbs free energy (G), pressure (P), volume (V), temperature (T), and internal energy (E). On the AP Chemistry exam, the most common quantities involve changes in enthalpy, entropy, and free energy between an initial state and a final state (ΔH, ΔS, and ΔG, respectively).

Standard State Conditions

Standard state conditions for state functions are indicated by the degree symbol (°). $\Delta H°$ represents the standard change in enthalpy; $\Delta S°$ represents the standard change in entropy; and $\Delta G°$ represents the standard change in free energy. Standard conditions are a very specific set of conditions:

- The temperature is 25°C, or 298 K.

- Gases are at 1 atmosphere of pressure.

- Solutions are 1 mole/liter (M) in concentration.

- Liquids and solids are pure.

TEST TIP

Do not confuse thermodynamic standard conditions, where the temperature is 298 K, with standard temperature and pressure (STP) for gases, where the temperature is 273 K.

Heats of Formation

The standard **heat of formation** ($\Delta H_f°$) refers to the energy associated with forming a compound from its elements in their standard states. The $\Delta H_f°$ for an element at standard conditions is zero, because by definition it requires no energy to create an element from itself. In addition to calorimetry, $\Delta H_f°$ values can be used to determine the enthalpy of a reaction based on the equation:

$$\Delta H° = \sum \Delta H_{ff}° \, products - \sum \Delta H \, ° \, reactants$$

 **EXAMPLE:** Using the following ΔH_f° values, determine the amount of energy released when sugar ($C_{12}H_{22}O_{11}$) is burned to produce gaseous carbon dioxide and water vapor.

Compound	ΔH_f° (kJ/mol)
$C_{12}H_{22}O_{11(s)}$	−2,221
$H_2O_{(g)}$	−241.8
$CO_{2(g)}$	−393.5

SOLUTION:

$$C_{12}H_{22}O_{11(s)} + 12\ O_{2(g)} \rightarrow 12\ CO_{2(g)} + 11\ H_2O_{(g)}$$

The enthalpy of formation for oxygen gas is not given because it is zero (all elements in their standard states are zero).

$$\Delta H^\circ = [12(-393.5) + 11(-241.8)] - [1(-2,221) + 12(0)] = \textbf{−5161 kJ/mol}$$

TEST TIP

If you encounter a problem where the ΔH_f° values are not given for one or more substances in a reaction, do not dismay. They are probably elements in their standards states, which have a value of zero.

Hess's Law

In addition to calorimetry and heats of formation, Hess's law is a third way to determine the ΔH° of a reaction. Hess's law takes advantage of the fact that enthalpy is a state function: you can find the ΔH° for a reaction by adding up the enthalpy values from multiple steps so that their sum results in the enthalpy change for the overall chemical reaction. When rearranging the thermochemical equations, it is important to remember that reversing a reaction causes the sign of ΔH to flip, and multiplying an equation by a coefficient will require the ΔH to be multiplied, as well.

$H_2CO_2 \rightarrow H_2O + CO_2$

■ **EXAMPLE:** From the following information, calculate the enthalpy of the formation of 1 mole of $SO_{3(g)}$ from its elements.

$$S_{(s)} + O_{2(g)} \rightarrow SO_{2(g)} \qquad \Delta H = -296.8 \text{ kJ}$$

$$2 SO_{2(g)} + O_{2(g)} \rightarrow 2 SO_{3(g)} \quad \Delta H = -197.8 \text{ kJ}$$

■ **SOLUTION:** The chemical equation should be:

$$S_{(s)} + 3/2 O_{2(g)} \rightarrow SO_{3(g)} \qquad \Delta H = ?$$

You can use the first equation in its original form, though you will have to multiply the second equation by one half, including the ΔH for its reaction.

$$S_{(s)} + O_{2(g)} \rightarrow SO_{2(g)} \qquad\qquad\qquad\qquad \Delta H = -296.8 \text{ kJ}$$

$$1/2 \, [2 SO_{2(g)} + O_{2(g)} \rightarrow 2 SO_{3(g)}] \qquad\qquad \Delta H = 1/2 \, [-197.8 \text{ kJ}]$$

$$\overline{S_{(s)} + 3/2 O_{2(g)} \rightarrow SO_{3(g)} \qquad \Delta H = (-296.8 + -98.9) = \textbf{-395.7 kJ}}$$

TEST TIP

When rearranging a set of equations for Hess's law, focus on getting the correct number of the correct compounds on the correct side of the equation.

Bond Energies

One final way to calculate $\Delta H°$ for a reaction is by using bond energies. **Bond energy** is the amount of energy required to break bonds for the reactants and the amount of energy released when bonds are formed for the products. Bond energies use an assumption that all of the bonds for the reactants and products are broken and reformed in the gaseous state under standard conditions. It is a common misconception, so make sure it is straight in your mind that breaking bonds is an *endothermic* process, whereas forming bonds is an *exothermic* process. Heats of reaction can be estimated by finding the difference between the energy required to break all of the bonds in a molecule and the energy released when the bonds are formed. You will first have to draw the molecular structures of the reactants and products, and then evaluate the types of bonds broken and formed during a reaction.

$$\Delta H^\circ = \sum \Delta H_{bonds\ broken} - \sum \Delta H_{bonds\ formed}$$

EXAMPLE: Use the following table of bond energies to approximate the change in enthalpy when 1 mole of hydrogen is combusted.

Bond	Enthalpy (kJ/mol)
H—H	436
O=O	495
H—O	464

SOLUTION:

$$H_2 + O_2 \rightarrow 2\ H_2O$$

There is (1) H—H bond and (1) O=O bond to break in the reactants.

There are a total of (4) O—H bonds formed in the products.

$$\Delta H^\circ = [1(436) + 1(495)] - [4(464)] = \mathbf{-925\ kJ/mol}$$

TEST TIP

For complex reactions, you can perform bond energy calculations just based on the bonds that are actually broken and the bonds that are formed. This will save you some precious time.

Energy and Phase Changes

When performing energy calculations, the state of matter of the reactants and products is highly important. Particles in the solid state have very little energy compared to those in the gaseous state. In addition, when a

DID YOU KNOW?

Disposable hand warmers are created from solid iron that is spread over an enormous surface area. When the iron-containing hand warmer is exposed to air, it undergoes a redox reaction that releases a lot of heat and forms iron (III) oxide, which is commonly known as rust.

substance changes phase, there is an energy associated with those transitions. For the solid–liquid phase change, the enthalpy of fusion (H_{fus}) is used to quantify the amount of heat required to melt a solid. This value also tells you how much energy is released when a particle freezes. Similarly, the enthalpy of vaporization (H_{vap}) describes the energy required for the liquid-gas phase change. This value also tells you the amount of energy released when a gas is condensed to the liquid state.

Entropy and the Second Law of Thermodynamics

Entropy (S) is another thermodynamic quantity that describes the amount of randomness or disorder in a system. When either matter or energy is dispersed, the entropy will increase. From a chemical reactions perspective, the entropy will increase when:

1. The temperature increases.

2. Phase changes are involved (solids have the least entropy; gases and aqueous solutions have the most).

3. The volume or amount of a gas increases.

4. The number of moles of product is greater than the reactants.

Entropy values are based off of a perfect crystal at 0 K; thus, every substance will have an entropy value. Standard entropy (S°) values can be used to determine the entropy change for a reaction.

$$\Delta S° = \sum \Delta S° \text{ products} - \sum \Delta S° \text{ reactants}$$

The **second law of thermodynamics** states that the entropy of the universe increases during a spontaneous process. Spontaneous processes occur on their own without any external intervention.

TEST TIP

You should be able to estimate the sign of ΔS qualitatively for a given chemical reaction.

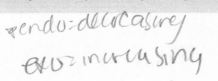

Gibbs Free Energy and Spontaneity

Whether or not a reaction is spontaneous or nonspontaneous comes down to one value: the Gibbs free energy (G). Free energy is the energy available to do work, and takes the enthalpy and entropy of a reaction into account. If ΔG is negative, the reaction will be spontaneous; positive ΔG values mean that the reaction is nonspontaneous; and when $\Delta G = 0$, the system is at equilibrium—meaning there is no preference. The Gibbs free energy value is related to the enthalpy and entropy according to the Gibbs-Helmholtz equation:

$$\Delta G° = \Delta H° - T\Delta S°$$

Alternatively, the Gibbs free energy value can be calculated from free energy of formation values ($\Delta G_f°$) acquired under standard conditions through the summation equation:

$$\Delta G° = \sum \Delta G° \ products - \sum \Delta G° \ reactants$$

EXAMPLE: Using the following values, determine whether or not the burning of sugar ($C_{12}H_{22}O_{11}$) will be a spontaneous process.

Compound	$\Delta H_f°$ (kJ/mol)	$\Delta S°$ (J/mol K)
$C_{12}H_{22}O_{11(s)}$	−2,221	392.4
$O_{2(g)}$	0	205.2
$CO_{2(g)}$	−393.5	213.6
$H_2O_{(g)}$	−241.8	188.1

SOLUTION:

$$C_{12}H_{22}O_{11(s)} + 12 O_{2(g)} \rightarrow 12 CO_{2(g)} + 11 H_2O_{(g)}$$

$$\Delta H° = [12(-393.5) + 11(-241.8)] - [1(-2,221) + 12(0)] = \textbf{−5161 kJ/mol}$$

$$\Delta S° = [12(213.6) + 11(188.1)] - [1(392.4) + 12(205.2)] = \textbf{+1778 (J/mol K)}$$

Because the units are not matching up, the $\Delta S°$ should be converted to kJ/mol.

$$\Delta S° = +1.778 \text{ (J/mol K)}$$

The Gibbs free energy is calculated using the Gibbs-Helmholtz equation, using the temperature of 298 K because the data is for standard conditions.

$$\Delta G° = -5{,}161 \text{ kJ/mol} - (298 \text{ K})(1.778 \text{ kJ/mol K}) = \mathbf{-5{,}691 \text{ kJ/mol}}$$

Because the $\Delta G°$ is negative, this reaction is *spontaneous*.

TEST TIP

Make sure the units are matching up when plugging into the Gibbs equation, which will likely require you to convert the temperature into Kelvin and the $\Delta S°$ in kJ/mol K.

Predicting Reaction Spontanaeity

On the AP Chemistry exam, you may be asked to predict the spontaneity of a reaction based solely on qualitative determinations. You should familiarize yourself with Table 10.1, which describes the possible scenarios for enthalpy, entropy, and free energy based on the signs of ΔH, ΔS, and ΔG and the equation: $\Delta G = \Delta H - T\Delta S$

Table 10.1. Reaction Spontaneity: Possible Scenarios for Enthalpy, Entropy, and Free Energy

ΔH	ΔS	ΔG	Result
−	+	−	Spontaneous at all temps
−	−	−	Spontaneous at low temps
−	−	+	Nonspontaneous at high temps
+	+	−	Spontaneous at high temps
+	+	+	Nonspontaneous at low temps
+	−	+	Nonspontaneous at all temps

Table 10.2. Thermo Signs and Symbols Summary

Sign and Symbol	Meaning
$-\Delta H$	Exothermic; heat given off
$+\Delta H$	Endothermic; heat absorbed
$-\Delta S$	Decrease entropy; more organized
$+\Delta S$	Increase entropy; more random/disordered
$-\Delta G$	Spontaneous
$+\Delta G$	Nonspontaneous

Time for a quiz
- Review strategies in Chapter 2
- Take Quiz 5 at the REA Study Center

(www.rea.com/studycenter)

Chemical Kinetics

Rates of Reaction

Chemical kinetics involves the measurement of how fast a chemical reaction occurs. Many of the reactions that are performed in AP Chemistry classes happen at a relatively fast rate: the reactants are mixed together and seconds, maybe minutes later, the products are formed and the reaction is over. Some reactions are spontaneous but still occur at a slow rate, such as the reaction of diamond with air to form carbon dioxide—which takes thousands of years to occur. There are a variety of factors that affect the rate of a chemical reaction, including concentration, the nature of the reactants, temperature, surface area, and the presence of a catalyst.

Measuring Reaction Rates

The reaction rate of a chemical reaction is a measure of the change in concentration per unit of time. Reaction rate can be expressed in terms of either the appearance of a product or the disappearance of a reactant. For example, the rate of the reaction below can be expressed as follows.

$$2\,HCl_{(g)} \rightarrow H_{2(g)} + Cl_{2(g)}$$

$$= -\frac{1}{2}\frac{\Delta[HCl]}{\Delta t} = +\frac{\Delta[H_2]}{\Delta t} = +\frac{\Delta[Cl_2]}{\Delta t}$$

In the preceding equation, the negative sign indicates that the reactant is decreasing in concentration. The multiplicative factor ½ in front of the HCl is utilized for stoichiometric reasons since 2 moles of HCl react for every 1 mole of products formed.

Effect of Concentration

In general, increasing the concentration of a reactant will increase the rate of a chemical reaction. One way to study the effect of concentration on reaction rate is through studying the rate using initial concentrations of the reactants (**method of** initial rates). The overall dependence of concentration of reactants on rate can be expressed as an experimental **rate law**. For the following hypothetical reaction, the rate law has the form:

$$A_{(aq)} + 2 B_{(aq)} \rightarrow C_{(aq)}$$
$$Rate = k[A]^x[B]^y$$

where k is the **rate constant**, x and y are the **orders of the individual reactants**, and [A] and [B] are the concentrations of A and B, respectively. The values for k, x, and y can only be determined experimentally; you cannot figure them out from the balanced chemical equation. The orders of reaction are an indication of how a given reactant actually reacts in a chemical reaction. For example, a reactant that reacts in a second-order fashion will quadruple the rate of reaction when the concentration of that reactant is doubled (rate = k [2]² = 4 times as fast). The sum of the individual orders of reaction will give the **overall order of the reaction**—which indicates how fast a reaction will proceed under specified conditions. Once you find the order of the reaction, you can determine the value of the rate constant (k), which is highly dependent upon reaction conditions such as temperature. A common question found on the AP Chemistry exam involves the determination of a rate law using experimental data.

EXAMPLE: Use the experimental data in the following table to determine the rate law for the reaction:

$$A_{(aq)} + 2 B_{(aq)} \rightarrow C_{(aq)}$$

Trial	Initial [A] (M)	Initial [B] (M)	Initial Rate (M/s)
1	0.20	0.20	2.5×10^{-3}
2	0.20	0.40	5.0×10^{-3}
3	0.40	0.20	1.0×10^{-2}

SOLUTION: In order to determine the rate law for this equation, you will need to use the method of initial rates, which allows you to compare the rates of reaction from two different experiments in an effort to ascertain what is happening with the orders of the reactants. The game plan should be this: first solve for the orders of the reactants (x and y), and once those variables are determined, follow up by finding the rate constant, k.

1. In order to solve for the orders of the reactant, find two trials whose concentrations remain constant for one of the reactants.

2. Write the ratio of the rate laws for these two trials and substitute the concentrations of A and B into the rate expression. With the preceding data, you will solve for the order of B first.

$$\frac{Trial\ 2}{Trial\ 1} = \frac{R_2 = k[0.20]^x[0.40]^y}{R_1 = k[0.20]^x[0.20]^y}$$

Since the rate constant is the same for all trials and the concentration of A remains constant, the ratio is reduced to $\frac{5.0\times10^{-3}}{2.5\times10^{-3}} = 2^y \text{ and } y = 1$.

3. The order of A can be found similarly as shown in the following expression. Using the same procedure as in the preceding example, the ratios of the concentrations for B are identical for Trials 1 and 3 and k is a constant, so they will be omitted from the calculation.

$$\frac{Trial\ 3}{Trial\ 1} = \frac{1.0\times10^{-2} = [0.40]^x}{2.5\times10^{-3} = [0.20]^x}$$

Upon solving this equation, the order with respect to A is 2.

4. The value of the rate constant, k, can be calculated using any experimental trial. For example, choose Trial 1 and substitute the concentrations of A and B into the rate expression and solve for the rate constant.

$$2.5\times10^{-3} = k[0.20]^2[0.20]^1$$

Solving for $k = 0.31$ M^{-2} s^{-1}.

5. The units for the rate constant will vary depending on the overall order of the reaction. In the preceding rate expression, the units are determined through a unit analysis based on the fact that the overall order is three for the rate law expression.

OVERALL RATE LAW: $Rate = 0.31\,M^{-2}s^{-1}[A]^2[B]^1$

TEST TIP

The units of the rate constant can be quickly determined by subtracting one from the overall order of the reaction and raising the concentration (M) to the inverse of this number multiplied by time^{-1}. This type of question is often found on the multiple-choice section of the test.

Collision Theory

For a chemical reaction to occur, there are three criteria that must be satisfied.

1. The two reactants must collide with one another.

2. The collision must occur with the reactants being in a specific orientation.

3. The two reactants must collide with sufficient energy known as the **energy of activation, E$_a$**.

In order to illustrate the energy of activation, a transition state diagram is utilized (see Figure 11.1). The figure represents both an **endothermic** and **exothermic** reaction.

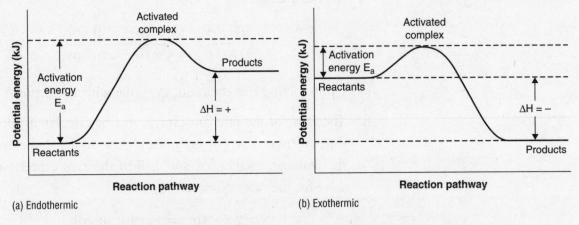

Figure 11.1. Endothermic and Exothermic Reactions

You should be able to identify the **E$_a$**, which is the difference in the potential energy between the reactants and the point of highest energy, which is the activated complex. The activated complex represents the halfway point in a reaction, where the reactants are transitioning into the final products. In addition, you can identify the diagram on the left as an endothermic reaction because the potential energy of the reactants is less than the potential energy of the products.

In contrast, the diagram on the right is exothermic due to the fact that the potential energy of the reactants is greater than the potential energy of the products.

TEST TIP

Remember there is no connection between the rate of a chemical reaction and the enthalpy (ΔH) for a chemical reaction. Kinetics and thermodynamics are two separate components involved with chemical reactions.

Integrated Rate Laws

For the AP Chemistry exam, you must be familiar with the integrated rate laws for rate expressions that are either first or second order with respect to a single reactant.

- For a first-order overall rate expression, $R = k[A]^1$, the integrated rate law takes the following form:

$$ln[A]_t - \ln[A]_0 = -kt$$

- A plot of the ln [A] vs. time will result in a straight line whose slope will be the negative of the rate constant.

- Note that all nuclear decay processes will follow a first-order decay and are discussed in further detail in Chapter 14, Nuclear Chemistry.

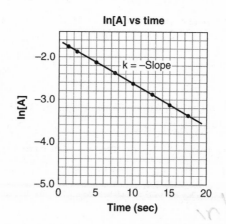

- For a second-order overall rate expression with respect to a single reactant $R = k[A]^2$, the integrated rate law takes the following form:

$$\frac{1}{[A]_t} - \frac{1}{[A]_0} = kt$$

- A plot of the 1/[A] vs. time will result in a straight line whose slope is the rate constant.

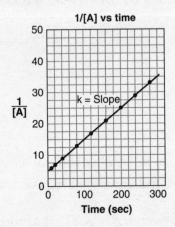

DIDYOU**KNOW?**

Nuclear decay processes can occur in fractions of a second but others, such as those that occur with nuclear waste, can take thousands of years!

Effect of Temperature on Rate

Temperature is a measure of the average kinetic energy of molecules. In general, raising the temperature will cause the reaction rate to increase. This is due to the fact that reactant molecules will be traveling at increased speed and will collide more frequently with greater kinetic energy. This results in an increased number of effective collisions that result in the formation of products. The Arrhenius equation represents the relationship between temperature and the rate constant of a reaction:

$$\ln k = -\frac{E_a}{R}\left(\frac{1}{T}\right) + \ln A$$

Note that since the Arrhenius equation deals with the energy of molecules, the value of R should be 8.31 J mol⁻¹ K⁻¹. If a plot of the natural log of k (ln k) versus the inverse of temperature (1/T) is created, it will produce a straight line whose slope allows for the calculation of the **energy of activation, E_a** for the reaction.

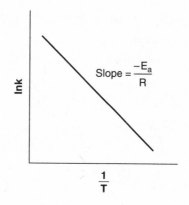

Reaction Mechanisms

A reaction mechanism represents the pathway by which reactants form products. Reaction mechanisms are classified by the number of steps involved, whether it is one (unimolecular), two (bimolecular), or three (termolecular). There are two criteria that must be met for a plausible mechanism of a chemical reaction.

1. The steps of the reaction mechanism must add up to and equal the overall reaction.

2. The experimental rate law must match the rate law derived from the mechanism.

Some reactions occur in one step and are known as **concerted reactions**. These types of reactions most often involve two reactants as shown in the following equation.

$$A + B \rightarrow C$$

When determining the rate law from a mechanism, the coefficients of the reactants represent the orders of the reactants. This is an extremely important point when determining rate law expressions from a reaction mechanism, because you can never use the coefficients to determine order, except for when determining a rate law from a reaction mechanism. For example, in the preceding mechanism, the rate law expression would be $Rate = k[A]^1[B]^1$. The orders are both one because of the coefficients in the balanced chemical equation.

TEST TIP

Orders of reaction must *always* be determined from experimental data except when working from a reaction mechanism!

When a chemical reaction involves more than two reactants, it is likely that the mechanism will contain more than one step. This can be traced back to the basic ideas of collision theory, because the likelihood of having three molecules simultaneously colliding in the correct orientation with sufficient activation energy would be quite rare. As a result, these reactions generally form **intermediates**. An intermediate in a mechanism is a short-lived, fast-reacting species that is formed in one step and quickly used up in a subsequent step. This is depicted in the following equations:

Overall reaction: $2A + B \rightarrow C + D$

Proposed mechanism: Step 1. $A + B \rightarrow I$ slow step

Step 2. $A + I \rightarrow C$ fast step

In this mechanism, Steps 1 and 2 add up to give the overall reaction, and "I" represents the intermediate. Step 1 is labeled the slow step, which makes it the **rate-determining step**. The rate-determining step is always used for determining the rate law for a chemical reaction. Therefore, the rate law for this reaction would be $Rate = k[A]^1[B]^1$. For this mechanism to be plausible, it must match the experimental rate law for the reaction.

To put a different twist on this problem and see the ramifications of the slow step, the next example makes the second step the slow step, and resultantly the first step would be in equilibrium.

Proposed mechanism: Step 1. $A + B \leftrightarrow I$ fast step

Step 2. $A + I \rightarrow C$ slow step

The rate law is written for the slow step, $R = k[A]^1[I]^1$. However, the rate law cannot contain an intermediate and must contain only reactants found in the overall reaction. Step 1 cannot be ignored since it occurs prior to the rate-determining step. By definition, the rate of the forward reaction equals the rate of the reverse reaction. Hence,

$$k_{forward}[A]^1[B]^1 = k_{reverse}[I]^1$$

and $[I] = \dfrac{k_{forward}}{k_{reverse}}[A]^1[B]^1$. Substituting into the rate-determining step from earlier, the new rate law becomes $R = k[A]^2[B]^1$.

In order to determine the rate law of a chemical reaction from a reaction mechanism, use the following guidelines:

1. The slow step rules the process.

2. Identify intermediates and make a determination as to whether they impact the rate of reaction.

3. The overall reaction must find agreement between the experimental rate law and the rate law derived from the reaction mechanism.

TEST TIP

When the rate-determining step is not the first step, all steps prior to the rate-determining step will be represented as an equilibrium between reactants and products.

Catalysts

A catalyst is a substance that increases the rate of reaction without being used up. Catalysts provide an alternative pathway for the reaction to follow, which is at a lower activation energy—thus increasing the reaction rate. As a result of the lower energy of activation, a greater number of molecules will have enough energy to form products when they collide. This is illustrated in Figure 11.2.

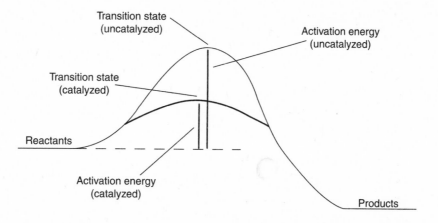

Figure 11.2. Potential Energy Diagram

In a chemical reaction, a catalyst is always recovered and only a small amount is required to increase the reaction rate. A **homogeneous catalyst** is in the same state of matter as the other reactants, while a **heterogeneous catalyst** is in a different state of matter than the reactants. A catalyst can be easily identified in a reaction mechanism because it is put in at the beginning of the reaction, and comes out on the products side at the very end. In the following mechanism, the catalyst is depicted by the letter C and the intermediate by the letter I.

Step 1. $A + C \leftrightarrow I$ fast step

Step 2. $A + I \rightarrow C + D$ slow step

The recovered catalyst will then be used again and again to speed up the chemical reaction.

DIDYOUKNOW?

A catalytic converter is a component used in the exhaust of automobiles to aid in the removal of pollutants such as nitrous oxides (NO_x), which are produced during the combustion of fossil fuels. Catalytic converters contain precious metals such as platinum because they can catalyze reactions that would otherwise take years to occur on their own in the environment.

Chapter 12

Equilibrium

Equilibrium Constants

- Equilibrium constants are ratios. See the following reaction:

$$aA + bB \leftrightarrow cC + dD$$

The ratio of the product concentrations raised to their stoichiometric coefficients, divided by the reactant concentrations raised to their stoichiometric coefficients, is the equilibrium constant, K_{eq}. This is also called the *law of mass action.*

$$K_{eq} = \frac{[C]^c[D]^d}{[A]^a[B]^b}$$

- Pure liquids or solids do not show up in the equilibrium expression because they do not change in concentration; only solutions measured as molar concentrations or pressures (as in the case of gases).

- The *equilibrium constant for a multi-step process* is equal to the product of the equilibrium constants for each step. Example: For a set of three reactions that add to equal a total reaction:

$$K_{total} = K_1 \times K_2 \times K_3$$

- The *equilibrium constant for a reverse reaction* is the inverse of the equilibrium constant for a forward reaction.

$$K_{reverse} = 1/K_{forward}$$

- There are different equilibrium constants for different types of reactions. See Table 12.1.

Table 12.1. Types of Equilibrium Constants

Constant	Used For	Example
K_c	Reactions in aqueous solution; reactants and products are expressed as molar concentrations (moles/liter)	$N_{2(aq)} + 3\ H_{2(aq)} \leftrightarrow 2\ NH_{3(aq)}$ $$K_c = \frac{[NH_3]^2}{[N_2][H_2]^3}$$
K_p	Gaseous reaction; reactants and products are expressed in units of pressure	$N_{2(g)} + 3\ H_{2(g)} \leftrightarrow 2\ NH_{3(g)}$ $$K_p = \frac{P_{NH_3}^2}{P_{N_2} P_{H_2}^3}$$
K_w	The autoionization (self-ionization) of water	$2\ H_2O_{(\ell)} \leftrightarrow H_3O^+_{(aq)} + OH^-_{(aq)}$ $K_w = [H_3O^+][OH^-] = 1.0 \times 10^{-14}$ @ 25°C
K_a	Reactions involving weak acids	$HA_{(aq)} + H_2O_{(\ell)} \leftrightarrow H_3O^+_{(aq)} + A^-_{(aq)}$ $$K_a = \frac{[H_3O^+][A^-]}{[HA]}$$
K_b	Reactions involving weak bases	$B_{(aq)} + H_2O_{(\ell)} \leftrightarrow HB^+_{(aq)} + OH^-_{(aq)}$ $$K_b = \frac{[HB^+][OH^-]}{[B]}$$
K_{sp}	Reactions involving the small amount of insoluble solid that will dissolve in water, known as the **solubility product**	$PbI_{2(s)} \leftrightarrow Pb^{+2}_{(aq)} + 2\ I^-_{(aq)}$ $K_{sp} = [Pb^{+2}][I^-]^2$

TEST TIP

The magnitude of the value of K indicates the strength of a particular species: Larger K_a values mean greater acid strength, larger K_b is a stronger base, and larger K_{sp} values mean that more solid is able to dissolve in a given amount of solvent.

Le Chatelier's Principle

- **Le Chatelier's principle** states that when a system at equilibrium is disturbed by a change in pressure, temperature, or the amount (concentration) of product or reactant, the reaction will shift to minimize the change and establish a new equilibrium.

- Change in concentration: Adding products to a reaction at equilibrium will shift the reaction to produce reactants; adding reactants will shift the reaction to produce products. In contrast, removing reactants will cause the reaction to shift to replace the reactants, while removing product will cause the reaction to shift to replace the products. See the following section on the reaction quotient, Q.

- Change in temperature: An increase in temperature causes the equilibrium to shift to use up the added heat energy. The direction of the shift depends on whether the reaction is exothermic or endothermic. For example, when energy is added to an exothermic reaction, it will cause the reaction to shift to the left to use up the additional energy added to the reaction. If the reaction was endothermic, the additional energy added to the reaction will shift the reaction to the right (form more products).

- Change in pressure: An increase in pressure causes the equilibrium to shift in the direction that contains the fewest number of gas moles.

- Addition of a catalyst or an inert gas will not cause the equilibrium to shift; the amounts of reactants and products would remain unchanged.

DIDYOUKNOW?

The carbonation of soda involves the equilibrium between carbon dioxide, water, and carbonic acid. When a can of soda is opened, the decrease in pressure causes the equilibrium to shift toward the formation of carbon dioxide (bubbles) and water.

Reaction Quotient, Q

- The reaction quotient, Q, can be used to calculate the direction a reaction will shift when products or reactants are either added or removed (Le Chatelier's principle).

- The reaction quotient for a reaction is found using the same ratio as the equilibrium constant, but at nonequilibrium conditions. For the reaction, $aA + bB \leftrightarrow cC + dD$.

$$Q = \frac{[C]^c [D]^d}{[A]^a [B]^b}$$

- If the reaction quotient is greater than the equilibrium expression, the ratio is too large. According to Le Chatelier's principle, the reaction will shift toward the left and create reactants. In summary, when $Q > K$, the reaction proceeds to the left toward reactants. When $Q < K$, the reaction proceeds to the right toward products. When $Q = K$, the reaction is at equilibrium.

EXAMPLE: See the following reaction:

$N_{2(g)} + 3 H_{2(g)} \leftrightarrow 2 NH_{3(g)}$, $K_{eq} = 5.9 \times 10^{-2}$. The molar concentrations of the species are: $[N_2] = 0.40$ M, $[H_2] = 0.80$ M, and $[NH_3] = 0.20$ M. In which direction will the reaction proceed as it begins to establish equilibrium?

SOLUTION:

$$Q = \frac{[0.20]^2}{[0.40][0.80]^3} = 0.20$$

Because $Q > K_{eq}$, the reaction will shift left toward the reactants.

Equilibrium Constants for Gaseous Reactions

- Concentrations of reactants and products in the gas phase may be expressed in units of molarity (moles/liter) or partial pressures (atm, Pa, mmHg).

- The ideal gas law (PV= nRT) is used to convert between the equilibrium constant expressed in moles/liter (K_c) to the equilibrium constant expressed in gas pressures (K_p).

$$K_p = K_c(RT)^{\Delta n}$$

$$\Delta n = \text{moles product gas} - \text{moles reactant gas}$$

$$R = \text{gas law constant (0.082 L atm / mol K)}$$

$$T = \text{Temperature (K)}$$

- The equilibrium expression for K_p only contains those species that are in the gas phase. For example, following is the K_p for the formation of ammonia from nitrogen gas and hydrogen gas:

EXAMPLE:

$$N_{2(g)} + 3 H_{2(g)} \leftrightarrow 2 NH_{3(g)}$$

$$K_p = \frac{P_{NH_3}^2}{P_{N_2} P_{H_2}^3}$$

DIDYOUKNOW?

All phase changes exist in a state of equilibrium. For example, at 100°C, water exists as both a liquid and a gas in equilibrium with one another.

TEST TIP

If pressures are given for products and reactants in an equilibrium, be sure to write the expression for K_p and not K_c.

EXAMPLE: The value of K_p for the following reaction is 8.3×10^{-3} at 700 K. What is the value for K_c?

$$N_{2(g)} + 3\,H_{2(g)} \leftrightarrow 2\,NH_{3(g)}$$

SOLUTION:

$$K_p = K_c\,(RT)^{\Delta n}$$

Δn = 2 moles gaseous product − 4 moles gaseous reactants = −2

$$8.3 \times 10^{-3} = K_c \left[\left(0.082\frac{L\ atm}{mol\ K} \right) (700\ K) \right]^{-2}$$

$$K_c = 27$$

The Dissociation of Weak Acids and Bases

- The water dissociation constant is shown in the following reaction:

$$K_w = 1.0 \times 10^{-14} = K_a \times K_b = [H_3O^+]\,[OH^-]$$

This relationship allows for computation of dissociation constants for conjugate acid–base pairs as well as concentrations of H_3O^+ and OH^- for use in pH and pOH calculations.

- The equilibrium constants K_a and K_b can be used to calculate the pH of a weak acid or weak base in aqueous solution.

EXAMPLE: What is the pH of a 0.10 molar solution of acetic acid, CH_3COOH, which has a $K_a = 1.8 \times 10^{-5}$?

SOLUTION:

1. Write the equation of the reaction that occurs when the weak acid or base is put in water, and its corresponding equilibrium expression.

$$CH_3COOH_{(aq)} + H_2O_{(\ell)} \leftrightarrow H_3O^+_{(aq)} + CH_3COO^-_{(aq)}$$

When the weak acid is placed in water, some number of moles will dissociate. For each mole of weak acid that dissociates, one mole of the proton and one mole of the weak base will be formed.

2. Construct a table to determine the amount of dissociation of the weak acid.

$$CH_3COOH_{(aq)} + H_2O_{(\ell)} \leftrightarrow H_3O^+_{(aq)} + CH_3COO^-_{(aq)}$$

Initial [ ]	0.10	—	0	0
Change	−x	—	+x	+x
Final [ ]	0.10−x	—	x	x

For the AP Chemistry exam, the simplifying assumption can always be made for all types of equilibrium problems.

3. Write the equilibrium expression using the final concentrations from the preceding table.

$$K_a = 1.8 \times 10^{-5} = \frac{x^2}{0.10}$$

4. Solve for x, which will be the $[H_3O^+]$ at equilibrium.

$$x = 1.3 \times 10^{-3} \, M$$

5. When calculating pH or % dissociation, always use the equilibrium $[H_3O^+]$.

$$pH = -\log[H_3O^+] \qquad \% \, dissociation = \frac{[H_3O^+]_{eq}}{[CH_3COOH]_{initial}}$$

$$pH = 2.87 \qquad \% \, dissociation = \frac{1.3 \times 10^{-3}}{0.10} \times 100 = 1.3\%$$

TEST TIP

For any problems that involve equilibrium, you must create a table as shown in step 2 of the previous problem in order to determine equilibrium concentrations. This will help you to organize the information and show your work for the equilibrium problem.

Hydrolysis

- Hydrolysis reactions occur when a salt containing the conjugate of either a weak acid or weak base is dissolved in solution, producing a solution that is either acidic or basic.

- Salts containing the conjugate base of a weak acid act as bases.

Example: $F^-_{(aq)} + H_2O_{(\ell)} \leftrightarrow HF_{(aq)} + OH^-_{(aq)}$

The equilibrium would have a K_b value calculated from the K_a value of HF.

- Salts containing the conjugate acid of a weak base act as acids.

Example: $NH_4^+_{(aq)} + H_2O_{(\ell)} \leftrightarrow NH_{3\,(aq)} + H_3O^+_{(aq)}$

The equilibrium would have a K_a value calculated from the K_b value of NH_3.

Solubility Product Constants

- The solubility product constant (K_{sp}) refers to the product of the molar concentration of soluble ions that exist at the saturation point of the solution. This is called the **molar solubility**.

- K_{sp} occurs for ionic compounds that are considered insoluble. Insoluble salts are soluble to some miniscule degree and the K_{sp} allows you to compute the concentrations of the ions that have dissolved.

- There are two basic types of problems that you will see that involve K_{sp}:

  1. Find the molar solubility of a compound based on the value of the K_{sp} for that compound.

  2. Determine whether a precipitate will form when two solutions are added together.

EXAMPLE: The K_{sp} for $BaCO_3$ is 2.58×10^{-9}. What is the molar solubility of barium carbonate?

SOLUTION:

$$BaCO_{3\,(s)} + H_2O_{(l)} \leftrightarrow Ba^{+2}_{(aq)} + CO_3^{-2}_{(aq)}$$

$$K_{sp} = [Ba^{+2}][CO_3^{-2}] = 2.58 \times 10^{-9}$$

$$x = \text{the molar solubility of } BaCO_3$$

$$K_{sp} = 2.58 \times 10^{-9} = (x)(x)$$

$$x = 5.08 \times 10^{-5}\ M = (BaCO_3)$$

- The following example shows how to determine whether a precipitate will form when two solutions are mixed together.

EXAMPLE: A student mixed 10.0 mL of 1.0×10^{-4} M lead (II) nitrate solution with 500. mL of 1.0×10^{-5} M potassium iodide solution. Will a precipitate form? The K_{sp} for lead (II) iodide is 1.8×10^{-8}.

SOLUTION: $PbI_{2\,(s)} + H_2O_{(\ell)} \leftrightarrow Pb^{+2}_{\,(aq)} + 2\,I^{-1}_{\,(aq)}$

1. Calculate the new molar concentrations of the Pb^{+2} and I^{-1}.

$$Pb^{+2} = \frac{(10.0\ mL)(1.0 \times 10^{-4}\,M)}{510.\ mL} = 2.0 \times 10^{-6}\,M$$

$$[I^{-1}] = \frac{(500.0\ mL)(1.0 \times 10^{-5}\,M)}{510.\ mL} = 9.8 \times 10^{-6}\,M$$

2. Calculate the value of Q_{sp}, where $Q_{sp} = [Pb^{+2}]\,[I^{-1}]^2$

$$Q_{sp} = [2.0 \times 10^{-6}][9.8 \times 10^{-6}]^2 = 1.9 \times 10^{-16}$$

3. Compare Q_{sp} to K_{sp}. If $Q_{sp} < K_{sp}$, then no precipitate will form because the reaction will shift to the right. If $Q_{sp} > K_{sp}$, then a precipitate will form because the reaction will shift to the left. Because $Q_{sp} < K_{sp}$, there will be no precipitate of PbI_2.

Common Ion Effect

- The solubility of a slightly soluble compound will be lowered when a common ion is introduced.

EXAMPLE: The K_{sp} for $Mg(OH)_2$ is 8.9×10^{-12}. What is the molar solubility of magnesium hydroxide in a solution that has a $[OH^-] = 0.0040$ M?

SOLUTION: $Mg(OH)_{2(s)} + H_2O_{(\ell)} \leftrightarrow Mg^{+2}_{\,(aq)} + 2\,OH^-_{\,(aq)}$

$K_{sp} = [Mg^{+2}][OH^-]^2$ where x = molar solubility of $Mg(OH)_2$

$8.9 \times 10^{-12} = [x][2x + 0.0040]^2$ which simplifies to

$8.9 \times 10^{-12} = [x][0.0040]^2$

$x = [Mg(OH)_2] = 5.6 \times 10^{-7} M$

Buffers

- A buffer is an aqueous solution consisting of a weak acid and its conjugate base, or a weak base and its conjugate acid.

- The pH of a buffer solution will not change appreciably when either an acid or base is added to it.

- The capacity of a buffer solution to maintain pH will be exhausted if either component of the buffer is exhausted.

- In order to calculate the pH of a buffer, you can utilize the Henderson-Hasselbach equation, which can be written in terms of an acidic buffer or a basic buffer.

Acidic Buffer: $pH = pK_a + \log \dfrac{[salt]}{[acid]}$

Basic Buffer: $pOH = pK_b + \log \dfrac{[salt]}{[base]}$

$pK_a = -\log K_a$

$pK_b = -\log K_b$

[salt] = concentration of the salt (conjugate base or conjugate acid)

[acid] = concentration of the acid if it is an acidic buffer

[base] = concentration of the base if it is a basic buffer

EXAMPLE: What is the pH of the buffer solution created by combining 100. mL of 0.20 M acetic acid and 400. mL of 0.10 M sodium acetate? $K_a = 1.8 \times 10^{-5}$ for acetic acid.

SOLUTION:

1. Write the dissociation equation for the weak acid.

$$CH_3COOH_{(aq)} + H_2O_{(\ell)} \leftrightarrow H_3O^+_{(aq)} + CH_3COO^-_{(aq)}$$

2. Calculate the new concentrations of the weak acid and the salt of the weak acid.

$$[CH_3COOH] = \frac{(100.mL)(0.20\ M)}{500.mL} = 0.040\ M$$

$$[CH_3COO^-] = \frac{(400.mL)(0.10\ M)}{500.mL} = 0.080\ M$$

3. Use the Henderson-Hasselbach equation to determine the pH of the buffer.

$$pH = -\log(1.8 \times 10^{-5}) + \log \frac{[0.080]}{[0.040]}$$

$$pH = 5.04$$

TEST TIP

In titrations involving weak acids or weak bases, the pH is computed using the Henderson-Hasselbach equation for volumes of added titrant prior to reaching the equivalence point of the titration.

Time for a quiz
- Review strategies in Chapter 2
- Take Quiz 6 at the REA Study Center
  (www.rea.com/studycenter)

Electrochemistry

Application of Redox

Electrochemistry is the application of oxidation and reduction half reactions. There are numerous oxidation–reduction (redox) reactions that occur spontaneously, such as the displacement of silver metal when a copper wire is submerged in a silver nitrate solution.

$$2\,Ag^+ + Cu \rightarrow Cu^{+2} + 2\,Ag$$

Thermochemistry is closely associated with electrochemistry. The Gibbs free energy, ΔG, not only indicates whether a reaction is spontaneous or nonspontaneous, it also is a measure of the amount of work that can be done by a system on its surroundings. Although the preceding reaction is spontaneous, the free energy of this reaction cannot be harnessed.

In electrochemistry, there are two different types of electrochemical cells:

1. A **voltaic cell (galvanic cell)** is commonly called a *battery*. This type of cell contains a spontaneous chemical reaction that produces electricity and supplies it to an external circuit.

2. Nonspontaneous reactions give rise to an **electrolytic cell**. This cell uses electrical energy from an external source to force a nonspontaneous redox reaction to occur.

DIDYOU**KNOW?**

The coating of metals onto a second surface is accomplished through a process called *electroplating*. Chrome—which is found on car bumpers, motorcycle frames, and exhausts—is a thin layer of chromium plated onto steel. The chromium not only adds an attractive silvery shine, but also inhibits corrosion.

Voltaic Cells

Electrical conduction in chemistry occurs through the motion of electrons through a metallic medium or by the movement of ions in an aqueous solution or molten salt. In order to harness the free energy of a spontaneous redox reaction, the two half reactions of the redox reaction are separated into two half cells. These half cells consist of an **electrode** and a solution of the ion involved in either the oxidation or reduction process. Electrodes are surfaces upon which a reduction or oxidation half reaction occurs. They may participate in the reaction or simply serve as a medium through which electrons travel (inert electrode). The mnemonic **"Red Cat and An Ox"** is useful to help remember that reduction occurs at the cathode (positive electrode) and oxidation at the anode (negative electrode). See Figure 13.1 for a typical voltaic cell construction, illustrating a cell consisting of copper and zinc half cells.

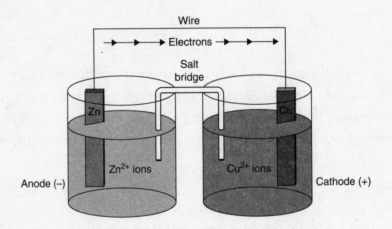

Figure 13.1. Typical Voltaic Cell Construction

- The anode consists of the oxidation of Zn to Zn^{+2}.

- The cathode involves the reduction of Cu^{+2} to Cu.

- The overall reaction is $Zn + Cu^{+2} \rightarrow Zn^{+2} + Cu$.

- Electrons are always generated at the anode and travel to the cathode.

- A salt bridge connects the two half cells and completes the circuit.

TEST TIP

When drawing a voltaic cell, always write the anode on the left and the cathode on the right. You read a book left to right, so keep it that way to remember electron flow in the cell.

Salt Bridge

A salt bridge is a device constructed using an agar solution containing an ionic salt. It is essential for the cell because it maintains charge neutrality in each beaker for each half cell as well as completing the circuit of the cell. You should remember that under no circumstances do electrons flow through the salt bridge—only ions!

DID YOU KNOW?

Bacteria can convert organic waste directly into carbon dioxide through a redox reaction, and it is possible to harness the electrons utilized during this process. These microbial fuel cells can produce a measurable amount of electricity and there is currently research to use these fuel cells in remote areas of the world to power homes and portable devices.

 EXAMPLE:

Anodic reaction	$Zn \rightarrow Zn^{+2} + 2\ e^-$
Cathodic reaction	$Cu^{+2} + 2e^- \rightarrow Cu$

Positive ions from the salt bridge will flow into the cathode half cell to replace the Cu^{+2} being reduced. Anions forming the salt bridge will flow into the anode half cell to provide counter ions for the Zn^{+2} ions that are formed.

Reduction Potentials

Every half reaction has a potential or voltage associated with it. For Part II of the exam, a table of standard reduction potentials will be supplied (see Figure 13.2). Reduction potentials indicate the tendency for a reduction half reaction to occur when compared to a second half reaction. Reduction potentials are relative and based on the standard hydrogen electrode having a potential of zero volts (0 V). Another key thing to remember is that if the reduction half reaction is reversed, the sign of the potential is changed and now represents the oxidation potential.

TEST TIP

You can use oxidation potentials to predict the reactivity of metals, thus creating an activity series that can determine which species are displaced in a single-replacement reaction.

Half-reaction			$E°(V)$
$F_{2(g)} + 2\,e^-$	$\rightarrow$	$2\,F^-$	2.87
$Co^{3+} + e^-$	$\rightarrow$	Co^{2+}	1.82
$Au^{3+} + 3\,e^-$	$\rightarrow$	$Au_{(s)}$	1.50
$Cl_{2(g)} + 2\,e^-$	$\rightarrow$	$2\,Cl^-$	1.36
$O_{2(g)} + 4\,H^+ + 4\,e^-$	$\rightarrow$	$2\,H_2O_{(\ell)}$	1.23
$Br_{2(\ell)} + 2\,e^-$	$\rightarrow$	$2\,Br^-$	1.07
$2\,Hg^{2+} + 2\,e^-$	$\rightarrow$	Hg_2^{2+}	0.92
$Hg^{2+} + 2\,e^-$	$\rightarrow$	$Hg_{(\ell)}$	0.85
$Ag^+ + e^-$	$\rightarrow$	$Ag_{(s)}$	0.80
$Hg_2^{2+} + 2\,e^-$	$\rightarrow$	$2\,Hg_{(\ell)}$	0.79
$Fe^{3+} + e^-$	$\rightarrow$	Fe^{2+}	0.77
$I_{2(s)} + 2\,e^-$	$\rightarrow$	$2\,I^-$	0.53
$Cu^+ + e^-$	$\rightarrow$	$Cu_{(s)}$	0.52
$Cu^{2+} + 2\,e^-$	$\rightarrow$	$Cu_{(s)}$	0.34
$Cu^{2+} + e^-$	$\rightarrow$	Cu^+	0.15
$Sn^{4+} + 2\,e^-$	$\rightarrow$	Sn^{2+}	0.15
$S_{(s)} + 2\,H^+ + 2\,e^-$	$\rightarrow$	$H_2S_{(g)}$	0.14
$2\,H^+ + 2\,e^-$	$\rightarrow$	$H_{2(g)}$	0.00
$Pb^{2+} + 2\,e^-$	$\rightarrow$	$Pb_{(s)}$	−0.13
$Sn^{2+} + 2\,e^-$	$\rightarrow$	$Sn_{(s)}$	−0.14
$Ni^{2+} + 2\,e^-$	$\rightarrow$	$Ni_{(s)}$	−0.25
$Co^{2+} + 2\,e^-$	$\rightarrow$	$Co_{(s)}$	−0.28
$Tl^+ + e^-$	$\rightarrow$	$Tl(s)$	−0.34
$Cd^{2+} + 2\,e^-$	$\rightarrow$	$Cd_{(s)}$	−0.40
$Cr^{3+} + e^-$	$\rightarrow$	Cr^{2+}	−0.41
$Fe^{2+} + 2\,e^-$	$\rightarrow$	$Fe_{(s)}$	−0.44
$Cr^{3+} + 3\,e^-$	$\rightarrow$	$Cr_{(s)}$	−0.74
$Zn^{2+} + 2\,e^-$	$\rightarrow$	$Zn_{(s)}$	−0.76
$Mn^{2+} + 2\,e^-$	$\rightarrow$	$Mn_{(s)}$	−1.18

Figure 13.2. Standard Reduction Potentials in Aqueous Solution at 25°C

Half-reaction			$E°(V)$
$Al^{3+} + 3\,e^-$	$\rightarrow$	$Al_{(s)}$	-1.66
$Be^{2+} + 2\,e^-$	$\rightarrow$	$Be_{(s)}$	-1.70
$Mg^{2+} + 2\,e^-$	$\rightarrow$	$Mg_{(s)}$	-2.37
$Na^+ + e^-$	$\rightarrow$	$Na_{(s)}$	-2.71
$Ca^{2+} + 2\,e^-$	$\rightarrow$	$Ca_{(s)}$	-2.87
$Sr^{2+} + 2\,e^-$	$\rightarrow$	$Sr_{(s)}$	-2.89
$Ba^{2+} + 2\,e^-$	$\rightarrow$	$Ba_{(s)}$	-2.90
$Rb^+ + e^-$	$\rightarrow$	$Rb_{(s)}$	-2.92
$K^+ + e^-$	$\rightarrow$	$K_{(s)}$	-2.92
$Cs^+ + e^-$	$\rightarrow$	$Cs_{(s)}$	-2.92
$Li^+ + e^-$	$\rightarrow$	$Li_{(s)}$	-3.05

Figure 13.2. (*continued*)

TEST TIP

The chart of standard reduction potentials (Figure 13.2) can be helpful when you are completing the section of the exam pertaining to predicting products, especially if you forget the oxidation state of a transition metal.

Calculation of the Cell Potential

If we look at the electric cell discussed previously, we can calculate the overall cell potential of a redox reaction. Following are the two reduction reactions that you must examine:

$$Cu^{+2} + 2e^- \rightarrow Cu \qquad E^°_{red} = +0.34V$$

$$Zn^{+2} + 2e^- \rightarrow Zn \qquad E^°_{red} = -0.76V$$

The magnitude of the reduction potential indicates the likelihood that a reduction reaction will occur. Every reduction reaction requires an oxidation reaction, so in this case zinc will be oxidized and the reaction must be flipped because it has a lower reduction potential. When reversing the reaction, the sign of the potential is changed as well. The equation now represents an oxidation potential.

$$Zn \rightarrow Zn^{+2} + 2e^- \qquad E^°_{ox} = +0.76V$$

In order to calculate the overall cell potential for the redox reaction, the oxidation and reduction half reactions are added:

$$E^{\circ}_{cell} = E^{\circ}_{Oxidation} + E^{\circ}_{Reduction}$$

EXAMPLE:

$$Cu^{+2} + 2e^- \rightarrow Cu \qquad\qquad E^{\circ}_{red} = +0.34V$$

$$Zn \rightarrow Zn^{+2} + 2e^- \qquad E^{\circ}_{ox} = +0.76V$$

$$Cu^{+2} + Zn \rightarrow Zn^{+2} + Cu \qquad E^{\circ}_{cell} = +1.10V$$

Remember when adding the two half reactions, the number of electrons lost during the oxidation must equal the number of electrons gained by the reduction. The overall cell potential is computed by adding the reduction and oxidation cell potentials. However, if one or both of the half reactions require a multiplicative factor to balance electrons, *do not* multiply the cell potential and sum the reduction and oxidation cell potentials as described previously.

EXAMPLE: For the following equation, calculate the standard cell potential for the following reaction.

$$3\ Sn^{+4} + 2\ Cr \rightarrow 3\ Sn^{+2} + 2\ Cr^{+3}$$

SOLUTION:

$$3\ (Sn^{+4} + 2e^- \rightarrow Sn^{+2}) \qquad\qquad E^{\circ}_{red} = +0.15V$$

$$2\ (Cr \rightarrow Cr^{+3} + 3e^-) \qquad E^{\circ}_{ox} = +0.74V$$

$$3\ Sn^{+4} + 2\ Cr \leftrightarrow 3\ Sn^{+2} + 2\ Cr^{+3} \qquad E^{\circ}_{cell} = +0.89V$$

Note that the reduction and oxidation potentials were not multiplied by the coefficients.

Relationship of Cell Potential to Gibbs Free Energy

For a voltaic cell, the overall cell potential will always be positive and signifies a spontaneous redox reaction. The relationship between the overall cell potential and the free energy is shown in the following equation:

$$\Delta G^\circ = -nFE^\circ$$

n = number of electrons lost or gained

F = Faraday's constant; 96,500 coulombs/mole

E° = standard cell potential

The free energy of the reaction can also be used to calculate the equilibrium constant, K, for a reaction.

$$\Delta G^\circ = -RTlnK = -2.303RTlogK$$

R = gas constant, 8.31 J/mol K

T = absolute temperature, K

K = equilibrium constant

The combination of the two equations can be used to relate the cell potential of a redox reaction to its equilibrium constant.

$$nFE^\circ = RTlnK$$

TEST TIP

You should make sure that the units of ΔG are in Joules, not kilojoules, when calculating an equilibrium constant.

$Sn^{+4} \rightarrow Sn^{+2} \rightarrow$ reduced cath

$Cr \rightarrow Cr^{+3} \rightarrow$ oxidized an

$.15 + .74 = .89$

EXAMPLE: For the following equation, calculate the standard cell potential, the free energy, and the equilibrium constant.

$$3\ Sn^{+4} + 2\ Cr \leftrightarrow 3\ Sn^{+2} + 2\ Cr^{+3}$$

SOLUTION:

$$3\ (Sn^{+4} + 2e^- \rightarrow Sn^{+2}) \qquad E^°_{red} = +0.15V$$

$$2\ (Cr \rightarrow Cr^{+3} + 3e^-) \qquad E^°_{ox} = +0.74V$$

$$3\ Sn^{+4} + 2\ Cr \leftrightarrow 3\ Sn^{+2} + 2\ Cr^{+3} \qquad E^°_{cell} = +0.89V$$

$$G^° = -(6\ mole\ e^-)(96,500C\ /\ mole\ e^-)(0.89V) =$$
$$G^° = -5.2 \times 1^5 J$$

$$-5.2 \times 10^5 J = -\left(8.31\frac{J}{mol\ K}\right)(298\ K)\ln K$$

$$K = 1.6 \times 10^{91}$$

Nernst Equation

Often, chemical reactions are not carried out under standard conditions (1 atm, 25°C, and 1 M solution concentration). Under nonstandard conditions, the cell potential (E_{cell}) can be computed using the Nernst equation.

$$E_{cell} = E^°_{cell} - \frac{RT}{nF}lnQ$$

E_{cell} = cell potential for nonstandard conditions

$E^°_{cell}$ = standard cell potential

R = 8.31 J/mol K

T = absolute temperature, K

F = Faraday, 96,500 C/mole e$^-$

n = number of electrons lost or gained

Q = reaction quotient

The reaction quotient is depicted as follows for a reaction occurring in both the forward and reverse directions.

$$Q = \frac{[C]^c[D]^d}{[A]^a[B]^b}, \text{ where } a\,A + b\,B \leftrightarrow c\,C + d\,D$$

At 25°C, the Nernst equation reduces to the following:

$$E_{cell} = E_{cell}^\circ - \frac{0.0592}{n} \log Q \text{ at } 25\,^\circ C$$

prod
reac

EXAMPLE: Calculate cell potential (E) for an Al–Cu cell in which the temperature is 25.0 °C and the $[Cu^{+2}] = 0.25$ M and $[Al^{+3}]$ is 0.75 M.

SOLUTION:

$$3\,(Cu^{+2} + 2e^- \rightarrow Cu) \qquad\qquad E_{red}^\circ = +0.34V$$

$$2\,(Al \rightarrow Al^{+3} + 3e^-) \qquad\qquad E_{ox}^\circ = +1.66V$$

$$\overline{3\,Cu^{+2} + 2\,Al \rightarrow 2\,Al^{+3} + 3\,Cu \qquad E_{cell}^\circ = +2.00V}$$

$$E_{cell} = 2.00V - \frac{0.0592}{6} \log \frac{[0.75]^2}{[0.25]^3}$$

$$E_{cell} = 1.98V$$

ΔG and Nonstandard Conditions

Although the data for standard conditions is prevalent, most reactions do not occur under these specific circumstances. It is still important to predict spontaneity though, so it will be necessary to calculate ΔG rather than ΔG°. Following is the relationship between ΔG and ΔG°:

$$\Delta G = \Delta G^\circ + RT \ln Q = \Delta G^\circ + 2.303\,RT \log Q$$

$R = 8.31\,\text{J/mol K}$

T = absolute temperature, K

Q = reaction quotient

ΔG° = Gibbs free energy under standard conditions

ΔG can be related to the cell potential at nonstandard conditions, as well.

$$\Delta G = -nFE$$

Here, E is calculated using the Nernst equation.

Electrolytic Cell

In addition to Voltaic cells, there is another type of electrochemical cell called an **electrolytic cell.** An electrolytic cell is a nonspontaneous redox reaction that requires energy from an external source. Similar to before, reduction still takes place at the cathode and oxidation at the anode.

Electrolysis of a Molten Salt

Figure 13.3 shows an electrolytic cell used to separate the components of a molten salt: NaCl. You will notice that unlike the voltaic cells from before, there is an external source of electricity (a battery).

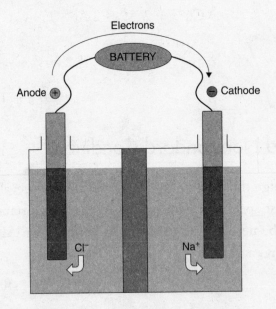

Figure 13.3.   Electrolysis of a Molten Salt

$$2 \, (Na^+ + e^- \rightarrow Na) \qquad E^{\circ}_{red} = -2.71V$$

$$2 \, Cl^- \rightarrow Cl_2 + 2e^- \qquad E^{\circ}_{ox} = -1.36V$$

$$2 \, Cl^{-1} + 2 \, Na^+ \rightarrow 2 \, Na + Cl_2 \qquad E^{\circ}_{cell} = -4.07V$$

Based on the preceding half reactions, you will note that there are negative voltages for both reactions. Since there is no such thing as a negative voltage, the negative sign simply means it is a nonspontaneous process and 4.07 V must be supplied for the reaction to take place.

Electrolysis of Aqueous Salts

The electrolysis of aqueous solutions also introduces the possibility of the oxidation and reduction of water in addition to the cation and anion of the salt. The following equations demonstrate the electrolysis of water:

$$2\,H_2O + 2\,e^- \rightarrow H_2 + 2\,OH^- \qquad E^{\circ}_{red} = -0.83V$$

$$2\,H_2O \rightarrow O_2 + 4\,H^+ + 4\,e^- \qquad E^{\circ}_{ox} = -1.23V$$

In order to determine which oxidation or reduction reaction occurs, you must compare the oxidation and reduction cell potentials. The cell potential that is the largest will be the half reaction that occurs.

EXAMPLE: What is produced at the anode and cathode with the electrolysis of $CuF_{2(aq)}$?

SOLUTION: **Anode**

$$2\,H_2O \rightarrow O_2 + 4\,H^+ + 4\,e^- \qquad E^{\circ}_{ox} = -1.23V$$

$$2\,F^- \rightarrow F_2 + 2\,e^- \qquad E^{\circ}_{ox} = -2.23V$$

- The oxidation of water occurs at the anode because the oxidation potential for water is larger (less negative).

Cathode

$$2\,H_2O + 2\,e^- \rightarrow H_2 + 2\,OH^- \qquad E^{\circ}_{red} = -0.83V$$

$$Cu^{+2} + 2\,e^- \rightarrow Cu \qquad E^{\circ}_{ox} = +0.34V$$

- The reduction of copper will occur at the cathode because its reduction potential is larger. The overall reaction would be as follows:

$$2\,H_2O + 2\,Cu^{+2} \rightarrow 2\,Cu + O_2 + 4\,H^+ \qquad E^{\circ}_{cell} = -0.89V$$

- The negative sign simply means it is a nonspontaneous process and 0.89 V must be supplied for the reaction to take place.

Electrolysis Stoichiometry

The amount of substance reduced or oxidized in an electrolytic cell can be computed through stoichiometry. The number of coulombs of charge can be calculated if you know both the number of amps and how long the electrolysis reaction was run as depicted in the following equation:

$$I = \frac{q}{t}$$

I = current (amps)

t = time (seconds)

q = charge (coulombs)

In order to determine the amount of reduced or oxidized product, the amount of charge involved with the reaction is computed. Utilizing Faraday's constant and the reduction half reaction, the amount of product can be calculated.

EXAMPLE: What is the amount of copper that can be produced if an aqueous solution of copper (II) chloride is subjected to a 5.00 A current for 2.0 hours?

SOLUTION:

$$Cu^{+2} + 2\,e^- \rightarrow Cu$$

$$q = 5.00\,A \times 7200\,s = 36,000\,C$$

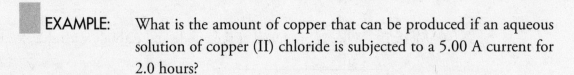

$$36,000\,C \times \frac{1\ mole\ e^-}{96,500\ C} \times \frac{1\ mole\ Cu}{2\ mole\ e^-} \times \frac{63.55\ g\ Cu}{1\ mole\ Cu} = 12\ g\ Cu$$

Nuclear Chemistry

Chapter 14

Fundamentals of Nuclear Chemistry

Nuclear chemistry involves chemical reactions that deal with the loss and gain of particles found within the nucleus—protons and neutrons. In these reactions, the nucleus undergoes a fundamental change that alters its identity. In radioactive atoms, the nuclei are unstable and may emit particles or energy called **radiation**. You should know that only certain isotopes of elements are radioactive (**radioisotopes**). There is also a variety of decay processes that can occur that transform an unstable nucleus in a high energy state into a more stable nucleus. These decay processes result in a net release of energy and occur as first-order rate expressions.

Types of Decay Processes

Alpha Decay

Alpha decay involves the emission of an alpha (α) particle, which is essentially a helium nucleus: ^4_2He or $^4_2\alpha$. This type of decay occurs for unstable radioisotopes having an atomic number greater than 82. Alpha particles are relatively harmless and cannot even penetrate a piece of paper.

EXAMPLE:

$$^{226}_{88}Ra \rightarrow ^4_2He + ^{222}_{86}Rn$$

Mass number | $226 = 4 + 222$

Atomic number | $88 = 2 + 86$

Beta Decay

Beta decay involves the emission of a beta (β) particle, $_{-1}^{0}e$. This type of decay process occurs when the proton-to-neutron ratio within the nucleus is too low for the radioisotope. Beta particle emission involves the splitting of a neutron into a proton and high-speed electrons that are ejected from the nucleus. As a result, the emission of the beta particle will cause the number of neutrons to decrease and the number of protons to increase. Beta particles have more penetrating power than alpha particles, but are stopped readily by dense materials such as lead.

EXAMPLE: beta decay: $_{0}^{1}n \rightarrow {}_{1}^{1}p + {}_{-1}^{0}e$

$$_{53}^{131}I \rightarrow {}_{54}^{131}Xe + {}_{-1}^{0}e$$

For beta decay, the mass number will stay the same but the atomic number (# of protons) will increase. Because the number of protons is increasing, the element (and thus the atomic symbol) changes.

Gamma Radiation

Gamma radiation or gamma rays, $_{0}^{0}\gamma$, is a form of extremely high-energy electromagnetic radiation of small wavelength. Unlike alpha and beta decay, gamma radiation is not a particle—but rather the most powerful form of electromagnetic radiation. Gamma radiation is often emitted during the alpha and beta decay processes. Table 14.1 summarizes these decay processes.

Table 14.1   Characteristics of α, β, and γ Radiation

Name	Symbols	Charge	Nature of Radiation	Mass(g)
Alpha	$_{2}^{4}He$ or $_{2}^{4}\alpha$	+2	Helium atoms	6.64×10^{-24}
Beta	$_{-1}^{0}e$ or $_{-1}^{0}\beta$	−1	High-speed electrons	9.11×10^{-28}
Gamma	$_{0}^{0}\gamma$	0	High-energy photons	0

Positron Emission

A radioisotope can also have a neutron-to-proton ratio that is too low. This is the case with positron emission. A positron, $_{+1}^{0}e$, is a positively charged particle having the same mass of an electron. When a nucleus emits a positron, it allows for a proton to be converted to a neutron.

EXAMPLE: $_{1}^{1}p \rightarrow {}_{0}^{1}n + {}_{+1}^{0}e$

$_{6}^{11}C \rightarrow {}_{5}^{11}B + {}_{1}^{0}e$

Electron Capture

Electron capture is similar to positron emission because the neutron-to-proton ratio in the nucleus is too low. However, in this process, a proton captures an electron from the electron cloud and combines to form a neutron.

DIDYOU**KNOW?**

Radioisotopes are often utilized in medical diagnostics. For example, iodine-131 is used to test the activity of the thyroid gland.

EXAMPLE: $_{1}^{1}p + {}_{1}^{0}e \rightarrow {}_{0}^{1}n$

$_{37}^{81}Rb + {}_{-1}^{0}e \rightarrow {}_{36}^{81}Kr$

TEST TIP

There is an easy way to determine which decay process will occur for a particular radioisotope:

- if the atomic mass of the radioisotope is greater than 82, alpha decay will most likely occur;
- if the radioisotope mass is greater than the atomic mass of the element, beta decay will most likely occur;
- if the radioisotope mass is less than the atomic mass of the element, either electron capture or positron emission will occur.

Half-Life

The time it takes for one half of a radioisotope to decay is known as the *half-life*. The half-life of a particular isotope can vary from a fraction of a second to thousands of years. Figure 14.1 illustrates the concept of a half-life for ^{15}O.

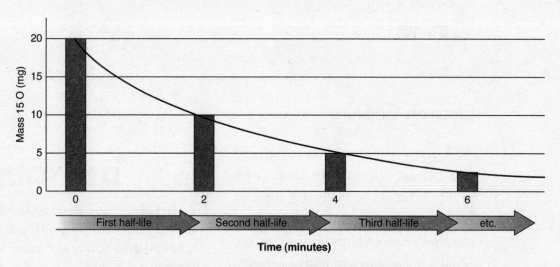

Figure 14.1   Graph of Half-Life Nuclear Decay

Because all nuclear decay processes occur via first-order kinetics, you can utilize the integrated first-order rate equation to follow the decay process. If you recall, the integrated first-order rate law takes the form:

$$ln\frac{[A]_t}{[A]_0} = kt$$

$[A]_t$ = concentration at time t

$[A]_0$ = initial concentration

k = rate constant

The half-life of a radioisotope can be computed by substituting $\frac{1}{2}[A]_0 = [A]_t$ because half of the original amount of the radioisotope will have disappeared. This reduces the integrated rate equation to:

$$t_{1/2} = \frac{0.693}{k}$$

EXAMPLE: A 1.00 g of ^{90}Sr is initially present. After 2 years, 0.953 g remains. What is the half-life of ^{90}Sr?

SOLUTION:

First, solve for the rate constant.

$$ln\frac{0.953}{1.00} = -k(2\ years)$$

$$k = 0.0241 yr^{-1}$$

Then solve for the half-life.

$$t_{1/2} = \frac{0.693}{0.0241\ yr^{-1}}$$

$$t_{1/2} = 28.8\ years$$

TEST TIP

Even though you do not have a calculator on the multiple-choice section of the test, you can still determine an amount of substance left after a given amount of half-lives by taking half of the original amount for each half-life. Show your work next to the multiple-choice question to avoid confusion.

Time for a quiz
- Review strategies in Chapter 2
- Take Quiz 7 at the REA Study Center
  (www.rea.com/studycenter)

Descriptive and Organic Chemistry

Colors of Aqueous Solutions

Many aqueous solutions are clear, while others have a distinct color. The colors of popular species are given in the following table:

Species	Color
Ni^{+2}	Green
Mn^{+2}	Pinkish/purple
Cr^{+3}	Navy blue
Cu^{+2}	Royal blue
Co^{+2}, Co^{+4}	Blue/pink
Fe^{+2}	Rusty yellow/orange
CrO_4^{-2}	Yellow
$Cr_2O_7^{-2}$	Orange
MnO_4^-	Purple
I^-	Yellow
Br^-	Colorless
$Br_{2\,(\ell)}$	Brownish
$I_{2\,(s)}$	Purple
$Cl_{2\,(g)}$	Yellowish-green

TEST TIP

On the AP Chemistry exam you should be able to identify the color associated with a particular molecule or ion. This is a popular subject for questions in the multiple-choice section.

Colors of Ions in a Flame Test

When metallic ions are placed in a flame, the electrons are promoted to excited states and subsequently fall back down to the ground state, giving off specific wavelengths of light. These different wavelengths result in colors that correspond to the primary and dominant electron transitions. Flame tests are useful as a means for identifying ions in unknown compounds because the color of the flame is much like a fingerprint for an ionic compound. The colors associated with popular cations are listed in the following table.

Ion	Color
Li^+	Red
Na^+	Yellow
K^+	Purple
Cu^{+2}	Teal
Ca^{+2}	Orange
Ba^{+2}	Green
Sr^{+2}	Red

DIDYOUKNOW?

The active ingredients in sunscreens are organic molecules that absorb ultraviolet light from 290–400 nm. In general, it is the presence of benzene rings and other double bonds that absorb these specific energies of light—acting as a barrier between harmful UV rays and your skin.

TEST TIP

Similar to the colors of aqueous solutions, flame test colors would most likely show up in the multiple-choice section. They are also a valuable way of distinguishing compounds in a qualitative analysis.

Organic Chemistry

- Organic chemistry pertains to the chemistry of carbon-containing compounds.

- There is very little organic chemistry on the AP Chemistry exam; however, a basic knowledge of nomenclature and reactions is highly beneficial.

- The organic chemistry section can be separated into three basic components: hydrocarbons, functional groups, and chemical reactions.

Hydrocarbons

Hydrocarbons are molecules that contain only carbon and hydrogen. There are three different classifications of linear hydrocarbons, which will be discussed.

Alkanes

Alkanes are saturated hydrocarbons that contain only single bonds and have the formula C_nH_{2n+2}. In order to name hydrocarbons, you must know the prefixes associated with the number of carbon atoms in the carbon backbone of the molecule, as shown in the following table.

Number	Prefix	Number	Prefix
1	meth-	6	hex-
2	eth-	7	hept-
3	prop-	8	oct-
4	but-	9	non-
5	pent-	10	dec-

When naming hydrocarbons, you must first determine the longest, continuous chain of carbon atoms in the molecule. This is called the *carbon backbone* and determines the correct prefix. The suffix of the alkane ends in *–ane* because it contains only single bonds.

Molecule	Name
CH_4	Methane
CH_3CH_3	Ethane
$CH_3CH_2CH_3$	Propane
$CH_3CH_2CH_2CH_3$	Butane

Alkenes

Alkenes are unsaturated hydrocarbons that contain a double bond between at least two carbon atoms in the carbon backbone. Alkenes have the general formula C_nH_{2n}. When naming alkenes, count the longest carbon chain containing the double bond to determine the prefix and end the name in the suffix *–ene*. Remember that you must indicate which carbon atom contains the double bond.

Molecule	Name
CH_2CH_2	Ethene
CH_2CHCH_3	Propene
$CH_2CHCH_2CH_3$	1-Butene
$CH_3CHCHCH_3$	2-Butene

Alkynes

Alkynes are unsaturated hydrocarbons that contain a triple bond between at least two carbon atoms in the carbon backbone. Alkynes have the general formula C_nH_{2n-2}. When naming alkynes, count the longest carbon chain containing the triple bond to determine the prefix and end the name in the suffix *–yne*, as shown in the following table. Remember that you must indicate which carbon atom contains the triple bond.

Molecule	Name
CHCH	Ethyne
$CHCCH_3$	Propyne
$CHCCH_2CH_3$	1-Butyne
CH_3CCCH_3	2-Butyne

Sigma and Pi Bonding for Organic Molecules

- Covalent bonds formed from hybridized orbitals are called **sigma bonds** (σ). Alkanes contain only σ type bonds because sigma bonds are essentially single bonds.

- Bonds formed from overlap of unhybridized orbitals are called **pi bonds** (π). A carbon–carbon double bond consists of one σ bond and one π bond. A carbon–carbon triple bond contains one σ bond and two π bonds.

- Pi bonds react more easily than sigma bonds. Therefore, alkenes and alkynes are generally more reactive than alkanes.

DIDYOU**KNOW?**

Hemoglobin is a molecule in blood that carries oxygen to cells. Each hemoglobin molecule contains four iron atoms, which, when bonded to oxygen, has a red color.

Organic Functional Groups

There is a variety of organic functional groups that illicit a wide range of chemical properties and characteristics. You should be able to identify an organic functional group as well as name it. See the following table.

Type	Functional Group (R = hydrocarbon chain)	Example	Name
Alkyl halide	R-X	CH_3Cl	Chloromethane
Alcohol	R-OH	CH_3CH_2OH	Ethanol
Ether	R-O-R	CH_3OCH_3	Dimethyl ether
Aldehyde		CH_3CH_2CHO	Propanal
Ketone		CH_3COCH_3	Propanone
Carboxylic acid		CH_3CH_2COOH	Propanoic acid
Ester		CH_3COOCH_3	Methylethanoate
Amine	R-NH$_2$	CH_3NH_2	Methylamine

TEST TIP

Questions on the AP Chemistry exam typically will involve basic organic nomenclature in the predicting products section of the exam. It is also often found with questions involving empirical formulas.

Organic Reactions

For the predicting products section of the exam, organic reactions will sometimes appear. The most common type of reaction is the combustion of a hydrocarbon.

EXAMPLE: $CH_4 + 2 O_2 \rightarrow CO_2 + 2 H_2O$

TEST TIP

When balancing combustion reactions, if there is an odd number of oxygen atoms, first balance the reaction using a fractional number of O_2 molecules, and then multiply the entire equation by 2. This method will allow you to quickly balance the reaction and find the smallest whole number ratio between the atoms in the equation.

Reactivity Series of Metals

The reactivity series of metals can be very helpful when determining how reactive a metal is when compared to other metals. Although it may be beneficial to memorize the reactivity series, it may also be derived from an examination of reduction potentials. Remember that the reduction potentials of various metals are given on the problem section of the AP Chemistry exam. As an example, the oxidation potential (reverse of reduction potential) of aluminum is much larger than that of copper and thus would be more reactive. See Figure 15.1.

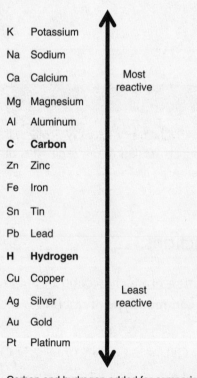

K	Potassium
Na	Sodium
Ca	Calcium
Mg	Magnesium
Al	Aluminum
C	**Carbon**
Zn	Zinc
Fe	Iron
Sn	Tin
Pb	Lead
H	**Hydrogen**
Cu	Copper
Ag	Silver
Au	Gold
Pt	Platinum

Most reactive

Least reactive

Carbon and hydrogen added for comparison.

Figure 15.1 Reactivity Series of Metals

Making a Solution

When making an aqueous solution, the process can either be endothermic or exothermic depending on the solute. It should be noted that in diluting acid solutions, the reactions can be highly exothermic depending on the concentration being made, e.g. H_2SO_4. As a safety reminder, always add the acid to water so that water (with its high heat capacity) may absorb the heat attributed to the dilution process.

Laboratory Experiments

Laboratory Safety

There are some key safety concepts that you should not only know for the AP Chemistry exam, but also practice when you are in the lab:

- Always wear safety goggles. This should become a habit during lab.

- Never put chemicals in your mouth or eyes. That also means that you should not touch your eyes or mouth when you are working in the laboratory.

- Work in a well-ventilated area because many chemicals are toxic.

- Heat substances slowly, which will prevent substances from burning or spattering. Also be sure to point the mouth of test tubes away from yourself and others while heating.

- Always add acid to water when making an acid solution.

- If you spill an acid on your skin, immediately flush the area with copious amounts of water.

TEST TIP

Laboratory safety questions are sometimes found in the multiple-choice section on the AP Chemistry exam.

Collecting Accurate and Precise Data

The entire discipline of chemistry is based upon the empirical evidence collected from a plethora of experiments. We would not be where we are today in chemistry without the accurate collection of data from these experiments. Keep in mind that the data you collect could be either quantitative (numeric) or qualitative (sensory), and data is different from calculations or interpretations of the information. Here are some useful tips for collecting accurate and precise data:

- Always record one uncertain digit in your measurements. For example, an uncertain digit would be the number that you guess between two lines on a graduated cylinder. A thorough set of laboratory measurements will include +/− values, which create a range of acceptable error for every measurement.

- When measuring mass, be sure to allow objects to return to room temperature before weighing. Don't forget to subtract the mass of the weighing paper or container when recording the mass of a compound.

- When measuring the volume of a liquid in a graduated cylinder, take the measurement at eye level on the bottom of the meniscus—the downward curve caused by intermolecular forces between the glass and the liquid.

- Never place chemicals back in the stock bottle since this can contaminate the stock chemicals and solutions. Another source of contamination is when the tips of droppers or wash bottles touch other surfaces.

- When collecting a gas over water with a eudiometer, make sure you take the vapor pressure of water into account when performing calculations.

- Use a lab sheet or lab notebook to record data. Your measurements, procedure, and analysis should be clearly written so that someone else could replicate the same experiment from your notebook.

- Give careful thought to sources of error in an experiment. For example, when using a coffee cup calorimeter to measure the enthalpy of a reaction, there is a high probability that some heat will escape into the surroundings, thereby resulting in a measured value that is less than the expected value.

- The following traits can be measured by the corresponding methods.

  — Concentration: titration, spectrophotometer

  — Mass: balance/scale

  — Volume: graduated cylinder, buret, eudiometer, pipet, volumetric flask

  — Temperature: thermometer

— pH: litmus paper, pH electrode

— Volts: voltmeter

— Amps: ammeter

TEST TIP

Be familiar with sources of error in the required experiments. Many questions on the AP Chemistry exam that pertain to laboratory experiments involve the effects of error on experimental outcomes.

Laboratory Equipment

Figure 16.1 shows the items that are used when performing the required chemistry experiments. Familiarize yourself with their names and usages.

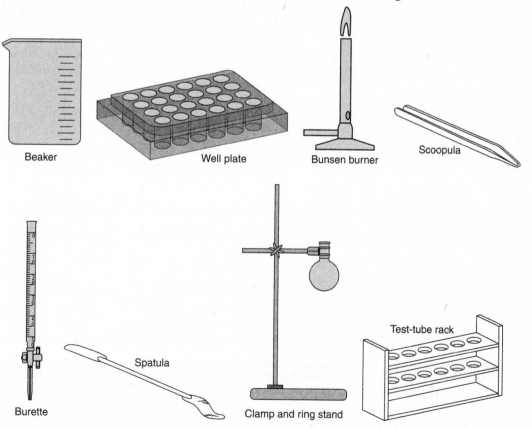

Figure 16.1 Standard Laboratory Equipment

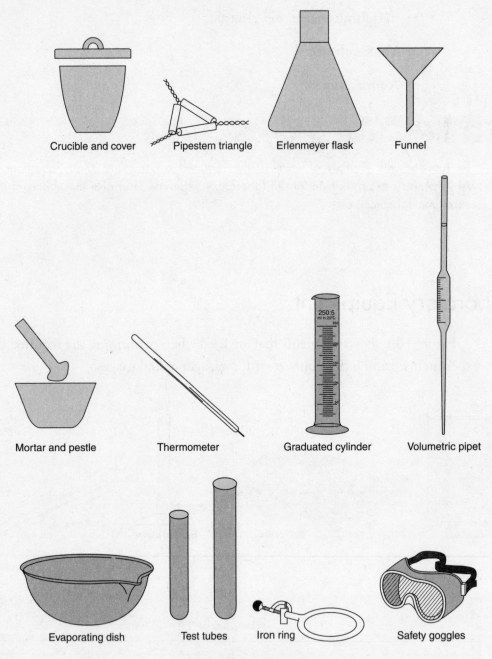

Crucible and cover   Pipestem triangle   Erlenmeyer flask   Funnel

Mortar and pestle   Thermometer   Graduated cylinder   Volumetric pipet

Evaporating dish   Test tubes   Iron ring   Safety goggles

Figure 16.1 (*continued*)

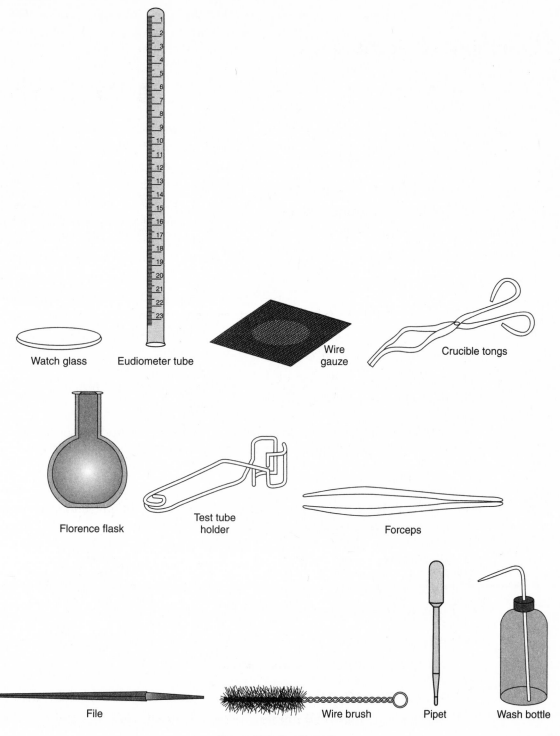

Watch glass　　Eudiometer tube　　Wire gauze　　Crucible tongs

Florence flask　　Test tube holder　　Forceps

File　　Wire brush　　Pipet　　Wash bottle

Figure 16.1 (*continued*)

Common Lab Techniques

There are a few laboratory techniques that are common to most chemistry labs. You should familiarize yourself with each of the following:

- **CHROMATOGRAPHY:** separates components of a mixture based on the intermolecular forces of the stationary phase with the substance

- **CONDUCTIVITY:** measures the concentration of ions in solution; greater ion concentrations mean that the solution will conduct electricity better

- **DISTILLATION:** used to separate a mixture of liquids based on their different volatilities/boiling points; requires heating the mixture followed by condensation of the components

- **FILTRATION:** technique that separates solids from liquids/aqueous solutions by using a filter

- **FLAME TEST:** qualitative test on metal compounds that when placed in a flame, produce different colors due to the different excited state to ground state transitions

- **PRECIPITATION:** formation of an insoluble solid that can remove ions from solution; usually used in tandem with filtration

- **SPECTROPHOTOMETRY:** measuring the amount of light that passes through a sample; used to measure concentration via Beer's law

- **TITRATION:** technique in which substances, such as acids or bases, are reacted in perfect stoichiometric ratios; makes use of an indicator, that is, a compound that changes color when there is an excess of one reactant; alternatively, a redox reaction results in a color change

TEST TIP

You should be familiar with these laboratory techniques and their usage not only for multiple-choice questions but definitely for Part B of the free-response section of the AP Chemistry exam.

Example Problems for the Recommended Experiments

The following experiments are recommended by the College Board for AP Chemistry courses. For each of the experiments, a sample question is given along with the corresponding calculations. The sample problem listed here is not the only example of the experiment, but it does represent the most common types of calculations involved in the experiment and the common questions that are asked in Part B of the free-response section of the AP Chemistry exam.

DIDYOUKNOW?

Crude oil is a viscous mixture of hydrocarbons. In order to get usable components such as gasoline, the mixture is distilled at refineries. The short-chain alkanes are the most volatile and quickly rise to the top, while the long-chain alkanes stay near the bottom. The part of the mixture that is separated containing alkanes with 6–8 carbon atoms is pumped off for use as gasoline.

1. Determination of the Formula of a Compound

EXAMPLE: A student cut a 5.30 g magnesium ribbon into small pieces, then began to heat it in a 14.20 g crucible. Over time, the magnesium ignited and burned to form a grayish-white powdery substance. After the crucible cooled, the student measured the mass of the crucible that contained the powder and found it to be 22.70 g.

A. What is the mass of the powder in the crucible?

22.70 g − 14.20 g = **8.50 g powder** (5.30 g Mg and 3.20 g O)

B. What is the formula of the oxide formed?

$$\# \, mol \, Mg = \frac{5.30 \, g \, Mg}{1} \times \frac{1 \, mol \, Mg}{24.30 \, g \, Mg} = \frac{0.218 \, mol \, Mg}{0.200} = 1.09 = 1 \, mol \, Mg$$

$$\# \, mol \, O = \frac{3.20 \, g \, O}{1} \times \frac{1 \, mol \, O}{16.00 \, g \, O} = \frac{0.200 \, mol \, O}{0.200} = 1 \, mol \, O$$

Divide the moles of Mg and O by the smallest number of moles to find the simplest whole-number ratio between the elements, which is the empirical formula.

empirical formula = MgO

C. What is the mass percent of oxygen in the compound?

$$Mass \, \% \, O = \frac{3.20 \, g \, O}{8.50 \, g \, MgO} \times 100 = 37.6 \, \% \, Oxygen$$

D. What is the most likely source of error in the experiment, and how do these results demonstrate that error?

It is likely that some of the magnesium did not combine with the oxygen, and therefore there would be slightly fewer moles of oxygen than magnesium. The experimental observations substantiate this type of error (0.200 mol O vs. 0.218 mol Mg).

2. Determination of the Percentage of Water in a Hydrate

EXAMPLE: A student obtained 4.23 g of a vibrant blue copper (II) sulfate hydrate from a teacher. The hydrate was heated in a 16.80 g crucible over moderate heat for several minutes. Over time, the entire substance appeared to turn white, at which time the student removed the crucible from the heat. The student measured the mass of the crucible and substance together and found it to be 19.50 g.

A. What mass of water was removed from the hydrate?

19.50 total − 16.80 g crucible = 2.70 g anhydrous $CuSO_4$

4.23 g $CuSO_4 \bullet x \, H_2O$ − 2.70 g $CuSO_4$ = 1.53 g H_2O

B. How many moles of water were removed from the hydrate?

$$\# \, mol \, H_2O = \frac{1.53 \, g \, H_2O}{1} \times \frac{1 \, mol \, H_2O}{18.02 \, g \, H_2O} = 0.0849 \, mol \, H_2O$$

C. How many moles of the anhydrous copper (II) sulfate were left in the container after heating?

$$\# \, mol \, CuSO_4 = \frac{2.70 \, g \, CuSO_4}{1} \times \frac{1 \, mol \, CuSO_4}{159.55 \, g \, CuSO_4} = 0.0169 \, mol \, CuSO_4$$

D. What is the formula of the hydrate of copper sulfate?

To find the empirical ratio between the anhydrous salt and water, you need to divide by the smallest number of moles (.0169). Since 0.0849 moles of water is approximately five times the 0.0169 moles of copper (II) sulfate, the formula of the hydrate would be $CuSO_4 \cdot 5H_2O$.

E. What is the percentage of water in the hydrate?

$$Mass \, \% \, H_2O = \frac{1.53 \, g \, H_2O}{4.23 \, g \, CuSO_4 \cdot 5 \, H_2O} \times 100 = 36.2 \, \% \, H_2O$$

F. What would be the effect on the final results if the student did not heat the copper (II) sulfate long enough to remove all the water?

If less than the entire amount of water were removed, the student would have attributed a greater amount of the original mass to copper sulfate, and less to water. The student would probably end up concluding that the coefficient for water would have been some integer less than 5.

3. Determination of the Molar Mass by Vapor Density

EXAMPLE: A student in a laboratory with an atmospheric pressure of 1.00 atm puts 5.00 g of a volatile liquid in a flask that has a single-hole stopper. The flask is immersed in a boiling water bath at 373 K. At the point where the last small bit of the liquid evaporates, the flask is plunged into cold water and 0.789 g of the volatile liquid condenses.

Afterward, the flask is cleaned out and the interior volume of the flask is found to be 287 mL.

A. What is the pressure at which the volatile liquid both evaporated and condensed?

1.00 atm

B. Use the vapor pressure of the volatile liquid to determine its molar mass.

$$M = \frac{m}{PV}RT = \frac{0.789\,g}{1.00\,atm \times 0.287\,L} \times 0.0821\,L\,atm\,mol^{-1}K^{-1} \times 373\,K$$

molar mass (M) = 84.2 g/mol

C. The volatile liquid is found to be 14.37% hydrogen and 85.63% carbon. What is the empirical formula of the volatile liquid?

$$\# \, mol\,H = \frac{14.37\,g\,H}{1} \times \frac{1\,mol\,H}{1.0079\,g\,H} = \frac{14.25\,mol\,H}{7.129} = 2\,mol\,H$$

$$\# \, mol\,C = \frac{85.63\,g\,C}{1} \times \frac{1\,mol\,C}{12.011\,g\,C} = \frac{7.129\,mol\,C}{7.129} = 1\,mol\,C$$

empirical formula = CH_2

D. What is the molecular formula of the compound?

Since the molar mass of the empirical formula is one-sixth the molar mass of the experimentally determined molar mass, then the molecular formula is six times the empirical formula, or C_6H_{12}.

4. Determination of the Molar Mass by Freezing Point Depression

EXAMPLE: A student is given a 3.80 g sample of an unknown nonelectrolyte solid and is asked to find its molar mass by freezing point depression. The student decides to use 40.00 g of benzene as a solvent, which has a melting point of 5.5 °C and molal freezing point constant of 5.12 °C kg/mol.

A. What is the significance of the unknown solute being a nonelectrolyte? How could the student have figured that property out if she had not been told this information?

Freezing point depression is given by the equation $\Delta T = k_f mi$. The van 't Hoff factor (i) refers to the degree of ionization of the solute in the solvent. If the unknown solute is a nonelectrolyte, then it is not ionized and $i = 1.0$. If she had not been told whether the solute was a nonelectrolyte, she could perform conductivity tests to verify the presence of ions in solution.

B. Describe how the student should find the freezing point of the unknown/ solvent mixture using graphical means.

The student should place the solution in a test tube, immerse the tube in ice, and then measure and record the temperature at regular intervals of time. When the temperature values are plotted vs. time, the slope of the resulting best-fit line will decrease sharply, and then change abruptly—and more or less form a plateau. The new melting point of the solution is the temperature that corresponds to this plateau of temperatures on the cooling curve.

C. The student measures the ΔT to be 3.2 °C. What is the molality of the solution that contains the unknown?

$$T = k_f mi = 3.2^0 C = 5.12 \frac{^0 C\, kg}{mol} \times m \times 1.0$$

$$m = 0.63 \text{ molal}$$

D. How many moles of the unknown were in the test solution?

$$\# mol\, Unknown = \frac{40.00\, g\, benezene}{1} \times \frac{1\, kg}{1000\, g} \times \frac{0.63\, mol\, unknown}{1\, kg\, benzene} =$$

$$0.025\ mol\ Unknown$$

E. What is the molar mass of the unknown substance?

$$M = \frac{3.80\, g\, unknown}{0.025\, mol\, unknown} = 150\, g/mol$$

5. Determination of the Molar Volume of a Gas

EXAMPLE: A 0.035 g sample of magnesium ribbon is placed in a stoppered flask that is connected to a eudiometer tube—collecting the gas by water displacement. When concentrated HCl is placed in the flask with the magnesium, 32.42 mL of hydrogen gas is produced in the eudiometer tube. The reaction was carried out at a temperature of 22 °C.

A. Write the balanced chemical reaction that occurs when the magnesium is combined with the HCl.

$$Mg_{(s)} + 2\,H^+_{(aq)} \rightarrow Mg^{+2}_{(aq)} + H_{2\,(g)}$$

B. How many moles of hydrogen gas are expected to be produced from this amount of magnesium in this reaction?

$$\# \,mol\,H_2 = \frac{0.035\,g\,Mg}{1} \times \frac{1\,mol\,Mg}{24.30\,g\,Mg} \times \frac{1\,mol\,H_2}{1\,mol\,Mg} = 0.0014\,mol\,H_2$$

C. How many moles of water also exist with the collected hydrogen gas in the eudiometer tube? (Vapor pressure of water at 22 °C = 0.030 atm.)

$$PV = nRT = .030\,atm \times 0.03242L = n \times 0.0821\frac{L\,atm}{mol\,K} \times 295\,K$$

$$n = 4.0 \times 10^{-5}\,mol\,H_2O$$

D. What is the mole fraction for the water vapor that exists in the eudiometer tube?

$$X = \frac{0.000040}{0.0014 + 0.000040} = 0.028$$

E. What is the percent error between the number of moles of hydrogen gas actually produced at 1.00 atm and 22°C and the expected yield of hydrogen gas?

According to Dalton's law of partial pressures, the pressure due to hydrogen gas inside the eudiometer is proportional to the total pressure multiplied by its mole fraction—thus the pressure of hydrogen gas is 0.97 atm.

$$PV = nRT = 0.97\,atm \times 0.03242\,L = n \times 0.0821\frac{L\,atm}{mol\,K} \times 295\,K$$

$$n = 0.0013 \text{ mol } H_2$$

$$\%\,Error = \frac{(0.0014 - 0.0013)}{0.0014} \times 100 = 7\%\,Error$$

6. Standardization of a Solution Using a Primary Standard

EXAMPLE: A student wishes to use a known concentration of $KMnO_4$ for an oxidation–reduction titration. However, to do this experiment, the student must know the exact concentration of a stock solution of $KMnO_4$ that is in the storeroom. She carefully mixes a solution of 0.10 M oxalic acid to react with the $KMnO_4$ in the following reaction:

$$5\,H_2C_2O_4 + 2\,MnO_4^- + 6\,H_3O^+ \rightarrow 2\,Mn^{+2} + 10\,CO_2 + 14\,H_2O$$

A. How does the student know when the oxalic acid completely consumes the permanganate ion in the sample?

The permanganate ion is a deep purple color. When the ion is used up, the solution in the beaker will be clear.

B. Is the oxalic acid oxidized or reduced?

During the reaction, the carbon atom in the oxalic acid molecule goes from an oxidation state of +3 to an oxidation state of +4. Since the oxidation state of the carbon increases during the reaction, then the carbon in the oxalic acid is oxidized (reducing agent).

C. 50.0 mL of the oxalic acid solution is required to titrate 100.0 mL of the permanganate solution. What is the concentration of the permanganate solution?

$$\#\,M = \frac{0.0500\,L\,H_2C_2O_4}{0.1000\,L\,MnO_4^-} \times \frac{0.10\,mol\,H_2C_2O_4}{1\,L\,H_2C_2O_4} \times \frac{2\,mol\,MnO_4^-}{5\,mol\,L\,H_2C_2O_4} = 0.020\,M\,MnO_4^-$$

7. Determination of Concentration by Acid–Base Titration, Including a Weak Acid or Weak Base

EXAMPLE: A student wishes to find the concentration of acetic acid ($K_a = 1.8 \times 10^{-5}$) by titrating it with a standardized solution of 0.10 M NaOH in the following reaction:

$$CH_3COOH + OH^- \leftrightarrow H_2O + CH_3COO^-$$

A. Will the equivalence point be an acidic or basic pH? Give an explanation for your answer.

When the equivalence point is reached (moles acid = moles base), the pH will be basic. Inspection of the titration equation indicates that the only species left at the equivalence point are water and the acetate ion. Water is neutral, and the acetate ion—being the conjugate base of a weak acid—is basic due to hydrolysis. Therefore, at the equivalence point the solution will be basic.

B. The titration requires 40.00 mL of 0.10 M NaOH to titrate 100.00 mL of the acetic acid solution. What is the concentration of the weak acid?

At the equivalence point, the moles of acid in the solution equal the moles of base in the solution. As a shortcut, you can use the following equation:

$$(\#H^+)M_aV_a = M_bV_b(\#OH^-)$$

In this equation, the number of H^+ and OH^- correspond to how many protons or hydroxide ions are given off by the acid and base (respectively).

$$(1)(M_a)(0.1000\,L) = (0.10M)(0.0400\,L)(1)$$

$$M_a = 0.040 \text{ M}$$

C. What is the pH at the equivalence point?

This question seems straightforward, but is pretty labor intensive. You need to perform an equilibrium calculation based on the conjugate base that formed using an Initial/Change/Final table. Also, due to the one-to-one stoichiometric ratio of the acid and base, the moles of the conjugate base are the same as the moles of the base added (0.10 M × 0.040 L = .004 mol). Based on the new volume of the solution (140 mL) the concentration of the conjugate base CH_3COO^- is 0.029 M.

	CH_3COO^-	+	H_2O	$\leftrightarrow$	OH^-	+	CH_3COOH
Initial [ ]	0.029		—		0		0
Change	$-x$		—		$+x$		$+x$
Final [ ]	0.029–x		—		x		x

Since this is a hydrolysis of the conjugate base of a weak acid, you need to find the corresponding K_b value, which can be found by the following equation:

$$K_a \times K_b = K_w = 1 \times 10^{-14}$$

$$K_b = \frac{1 \times 10^{-14}}{1.8 \times 10^{-5}} = 5.6 \times 10^{-10}$$

Based on the calculated K_b value, we can solve the equilibrium using the simplifying assumption for x, which is the concentration of OH^- in solution.

$$K_b = \frac{x^2}{0.029} = 5.6 \times 10^{-10}$$

$$x = [OH^-] = 4.0 \times 10^{-6}\,M$$

The corresponding pOH and later the pH can then be calculated.

$$pOH = -\log[4.0 \times 10^{-6}\,M] = 5.40$$

$$pH = 14 - 5.40 = 8.60$$

8. Determination of a Concentration by Oxidation–Reduction Titration

EXAMPLE: A student wishes to analyze an ore sample for Fe^{+2} content. To do this, she crushes the ore sample and then soaks it in concentrated HCl to dissolve the Fe^{+2}. Then she oxidizes the Fe^{+2} ion to Fe^{+3} using a standardized solution of potassium permanganate.

A. Write the balanced oxidation–reduction reaction that the student will undergo in this titration.

Balancing this equation will require you to use your redox balancing skills.

$$5\,Fe^{2+} + 8\,H^+ + MnO_4^{-1} \rightarrow 5\,Fe^{+3} + Mn^{+2} + 4\,H_2O$$

B. To analyze the sample, the student creates a standardized solution of potassium permanganate by combining 3.20 g of $KMnO_4$ with enough water to yield 200.0 mL of solution. What is the molar concentration of the standardized solution?

$$M = \frac{\dfrac{3.20\,g\,KMnO_4}{1} \times \dfrac{1\,mol\,KMnO_4}{158.04\,g}}{0.200\,L} = 0.101\,M\,KMnO_4$$

C. How does the student know when she reaches the end point, when all the iron (II) has been converted into iron (III)?

As long as there is iron (II) in the solution that is analyzed, the otherwise dark purple permanganate ion will be used up and turn clear. However, when the iron (II) has been used up—such as at the end point—any additional permanganate ion added will remain unreacted and the sample solution will turn purple.

D. A 10.00 gram sample of the ore is crushed and titrated with the standardized solution. It takes 6.32 mL of the standardized solution to reach the end point. How many moles of iron (II) are in the sample that was analyzed?

$$\#\,mol\,Fe^{+2} = \frac{0.00632\,L\,KMnO_4}{1} \times \frac{0.101\,mol\,KMnO_4}{1\,L} \times \frac{5\,mol\,Fe^{+2}}{1\,mol\,KMnO_4} = 0.00319\,mol\,Fe^{2+}$$

E. What is the mass percent of iron (II) in the sample?

$$\%\,Fe^{+2} = \frac{\dfrac{0.00319\,mol\,Fe^{2+}}{1} \times \dfrac{55.85\,g\,Fe^{+2}}{1\,mol\,Fe^{+2}}}{10.00} \times 100 = 1.78\%\,Fe^{+2}$$

9. Determination of Mass and Mole Relationships in a Chemical Reaction

This experiment can be done separately or in conjunction with some of the other recommended experiments. For example, the mass–mole questions could easily accompany the first experiment with magnesium.

EXAMPLE: A student cut 2.80 g magnesium ribbon into small pieces, then began to heat it in a 14.20 g crucible. Over time, the magnesium ignited and burned to form a grayish-white powdery substance. After the crucible cooled, the student measured the mass of the crucible that contained the powder and found it to be 18.73 g.

A. What is the mass of the powder in the crucible?

$$18.73 \text{ g} - 14.20 \text{ g} = \textbf{4.53 g powder} \text{ (2.80 g Mg and 1.73 g O)}$$

B. How many moles of magnesium were in the crucible when the reaction began?

$$\# \, mol \, Mg = \frac{2.80 \, g \, Mg}{1} \times \frac{1 \, mol \, Mg}{24.30 \, g \, Mg} = 0.115 \, mol \, Mg$$

C. Approximately how many moles of oxygen were added to the magnesium during the reaction?

$$\# \, mol \, O = \frac{1.73 \, g \, O}{1} \times \frac{1 \, mol \, O}{16.00 \, g \, O} = 0.108 \, mol \, O$$

10. Determination of the Equilibrium Constant for a Chemical Reaction

EXAMPLE: A student is given a solution of acetic acid and is asked to find the equilibrium constant for the following equilibrium:

$$CH_3COOH_{(aq)} + H_2O_{(l)} \leftrightarrow H_3O^+_{(aq)} + CH_3COO^-_{(aq)}$$

A. Describe how the student can use this information and a pH meter to find the K_a of acetic acid.

The student can make a standardized solution of acetic acid and measure its pH. The pH can tell the student how much the acetic acid has dissociated. From the amount dissociated, the student can determine the concentrations of all species after equilibrium, and then calculate the equilibrium constant using the relationship:

$$K_a = \frac{[H_3O^+][CH_3COO^-]}{[CH_3COOH]}$$

B. Calculate the initial concentration (before equilibrium is established) of the sample of acetic acid if 2.0 mL of an initial 12.0 M stock solution is diluted to make 400 mL of solution.

The concentration is the molarity of the solution.

$$M_1V_1 = M_2V_2$$

$$(12.0\ M)(0.0020\ L) = M_2\ (0.400\ L)$$

$$M_2 = 0.060\ M$$

C. After equilibrium is established, the student measures the pH to be 2.98. What is the dissociation constant (K_a) for this reaction?

$$CH_3COOH_{(aq)} + H_2O_{(\ell)} \leftrightarrow H_3O^+_{(aq)} + CH_3COO^-_{(aq)}$$

Equilibrium concentrations: 0.060 M   — $10^{-2.98}$ $10^{-2.98}$

$$K_a = \frac{[10^{-2.98}]^2}{[0.060\ M]} = 1.8 \times 10^{-5}$$

D. What is a reasonable approximation for the standard free energy, $\Delta G°$, for this reaction?

$$\Delta G° = -RT\ln K = -(8.31\ \text{J mol}^{-1}\ \text{K}^{-1})\ (298\ \text{K})\ \ln(1.8 \times 10^{-5}) = 27{,}000\ \text{J}$$

11. Determination of Appropriate Indicators for Various Acid–Base Titrations—Determining pH

This experiment is often done in conjunction with the titration of acids and bases. In particular, it requires you to understand why you use particular indicators for a titration.

EXAMPLE: A student is given the following indicators, all of which change color at the end point listed.

Indicator	End Point pH
Methyl Orange	5.0
Methyl Red	5.0
Bromothymol Blue	7.0
Phenolphthalein	9.0
Thymol Blue	9.0

A student is assigned to find the appropriate indicator for each of the following titrations. Calculate the pH of the end point of each titration and decide which indicator to use.

Titration #1:   Titration of 20.0 mL of hydrochloric acid using a standard solution of sodium hydroxide, in which it takes 60.0 mL of 0.10 M sodium hydroxide solution to reach the end point.

Titration #2:   Titration of 100.0 mL of a solution acetic acid using a standard solution of sodium hydroxide, in which it takes 40.0 mL of 0.10 M sodium hydroxide solution to reach the end point; the ionization constant for acetic acid is 1.8×10^{-5}.

Titration #3:   Titration of 40.0 mL of ammonia solution using a standard solution of hydrochloric acid, in which it takes 20.0 mL of 0.20 M hydrochloric acid to reach the end point; the K_b for ammonia is 1.8×10^{-5}.

Titration #1:

$$H^+ + OH^- \leftrightarrow H_2O$$

When the moles of base added equal the moles of acid (the equivalence point), the remaining species in solution are water and a neutral salt. Thus, the solution would be a neutral pH 7. Bromothymol blue would be the best indicator.

Titration #2:

$$CH_3COOH + OH^- \leftrightarrow H_2O + CH_3COO^-$$

At the end point, the acid and base are used up and the acetate ion and water remain. Because acetate is the conjugate base of a weak acid, the pH of the resulting solution will be basic. The pH can be calculated using equilibrium principles.

$$(1)(M_a)(0.1000\ L) = (0.10\ M)(0.0400\ L)(1)$$

$$M_a = 0.040\ M$$

Due to the one-to-one stoichiometric ratio of the acid and base, the moles of the conjugate base are the same as the moles of the base added ($0.10\ M \times 0.040\ L = .004$ mol). Based on the new volume of the solution (140 mL), the concentration of the conjugate base CH_3COO^- would be 0.029 M.

$$CH_3COO^- + H_2O \leftrightarrow OH^- + CH_3COOH$$

Initial [ ]	0.029	—	0	0
Change	$-x$	—	$+x$	$+x$
Final [ ]	$0.029-x$	—	x	x

Since this is a hydrolysis of the conjugate base of a weak acid, you need to find the corresponding K_b value, which can be found by the following equation:

$$K_a \times K_b = K_w = 1 \times 10^{-14}$$

$$K_b = \frac{1 \times 10^{-14}}{1.8 \times 10^{-5}} = 5.6 \times 10^{-10}$$

Based on the calculated K_b value, we can solve the equilibrium using the simplifying assumption (since the K_b value is smaller than 10^{-5}) expression for x, which is the concentration of OH^- in solution.

$$K_b = \frac{x^2}{0.029} = 5.6 \times 10^{-10}$$

$$x = [OH^-] = 4.0 \times 10^{-6}\ M$$

The corresponding pOH and later the pH can then be calculated.

$$pOH = -\log[4.0 \times 10^{-6}\ M] = 5.40$$

$$pH = 14 - 5.40 = 8.60$$

Therefore, phenolphthalein or thymol blue would be the best indicator.

Titration #3:

$$NH_3 + H^+ \leftrightarrow NH_4^+$$

This titration is the complete opposite of Titration #2: the conjugate acid of the weak base will result in a slightly acidic solution once the end point is reached due to the hydrolysis of NH_4^+. The calculations are identical to Titration #2 except for the calculation which uses the K_a of NH_4^+ and determination of the concentration of H^+ at equilibrium. When these calculations are performed, you will find the resulting pH would be 4.70; thus, methyl orange or methyl red would be the best indicators for this titration.

12. Determination of the Rate of a Reaction and its Order

EXAMPLE: A student runs an experiment that measures the rate of the catalytic decomposition of hydrogen peroxide by potassium iodide according to the following reaction:

$$2 H_2O_2 + I^- \rightarrow 2 H_2O + O_2 + I^-$$

The student records the time it takes for the oxygen gas production to cease as a measure of the reaction rate.

Trial	Initial [H$_2$O$_2$] (M)	Initial [I⁻] (M)	Initial Rate (M/s)
1	0.20	0.20	2.5×10^{-3}
2	0.20	0.40	5.0×10^{-3}
3	0.40	0.20	1.0×10^{-2}

A. Determine the order of the reaction with respect to each chemical species tested.

$$\frac{Trail\,2}{Trail\,1} = \frac{R_2 = k[0.20]^x[0.40]^y}{R_1 = k[0.20]^x[0.20]^y}$$

Since the rate constant is the same for all trials and the concentration of H_2O_2 remains constant, the ratio is reduced to the following:

$$\frac{5.0 \times 10^{-3}}{2.5 \times 10^{-3}} = 2^y \ and \ y = 1 = \text{order of } I^-$$

The order of H_2O_2 can be found similarly as shown in the following calculation. Following the same procedure as the preceding procedure, the ratios of the concentrations for I^- are identical for Trials 1 and 3 and k is a constant, so they will be omitted from the calculation.

$$\frac{Trial\,3}{Trial\,1} = \frac{1.0 \times 10^{-2} = [0.40]^x}{2.5 \times 10^{-3} = [0.20]^x}$$

Upon solving this equation, the order with respect to H_2O_2 is 2.

B. What is the rate equation for this reaction?

$$\text{Rate} = \text{k}\,[H_2O_2]^2\,[I^-]^1$$

C. What are the value and units for the rate constant, k?

By plugging in the data for one of the trials, the rate constant can be found.

$$2.5 \times 10^{-3} = k[0.20]^2[0.20]^1$$

$$k = 0.31\ M^{-2}\,s^{-1}$$

13. Determination of the Enthalpy Change Associated With a Reaction

EXAMPLE: A student wishes to calculate the molar heat of combustion of butane, and is given only a beaker, a thermometer, and a small, disposable butane lighter.

A. Design an experiment and determine what needs to be measured in order to find the molar heat of combustion of butane.

The student can use the butane in the lighter and finds it to heat water and measure the temperature change in the water. Weighing the lighter before and after the reaction will allow the student to calculate the number of moles of butane used. Multiplying the change in temperature of the water by the mass and specific heat of water (4.18 J/g°C) will tell the student how much heat was absorbed by the water. This type of coffee-cup calorimetry is crude, but gives a reasonable approximation of the enthalpy of combustion.

The student weighs the lighter and finds it to be 8.72 grams before starting. The lighter is found to only weigh 6.88 g after the student held the lighter open for several minutes under the beaker that contained 400.0 g of water. During this time, the temperature of the water rose by 22.4 °C.

B. How many moles of butane were used up?

The mass of the butane can be found by subtracting the final mass of the lighter from the initial mass; the mass can then be converted to moles.

$$\# \, mol \, C_4H_{10} = \frac{1.84 \, g \, C_4H_{10}}{1} \times \frac{1 \, mol \, C_4H_{10}}{58.123 \, g \, C_4H_{10}} = 0.0317 \, mol \, C_4H_{10}$$

C. How much heat was absorbed by the water?

$$q = mc\Delta T = 400.0 \, g \times 4.18 \, J/g°C \times 22.4 \, °C = 3.75 \times 10^4 \, J$$

D. What is the molar heat of combustion for butane that can be calculated from these measurements?

$$\# \frac{kJ}{mol} = \frac{3.75 \times 10^1 \, kJ}{0.0317 \, mol} = 1.18 \times 10^3 \, kJ/mol$$

E. What is the most typical type of error that this student will get in her measurement, and in which direction will this error push the results?

While the majority of the heat emitted by the reaction will go into raising the temperature of the water, some will be lost to the surroundings. This will result in a measured enthalpy value that is significantly less than the expected value.

14. Separation and Qualitative Analysis of Anions and Cations

EXAMPLE: A student is given three flasks, labeled A through C, that contain soluble solutions of barium nitrate, nickel nitrate, and lead nitrate. However, the student does not know which solution is in which flask. The student is also given three flasks with solutions of known identity: sodium chloride, potassium sulfate, and sodium hydroxide.

A. When a sample from flask A is mixed with the sodium chloride and potassium sulfate solutions separately, both mixtures result in a cloudy white precipitate.

What is the composition of flask A? Write the net ionic reactions for the precipitation reactions that occur.

The flask contains a solution of lead nitrate.

$$Pb^{+2} + 2Cl^- \rightarrow PbCl_2$$

$$Pb^{+2} + SO_4^{-2} \rightarrow PbSO_4$$

B. When a sample from flask B is mixed with the sodium chloride and potassium sulfate solutions separately, only the mixture with potassium sulfate yields a precipitate, which is white. What is the composition of flask B? Write the net ionic reaction for the precipitation reaction that occurs.

The flask contains a solution of barium nitrate.

$$Ba^{+2} + SO_4^{-2} \rightarrow BaSO_4$$

C. A sample from flask C, when mixed with the sodium chloride and potassium sulfate, does not yield a precipitate in either case. However, a combination of a sample from flask C and sodium hydroxide yields a green precipitate. What is the composition of flask C? Write the net ionic reaction for the precipitation reaction that occurs.

The flask contains a solution of nickel nitrate.

$$Ni^{+2} + 2\,OH^- \rightarrow Ni(OH)_2$$

D. Which of the preceding precipitates formed in the preceding reactions will most likely dissolve upon the addition of concentrated HCl? Explain.

The nickel hydroxide precipitate will dissolve because the hydroxide ions will combine with the protons from the HCl to form water.

15. Synthesis of a Coordination Compound and its Chemical Analysis

EXAMPLE: A number of different coordination compounds can be formed in the laboratory. One of the most frequently synthesized coordination compounds is iron thiocyanate in the following reaction:

$$Fe^{+3} + SCN^- \rightarrow FeSCN^{+2}$$

The formation of the product is quickly evident as a blood-red/orange solution with no precipitate, which absorbs light at 445 nm. It is quite common to form this metal complex while performing a spectroscopic determination of iron (III).

16. Analytical Gravimetric Determination

EXAMPLE: A student is given 2.482 grams of a powdered mixture that contains both $MgCl_2$ and $CaCO_3$. She is then asked to find the mass percent of the magnesium chloride in the mixture. To begin the analysis, the student dissolves the solid in a strong acid solution, and then precipitates one of the compounds with lead nitrate.

A. What will happen to the calcium carbonate when the acid is added to the mixture?

    The acid will dissolve the calcium carbonate; carbon dioxide gas will be emitted, leaving the dissolved calcium in solution.

B. What will be the precipitate when the lead nitrate is added to the solution? Given the dependence on this reaction, which strong acid(s) should NOT be used in the first step?

    The soluble lead ions will combine with the chloride, iodide, bromide, and sulfate ions to form insoluble lead compounds. For this reason, HCl, HI, HBr, and H_2SO_4 should *not* be used in the first step. The insoluble lead salts would cause an inaccurately high value for the percent of magnesium chloride in the mixture. HNO_3 is the most preferable strong acid to use for this reaction.

C. When the lead nitrate is added, 5.280 g of precipitate is formed. What is the mass percent of magnesium chloride in the original mixture?

$$\# \, g \, MgCl_2 = \frac{5.280 \, g \, PbCl_2}{1} \times \frac{1 \, mol \, PbCl_2}{278.1 \, g} \times \frac{2 \, mol \, Cl}{1 \, mol \, PbCl_2} \times \frac{1 \, mol \, MgCl_2}{2 \, mol \, Cl}$$

$$\times \frac{95.206 \, g \, MgCl_2}{1 \, mol \, MgCl_2} = 1.808 \, g \, MgCl_2$$

$$\% \, MgCl_2 = \frac{1.808 \, g \, MgCl_2}{2.482 \, g \, Mixture} \times 100 = \mathbf{72.84\% \, MgCl_2}$$

17. Colorimetric or Spectrophotometric Analysis

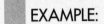 **EXAMPLE:** Beer's law makes it possible to use a spectrophotometer to measure the concentration of colored solutions. This is useful in experiments where concentrations are measured, such as kinetics, equilibrium, or quantitative analysis of colored ions in solution. There are two essential components to a spectrophotometric analysis: determining the ideal wavelength for analysis and constructing a calibration curve to determine an unknown concentration. There may be questions that arise on the AP exam on either of these topics.

A. Determine the optimal wavelength for the solution you are studying. This can be done by measuring the absorbance of a standard solution over the entire wavelength spectrum of the spectrophotometer. The wavelength where the solution shows the highest absorbance is the optimal wavelength, and should be used for the next step.

For example, a student generated the following data by using a spectrophotometer to analyze the absorbance of a 0.10 M solution of $CoCl_2$. What is the optimal wavelength to set up a calibration curve?

Wavelength (nm)	Absorbance
400	0.04
450	0.32
500	0.77
550	0.48
600	0.02
650	0.01

The ideal wavelength for this analysis is 500 nm since it demonstrates the highest absorbance.

B. Establish a calibration curve by measuring the absorbance of various known concentrations of the solution at the optimal wavelength. Use the resulting absorbance vs. concentration curve to interpolate the concentration of the unknown solutions in the study.

For example, a student measures the absorbance of various concentrations of cobalt chloride solution at 500 nm and obtains the following data:

Concentration (M)	Absorbance
0.020	0.11
0.040	0.21
0.060	0.33
0.080	0.44
0.100	0.55

What is the concentration of a solution for which the absorbance is measured to be 0.38?

Remember that there is a linear relationship between absorbance and concentration (Beer's law). Therefore, if the measured value of 0.38 is halfway between the standardized points of 0.33 and 0.44, then the concentration of the unknown solution is halfway between the respective standard concentrations of 0.060 M and 0.080 M, or 0.070 M.

18. Separation by Chromatography

Chromatography is a useful technique in qualitative identification of an unknown compound when compared with known compounds. For example, in Laboratory #22, students are asked to synthesize acetylsalicylic acid (aspirin). Chromatography gives a student the ability to test whether the synthesis reaction worked by developing the product on a chromatography plate alongside known compounds, such as the reactants in the reaction and a known sample of acetylsalicylic acid. The student can create a quantitative comparison by measuring the R_f value associated with each spot that has developed on the chromatography plate. The value is found in the following manner:

$$R_f = \frac{distance\ traveled\ by\ substance}{distance\ traveled\ by\ solvent}$$

Chromatography can easily separate different substances through minute differences in their physical properties. This is possible because different compounds demonstrate varied attraction to either the *stationary phase*—which is the thin layer of silica gel on the surface of a glass or plastic plate, and the *mobile phase*—which is the solvent that migrates up the plate via capillary action. Compounds that are more attracted to the mobile phase than the stationary phase will have a high R_f value. Conversely, compounds that are more attracted to the stationary phase than the mobile phase will have a low R_f value.

19. Preparation and Properties of Buffer Solutions

EXAMPLE:

A. Describe briefly how buffers work. Use specific chemical reactions with the acetic acid/acetate system to show how it minimizes a change in pH when either a strong acid or a strong base is added to the system.

A buffer is a combination of a weak acid and its conjugate base. When this combination exists, any additional protons added to the solution would react with the conjugate base to form water, and little change in pH results.

$$CH_3COO^- + H^+ \rightarrow H_2O$$

Likewise, any additional hydroxide ions added to the solution would react with the weak acid to form water, and little change in the pH results, except with the very slight increase in pH due to the addition of the conjugate base.

$$CH_3COOH + OH^- \rightarrow H_2O + CH_3COO^-$$

B. Use the Henderson–Hasselbach equation to describe why the ideal buffer pH for a buffer system equals the pK_a of the weak acid.

The Henderson–Hasselbach equation shows the relationship between the pK_a and the pH at different concentrations of the weak acid and the conjugate base.

$$pH = pK_a + log\frac{[A^-]}{[HA]}$$

The maximum buffering ability exists when the buffer system is equally equipped to neutralize acid or base, or where the molar concentration of the weak acid equals the concentration of its conjugate base $\left(\dfrac{[A^-]}{[HA]} = 1 \right)$. At this point, since the log of 1.0 is zero, the pH $=$ pK$_a$ of the acid.

C. Design an experiment to test the buffering ability of a buffer system. Be sure to identify what variable(s) you would keep constant, and what variable(s) you would change.

One way to test buffering ability is to test different buffer systems. Another type of test would be to look at buffering capacity when the members of the buffer are at different concentrations. For each of the different systems you would test, you would use an appropriate indicator that would change color when the buffer is exhausted, and then keep adding a measured amount of acid (or base) until the system reaches its endpoint. A comparison of the amount of acid (or base) added would give a measure of the system's ability to buffer changes in pH.

D. Given a 350 mL of a 0.20 M solution of acetic acid, what mass of solid sodium acetate would you add to the solution to achieve the maximum buffering ability of the solution?

$$\# \, g \, NaCH_3COO = \frac{0.350 \, L \, CH_3COOH}{1} \times \frac{0.20 \, mol \, CH_3COOH}{1 L \, CH_3COOH} \times \frac{1 \, mol \, NaCH_3COO}{1 \, mol \, CH_3COOH} \times$$

$$\frac{82.04 \, g}{1 \, mol \, NaCH_3COO} = 5.7 \, g NaCH_3COO$$

20. Determination of Electrochemical Series

EXAMPLE:

A. In the following figure, identify the following components of a galvanic (Voltaic) cell: voltmeter, anode, cathode, and salt bridge.

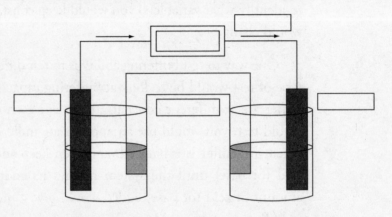

B. Where does reduction take place?

At the cathode.

C. The solution in the beaker on the right is 1.0 M $AgNO_3$, and the electrode in that beaker is solid silver (Ag). Use the chart of standard reduction potentials to calculate the total cell potential when the beaker on the left is separately filled with each of the following solutions and the electrode is composed of the corresponding solid metal:

a. 1.0 M $Al(NO_3)_3$

b. 1.0 M $Zn(NO_3)_2$

c. 1.0 M $Fe(NO_3)_2$

d. 0.001 M $Cu(NO_3)_2$

Based on the differences between the standard reduction potentials, the following voltage potentials are seen when these solutions are used to build a voltaic cell along with $AgNO_3$:

a. 2.46 Volts

b. 1.56 Volts

c. 1.24 Volts

d. 0.46 Volts

21. Measurements Using Electrochemical Cells and Electroplating

EXAMPLE: Two carbon rods, each with a mass of 8.000 g, are put into a 100.0 mL solution of 2.0 M $CuSO_4$. Electrodes from the two poles of a power source are placed at each electrode and the power is turned on for 20.0 minutes. An ammeter indicates that the current is 2.0 A for the entire time.

A. What is the reaction at the cathode?

$$Cu^{+2} + 2\ e^- \rightarrow Cu$$

B. What is the reaction at the anode?

$$2\ H_2O \rightarrow 4\ H^+ + O_2 + 4\ e^-$$

C. What is happening to the pH of the solution as the experiment proceeds?

Protons are being formed, so the pH decreases as the experiment proceeds.

D. How many moles of electrons were delivered to the cathode during the experiment?

$$\#\,mol\,e^- = \frac{2.00\,A \times 20.0\,min}{1} \times \frac{60\,s}{1\,min} \times \frac{C}{A\,sec} \times \frac{1\,mol\,e^-}{96,500\,C} = 0.0249\,mol\,e^-$$

E. What is the predicted new mass of the cathode when it is dried and reweighed after the experiment?

$$\#\,g\,Cu = \frac{0.0249\,mol\,e^-}{1} \times \frac{1\,mol\,Cu}{2\,mol\,e^-} \times \frac{63.55\,g\,Cu}{1\,mol\,Cu} = 0.791\,g\,Cu$$

Final mass electrode = initial mass + mass Cu added = 8.000 + 0.791 = 8.791 g Cu

22. Synthesis, Purification, and Analysis of an Organic Compound

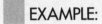 **EXAMPLE:** This laboratory usually entails performing a chemical reaction, purifying the product, and then measuring the physical properties of the product to confirm that the desired chemical change has taken place. One of the most common reactions used in high school for organic synthesis is the hydrolysis reaction. In a hydrolysis reaction, a strong acid, such as concentrated sulfuric acid, can be used to remove water from two molecules and convert the combination of an alcohol and a carboxylic acid into an ester. This is often done with salicylic acid and acetic acid to form acetylsalicylic acid, or aspirin. Aspirin is less water soluble than either salicylic acid or acetic acid. As a result, the product can be washed and extracted with a less polar solvent. The solvent can then be evaporated to yield the isolated product.

Another way to analyze the product is by using thin-layer chromatography. A student can dissolve both a sample of known acetylsalicylic acid and a sample of the product of the reaction that you ran in a mixture of solvents, such as toluene/ethyl formate/formic acid. Two plates can be spotted with each of the solutions and then allowed to develop. A student can compare the R_f value of the reaction product with the R_f value of the known solution of acetylsalicylic acid to confirm whether the reaction yielded the intended product.

Time for a quiz
- Review strategies in Chapter 2
- Take Quiz 8 at the REA Study Center
  (www.rea.com/studycenter)

Take Mini-Test 2
on Chapters 10–16
Go to the REA Study Center
(www.rea.com/studycenter)

Practice Exam

Also available at the REA Study Center *(www.rea.com/studycenter)*

This practice exam is available at the REA Study Center. Although AP exams are administered in paper-and-pencil format, we recommend that you take the online version of the practice exam for the benefits of:

- Instant scoring
- Enforced time conditions
- Detailed score report of your strengths and weaknesses

Practice Exam
Section I

(Answer sheets appear in the back of the book.)

TIME: 90 minutes

75 questions

50% of the entire test

Directions: Each set of lettered choices below refers to the numbered questions or statements immediately following it. Select the one lettered choice that best answers each question. A choice may be used once, more than once, or not at all in each set.

Part A

Questions 1–3 refer to the valence electron dot formulas in the figure below. The letters merely identify the different atoms. They do not stand for actual known elements.

$$\overset{\displaystyle\cdot}{H} \quad :\!\overset{\displaystyle\cdot\cdot}{\underset{\displaystyle\cdot}{A}}\!\cdot \quad \cdot\overset{\displaystyle\cdot\cdot}{\underset{\displaystyle\cdot}{D}}\!\cdot \quad \cdot\overset{\displaystyle\cdot}{\underset{\displaystyle\cdot}{Z}}\!\cdot \quad :\!\overset{\displaystyle\cdot\cdot}{\underset{\displaystyle\cdot\cdot}{Y}}\!:$$

1. The most active nonmetal is:

   (A) A   (D) Y

   (B) D   (E) Z

   (C) H

2. A likely bonding association is:

   (A) HA_2 (D) ZH_4

   (B) HD_4 (E) YZ

   (C) DH_5

3. Element D has a valence of:

   (A) 1   (D) 5

   (B) 3   (E) 7

   (C) 4

Questions 4–6

(A) Molecules are moving least rapidly and are closest together.

(B) Water is in this state at 12 degrees Centigrade.

(C) Mercury is in this state at room temperature.

(D) Molecules are moving most rapidly.

(E) Molecules maintain a definite volume but shape depends upon the contours of the container holding them.

4. Gas

5. Solid

6. Plasma

Questions 7–9

(A) sodium chlorate

(B) sodium chloride

(C) sodium chlorite

(D) sodium hypochlorite

(E) sodium perchlorate

7. NaC10

8. NaC10$_2$

9. NaC10$_3$

Questions 10–13

(A) alcohol

(B) alkane

(C) alkene

(D) alkyne

(E) amine

10. C$_2$H$_5$OH

11. C$_2$H$_6$

12. C$_2$H$_2$

13. C$_2$H$_4$

Part B

Directions: The following questions consist of questions or incomplete statements followed by five answers or completions. Select the best answer in each case.

14. Brønsted-Lowry acid and its conjugate base?

(A) Cu/Cu^{++}

(B) N$_2$/NH$_3$

(C) HC$_2$H$_3$O$_2$/C$_2$H$_3$O$_2$$^-$

(D) Al(OH)$_3$/[Al(OH)$_4$]$^-$

(E) PbI$_2$/Pb^{2+}

15. Which of the following sets of quantum numbers (listed in order of n, l, m_l, m_s) describe the highest energy valence electron of nitrogen in its ground state?

(A) 2,0,0, +½

(B) 2,1,1, −½

(C) 2,1,1, +½

(D) 2,1,−1, −½

(E) 2,1,−1, +½

16. Given the information in this chart, which of the following answers best represents the enthalpy of combustion for hydrogen gas, in kJ/mol?

Substance	ΔH_f° (kJ/mol)
$H_2(s)$	0
$CO_2(g)-$	393.5
$H_2O(l)-$	285.85
$O_2(g)$	0

(A) 0

(B) −393

(C) −107

(D) −285

(E) +107

17. Suppose that the reaction rate of an inorganic reaction mixture at 35 degrees Centigrade is double the reaction rate at an earlier temperature setting. All other environmental factors are held constant. This earlier temperature was most likely:

(A) 0 °C

(B) 10 °C

(C) 25 °C

(D) 40 °C

(E) 45 °C

18. For the reaction,

$$HCOO^- + H_2O \rightarrow HCOOH + OH^-$$

The rate expression is

$$Rate = k\,[HCOOH]\,[OH^-]$$

What is the overall order of this reaction?

(A) 1

(B) 2

(C) 4

(D) 5

(E) 6

19. Select the indicator that changes color at a pH of 1.

(A) congo red

(B) malachite green

(C) methyl violet

(D) phenophthalein

(E) thymol blue

20. Select the characteristic that is NOT a standard condition for comparing gas volumes:

(A) Pressure—1 atm

(B) Pressure—760 torr

(C) Temperature—0 degrees Centigrade

(D) Temperature—25 degrees Centigrade

(E) Temperature—273 degrees Kelvin

21. A recorded Fahrenheit value in lab is 122 degrees. Its corresponding Kelvin temperature value is:

    (A) 32

    (B) 52

    (C) 152

    (D) 273

    (E) 323

22. Consider the balanced equation:

    $$2H_2 + O_2 \rightarrow 2H_2O$$

    What volume of oxygen in liters must be available at STP to allow six grams of hydrogen to react and form water?

    (A) 2

    (B) 11.2

    (C) 16

    (D) 22.4

    (E) 33.6

23. Select the element with an atomic number of 19 and one electron in its valence shell:

    (A) calcium

    (B) chlorine

    (C) hydrogen

    (D) potassium

    (E) sodium

24. A certain element commonly has 8 protons, 8 neutrons, and 8 electrons. Select the combination of particles that denote an isotope of this particular atom.

    (A) 4 protons, 4 neutrons, 4 electrons

    (B) 8 protons, 8 neutrons, 4 electrons

    (C) 8 protons, 10 neutrons, 8 electrons

    (D) 10 protons, 8 neutrons, 8 electrons

    (E) 10 protons, 10 neutrons, 8 electrons

25. A probable compound formed from calcium and oxygen has the formula:

    (A) CaO

    (B) Ca_2O_2

    (C) Ca_2O

    (D) Ca_2O_3

    (E) Ca_3O_2

26. Select the INCORRECT statement about alpha, beta, and gamma rays of radiation.

    (A) All affect a photographic plate.

    (B) Alpha rays possess charged particles.

    (C) Beta rays move most rapidly.

    (D) Beta rays lack charged particles.

    (E) Gamma rays display high frequency waves.

27. The number of valence electrons in cobalt is:

    (A) 1

    (B) 2

    (C) 3

    (D) 4

    (E) 6

28. Among the choices given, the atom with the largest size is:

    (A) bromine

    (B) chlorine

    (C) fluorine

    (D) helium

    (E) iodine

29. The final stable, disintegration product in the decay of uranium, $^{238}_{9}U$, is:

    (A) $^{210}_{83}Bi$

    (B) $^{206}_{82}Pb$

    (C) $^{210}_{82}Pb$

    (D) $^{210}_{84}Po$

    (E) $^{234}_{90}Th$

30. The correct ranking of alkali metals from most reactive to least reactive is:

    (A) Be–Mg–Co–Sr–Ba

    (B) Cs–Rb–K–Na–Li

    (C) F–Cl–Br–I

    (D) I–Br–Cl–F

    (E) Li–Na–K–Rb–Cs

31. Select the most unreactive element:

    (A) Cl

    (B) H

    (C) Na

    (D) S

    (E) Xe

32. Each of the following is a statement of Dalton's laws EXCEPT:

    (A) Any gas in a mixture exerts its partial pressure.

    (B) Atoms are permanent and cannot be decomposed.

    (C) Each gas's pressure depends on other gases in a mixture.

    (D) Gases can exist in a mixture.

    (E) Substances are composed of atoms.

33. Consider the balanced equation:

    $$2KClO_3 \rightarrow 2KCl + 3O_2$$

    If 72 grams of oxygen gas are produced, the amount of potassium chlorate required in grams is:

    (A) 112

    (B) 224

    (C) 183

    (D) 448

    (E) 1020

34. In the following reaction, how would the equilibrium constant for the listed reaction be related to the acid ionization constant, K_a, for acetic acid?

    $$HC_2H_3O_2 + OH^- \leftrightarrow H_2O + C_2H_3O_2^-$$

    (A) K_a/K_w

    (B) K_w/K_a

    (C) $1/K_a$

    (D) K_a

    (E) $K_a K_b$

35. An atom has an atomic mass of 45 and an atomic number of 21. Select the correct statement about its atomic structure:

    (A) The number of electrons is 24.

    (B) The number of neutrons is 21.

    (C) The number of protons is 24.

    (D) The number of electrons and neutrons is equal.

    (E) The number of protons and neutrons is unequal.

36. Boron is bombarded by alpha particles. Complete the products formed in the following equation by transmutation.

$$^{11}_{5}B + ^{4}_{2}He$$

    (A) $^{12}_{6}C + ^{1}_{0}n$

    (B) $^{6}_{3}L + ^{1}_{0}n$

    (C) $^{14}_{7}N + ^{1}_{0}n$

    (D) $^{31}_{15}P + ^{1}_{0}n$

    (E) $^{28}_{14}Si + ^{1}_{1}H$

37. The least bond energy in kcals per mole is found with:

    (A) C–C

    (B) H–Br

    (C) H–Cl

    (D) H–F

    (E) O–H

38. The bond angles between carbon and hydrogen in methane are best labeled as:

    (A) covalent

    (B) ionic

    (C) linear

    (D) tetrahedral

    (E) trihybrid

39. Select the metal with the lowest melting point:

    (A) copper

    (B) iron

    (C) lithium

    (D) phosphorous

    (E) sulfur

40. HCl + NaOH $\rightarrow$ NaCl + H_2O is an example of a reaction classified as:

    (A) decomposition

    (B) double replacement

    (C) reversible

    (D) single replacement

    (E) synthesis

41. Consider this reaction under standard lab conditions:

$$FeS + 2HCl \rightarrow FeCl_2 + H_2S$$

If 22 grams of iron sulfide are completely reacted to form products, the volume of hydrogen sulfide gas produced is:

(A) 5.6

(B) 11.2

(C) 22.4

(D) 44.4

(E) 88.0

42. Compute the quantity in grams of sucrose $(C_{12}H_{22}O_{11})$ required to make a 1M strength solution of 500 mL.

(A) 85.5

(B) 171

(C) 342

(D) 684

(E) 982

43. Consider the following balanced equation:

$$2K + 2HCl \rightarrow 2KCl + H_2$$

The respective oxidation numbers for K, H, and Cl before and after reaction:

(A) go from 0, −1, +1 to −1, +1, 0

(B) go from 0, +1, −1 to +1, 0, −1

(C) go from 1, −1, 0 to −1, +1, −1

(D) go from 1, −1, 0 to −1, −1, 0

(E) go from 0, 0, 1 to 1, 1, −1

44. Enzymes, which are organic catalysts, always partly consist of:

(A) carbohydrates

(B) lipids

(C) nucleic acids

(D) proteins

(E) steroids

45. A correct ranking of elements in order of decreasing electronegativity is:

(A) Al−F−O−Cs−Na

(B) Cs−Na−Al−O−F

(C) F−O−Al−Na−Cs

(D) Na−F−Al−O−Cs

(E) O−Cs−Al−F−Na

46. The critical pressure of a substance is a value that is necessary to:

(A) convert a gas to a solid at its critical temperature

(B) convert a liquid to a solid at its critical temperature

(C) freeze a liquid at its critical temperature

(D) liquefy a gas at its critical temperature

(E) vaporize a liquid at its critical temperature

47. For the single-step reaction $PCl_5 \rightarrow PCl_3 + Cl_2$, the rate of the reaction is proportional to:

    (A) $[Cl_2] \times [PCl_3]$

    (B) $[PCl_5]$

    (C) $\dfrac{[Cl_2] \times [PCl_3]}{[PCl_5]}$

    (D) $\dfrac{[PCl_5]}{[Cl_3] \times [PCl_3]}$

    (E) $[PCl_5] \times [PCl_3] \times [Cl_2]$

48. What is the molar mass of C_2H_4O, in g/mol?

    (A) 12

    (B) 22

    (C) 32

    (D) 44

    (E) 60

49. Show phases, H_2 (g) + S (s) $\leftrightarrow$ H_2S (g) + energy

    $$H_2 + S \leftrightarrow H_2S \text{ (g) + energy}$$

    In this equilibrium, select the factor that will shift the reaction to the right:

    (A) adding heat

    (B) adding H_2S

    (C) removing hydrogen gas

    (D) removing hydrogen sulfide gas

    (E) removing sulfur

50. What mass in grams of sodium hydroxide, NaOH, would be needed to create 2.0 liters of a 0.40-molar solution of NaOH?

    (A) 0.8

    (B) 8.0

    (C) 16

    (D) 19.2

    (E) 32

51. Which of the following shows the highest conductivity in aqueous solution

    (A) alcohol

    (B) distilled H_2O

    (C) glucose

    (D) hydrochloric acid

    (E) sucrose

52. $HC_2H_3O_2 \leftrightarrow H^+ + C_2H_3O_2$

    Consider the above equation.

    0.5 moles/liter of acetic acid dissociates into hydrogen and acetate ions. The equilibrium concentration of the hydrogen ions is 2.9×10^{-3} moles/liter. The ionization constant for the acid is

    (A) 1.7×10^{-5}

    (B) 8×10^{-2}

    (C) 4×10^{-1}

    (D) 4×10^{-2}

    (E) 4×10^2

53. The pOH of a 1×10^{-4} M KOH solution is:

    (A) 1

    (B) 2

    (C) 4

    (D) 7

    (E) 11

54. Carbon's valence shell electron configuration can be symbolized as:

    (A) $2s^1 2p^1$

    (B) $2s^1 2p^2$

    (C) $2s^2 2p^2$

    (D) $2s^2 2p^4$

    (E) $2s^4 2p^2$

55. What is the approximate percent composition of oxygen in magnesium oxide, MgO?

    (A) 12%

    (B) 20%

    (C) 32%

    (D) 40%

    (E) 80%

56. What would be the most likely rate law for the mechanism below?

    Step one: $A + B \leftrightarrow I$ fast equilibrium

    Step two: $\underline{C + I \rightarrow D}$ slow step

    Total reaction: $A + B + C \rightarrow D$

    (A) Rate = k [A] [B]

    (B) Rate = k [A] [B] [C]

    (C) Rate = k [C]

    (D) Rate = k [C] [I]

    (E) Can't be determined from the information given

57. $\_\_H_2S + \_\_O_2 \rightarrow \_\_H_2O + \_\_SO_2$

    Balancing this equation yields the following coefficients from left to right:

    (A) 1-1-2-2

    (B) 2-3-2-2

    (C) 2-2-2-3

    (D) 3-2-2-2

    (E) 3-2-3-2

58. The volume in milliliters of a 0.3 M solution of NaOH needed to neutralize 3 liters of a 0.01M HCl solution is:

    (A) .1

    (B) 1

    (C) 10

    (D) 100

    (E) 1000

59. The outline for a molecular sub-unit for a saturated fat molecule is depicted at:

(A)

```
        O
        ||
    H – C
        |
    H – C – OH
        |
 HO – C – H
        |
    H – C – OH
        |
    H – C – OH
        |
    H – C – OH
        |
        H
```

(B)

```
        O
        ||
 HO – C – C = C = C = C = C – C –
```

(C)

```
    O   H   H   H   H
    ||  |   |   |   |
 HO – C – C –C – C – C
        |   |   |   |
        H   H   H   H
```

(D)

```
 H       H   O
  \      |   ||
     N – C – C – OH
  /      |
 H       R
```

(E)

```
        H   H
         \ /
    H     C     H
     \   / \   /
       C     C
     /         \
    H           H
```

60. An ice cube is placed in an open glass of water at room temperature. Describe the resultant effect on its energy content and entropy.

	Energy	Entropy
(A)	decrease	decrease
(B)	increase	increase
(C)	increase	decrease
(D)	increase	remains constant
(E)	remains constant	increase

61. The K_{sp} $PbCrO_4$ is 1.0×10^{-16}. What is the molar solubility of $PbCrO_4$ in a solution with pH 4?

(A) 1.0×10^{-4}

(B) 1.0×10^{-8}

(C) 1.0×10^{-16}

(D) 1.0×10^{-20}

(E) 1.0×10^{-22}

62. Solid zinc oxide, ZnO, has a heat of formation of about -84 kilocalories per mole. Select the correct statement for a reaction producing 162 grams of zinc oxide.

(A) 42 kilocalories are absorbed

(B) 81 kilocalories are absorbed

(C) 81 kilocalories are released

(D) 168 kilocalories are absorbed

(E) 168 kilocalories are released

63. One mole of a substance dissolved in 1000 grams of water elevates the boiling point by .52°C and depresses the freezing point by 1.86°C. 23 grams of an alcohol, C_2H_5OH, is dissolved in a kilogram of water. At standard conditions, water's new boiling and freezing points are respectively (in °C):

   (A) 100.26°, −.93°

   (B) .26°, −1.86°

   (C) .52°, −.93°

   (D) 100.52°, −1.86°

   (E) 101.04°, −1.86°

64. Select the correct solubility rule:

   (A) All ammonium salts are insoluble.

   (B) All nitrates are insoluble.

   (C) All silver salts, except $AgNO_3$, are insoluble.

   (D) All sodium salts are insoluble.

   (E) Sulfides of sodium, potassium, and magnesium are insoluble.

65. A salt formed by a neutralization reaction of a strong acid and weak base is:

   (A) HCl

   (B) NaCl

   (C) Na_2CO_3

   (D) NH_4Cl

   (E) NH_4CN

66. Substances are neither created nor destroyed, but simply changed from one form to another. This is the law of:

   (A) change of matter

   (B) conservation of energy

   (C) conservation of matter

   (D) multiple proportions

   (E) second law of thermodynamics

67. FeS_2 or "fool's gold" is also known as

   (A) hematite

   (B) lodestone

   (C) magnetite

   (D) pyrite

   (E) siderite

68. Members of a common horizontal row of the periodic table should have the same:

   (A) atomic number

   (B) atomic mass

   (C) electron number in the outer shell

   (D) number of energy shells

   (E) valence

69. The most common isotope of hydrogen has an atomic number and mass, respectively, of:

   (A) 1,0

   (B) 1,1

   (C) 1,2

   (D) 2,1

   (E) 2,2

70. 500 mL of a gas experiences a pressure change from 760 mm of mercury pressure to a barometric pressure of 800. If all other laboratory factors are held constant, its new volume in mL is:

    (A) 400 (D) 525

    (B) 425 (E) 595

    (C) 475

71. An atom's electron number is 11 while the number of neutrons is 12. Its atomic mass is:

    (A) 11/12 (D) 23

    (B) 11 (E) 132

    (C) 12

72. The following chart depicts the ionization constants (K_a) for a number of weak acids. If you had a 1.0-molar solution of each acid, which would have the highest pH?

Acid	K_a
HSO_2^-	1.2×10^{-2}
HNO_2	4.0×10^{-4}
HF	7.2×10^{-4}
HOCl	3.5×10^{-8}
HCN	6.2×10^{-10}

    (A) HSO_2^- (D) HOCl

    (B) HNO_2 (E) HCN

    (C) HF

73. What is the ratio of the rate of effusion of helium gas (molar mass = 4.0 g/mol) to the rate of effusion of oxygen gas (molar mass = 32.0 g/mol) at the same temperature and pressure?

    (A) 2

    (B) 4

    (C) 0.125

    (D) 8.0

    (E) 16.0

74. 44.8 liters of a gas are collected in a lab under standard conditions. The number of molecules in this volume is:

    (A) 112,000

    (B) 6.02×10^{23}

    (C) 12.04×10^{23}

    (D) 18.06×10^{23}

    (E) 1,112,000

75. The second law of Thermodynamics states that:

    (A) Energy is neither created nor destroyed, but changed from one form to another.

    (B) Gas pressures are determined independently in a mixture.

    (C) Heat flows to a more concentrated medium.

    (D) Matter is neither created nor destroyed.

    (E) Spontaneous processes tend toward increasing disorder.

Practice Exam
Section II

(Answer sheets appear in the back of this book.)

TIME: 95 minutes
6 free-response questions
50% of the entire test

The percentages given for the parts represent the score weightings for this section of the examination. You will be given 55 minutes for Part A and 40 minutes for Part B.

You may use a calculator on Part A, but not on Part B.

Be sure to write your answers in the space provided following each question. Pay attention to significant figures.

Part A

TIME: 55 minutes
3 free-response questions
60% (20% for each problem)

YOU MAY USE A CALCULATOR ON THIS PART.

Show your work clearly for full credit. Pay attention to significant figures in your answers.

Solve the following problems.

1. The value for the ionization constant, K_a, for hypochlorous acid, HOCl, is 3.2×10^{-8}.

   (a) Calculate the pH of a 0.030-molar solution of HOCl.

   (b) Calculate the percent dissociation of the solution in (A).

   (c) Calculate the hydrogen ion concentration of a solution prepared by mixing equal volumes of a 0.030-molar HOCl and a 0.020 molar solution of sodium hypochlorite, NaOCl.

   (d) Calculate the pH at which 50 mL of the 0.030 M HOCl solution is at the equivalence point after adding 50 mL of a standard NaOH solution.

   (e) What needs to be added to the solution in part (C) to create a solution of maximum buffering ability?

2. Iron reacts with oxygen gas to form rust according to the following equation,

$$2 \text{ Fe } (s) + 3/2 \text{ O}_2(g) \rightarrow \text{Fe}_2\text{O}_3(s) \qquad \Delta H°_f = -824 \text{ kJ/mol}$$

(a) 25.0 grams of Fe (s) is mixed with 20.0 L of oxygen gas at 3.00 atm and 25°C. What mass of iron oxide is produced?

(b) Identify the limiting reactant in this reaction. Support your conclusion with calculations.

(c) What further amount of mass of the limiting reactant would be needed to use up the remainder of the other reactant?

(d) What is the $\Delta S°$ for the reaction when it is just barely spontaneous?

3. The following data was collected for the reaction, $A \rightarrow B + C$.

Time (sec):	0	900	1800
[A] @ 25°C:	50.8	19.7	7.62
[A] @ 35°C:	80.0	26.7	8.90

(a) What is the rate law for the reaction?

(b) Calculate the specific rate constant and determine its units.

(c) Describe how to calculate the half-life from this information.

(d) Determine the energy of activation for this reaction.

(e) What will be the approximate concentration of A after 40 minutes (at 25 °C)?

Part B

TIME: 40 minutes
  3 free-response questions
  40% (10% for question 4; 15% for each essay)

YOU MAY NOT USE A CALCULATOR ON THIS PART.

4. For each of the following three reactions in part (i) write a BALANCED equation and in part (ii) answer the question about the reaction. In part (i), coefficients should be in terms of lowest whole numbers. Assume that solutions are aqueous unless otherwise indicated. Represent substances in solutions as ions if the substances are extensively ionized. Omit formulas for any ions or molecules that are unchanged by the reaction.

   a. A piece of zinc is placed in an aqueous solution of hydrochloric acid

       i. Write the balanced net ionic equation for this reaction.

       ii. Which reactant is oxidized, and how much does its oxidation state change?

   b. Boron triflouride is added to a solution of ammonia

       i. Write the balanced net ionic equation for this reaction.

       ii. Which species is the Lewis acid in this reaction, and why?

   c. Magnesium is burned in pure oxygen

       i. Write the balanced net ionic equation for this reaction.

       ii. Describe what a student would observe when seeing this reaction.

5. You are given three unlabeled bottles, each containing small samples of one of the following metals: magnesium, aluminum, and silver.

   You are also given samples of the following reagents: pure water, a 1.0-molar solution of HCl, and a solution of concentrated nitric acid.

   (a) Which metal can be easily identified because it is much softer than the others? What chemical test using the available reagents would you use to confirm your conclusion?

   (b) Determine a chemical test using an available reagent that would distinguish between the two remaining metals.

   (c) Write a balanced equation for the one metal that reacts with concentrated nitric acid.

   (d) Which of the reagent solutions could be used to identify the existence of Pb^{2+} ions in solution? Write a balanced chemical reaction that would identify the lead ions.

6. A student is given two vials of two isomers of 2,3-dichloro,2-butene, $C_4H_6Cl_2$, and is asked to distinguish between the two molecules.

(a) Draw the two possible isomers of this molecule.

(b) Compare the hybridization of each of the four carbon atoms in the molecule.

(c) How many pi bonds occur in this molecule, and where is (are) it (they) located?

(d) Pi bonds are broken upon heating before sigma bonds. The student heats a mixture of the two isomers, the pi bond is broken, and at high temperatures the molecule freely rotates around each sigma bond. Which of the two isomers will naturally re-form in greatest abundance, and why?

(e) How can the student use melting points to distinguish between the two isomers?

Answer Key

Section I

1. (D)	20. (D)	39. (C)	58. (D)
2. (D)	21. (E)	40. (B)	59. (C)
3. (B)	22. (E)	41. (A)	60. (B)
4. (D)	23. (D)	42. (B)	61. (B)
5. (A)	24. (C)	43. (B)	62. (E)
6. (B)	25. (A)	44. (D)	63. (A)
7. (D)	26. (D)	45. (C)	64. (C)
8. (C)	27. (B)	46. (D)	65. (D)
9. (A)	28. (E)	47. (B)	66. (C)
10. (A)	29. (B)	48. (D)	67. (D)
11. (B)	30. (B)	49. (D)	68. (D)
12. (D)	31. (E)	50. (E)	69. (B)
13. (C)	32. (C)	51. (D)	70. (C)
14. (C)	33. (C)	52. (A)	71. (D)
15. (C)	34. (A)	53. (C)	72. (E)
16. (D)	35. (E)	54. (C)	73. (B)
17. (C)	36. (C)	55. (D)	74. (C)
18. (B)	37. (A)	56. (B)	75. (E)
19. (C)	38. (D)	57. (B)	

Detailed Explanations of Answers

Section I

1. **(D)**

    Nonmetals tend to accept electrons to obey the octet rule. They have five or more electrons in their valence shell. Atom Y has seven, being very active and close to fulfillment.

2. **(D)**

    Z has four electrons. Four hydrogens, each with one electron, can share and fulfill Z with its remaining four. Hydrogen is also satisfied, gaining a second electron for fulfillment of its only energy shell. Four covalent bonds are formed.

3. **(B)**

    With 5 valence electrons, D is in need of 3 more for octet fulfillment.

4. **(D)**   5. **(A)**   6. **(B)**

    The two choices are general principles comparing solids and liquids for rapidity of particle movement and intermolecular distance. Liquid water does not freeze and become a solid until 0° C. Mercury, unlike most metals, is a liquid at room temperature.

7. **(D)**   8. **(C)**   9. **(A)**

    The most common oxygen-containing salt ends in the suffix "ate": $NaClO_3$ = sodium chlorate. Chlorine's oxidation state is $+5$, as sodium's is $+1$, and oxygen's total is -6 (3×-2). $+5$ and $+1$ balance the -6 oxidation state. The next lowest chlorine oxidation state ends in "ite": sodium chlorite, $NaClO_2$. Chlorine's oxidation state here is $+3$, along with sodium's $+1$ and oxygen's total -4. The next lowest chlorine oxidation state uses the "hypo. . .ite" prefix-suffix: $NaClO \rightarrow$ Na is $+1$, Cl is $+1$ and O is -2. The next lowest state uses the "ide" suffix: NaCl, sodium chloride. Chlorine's oxidation state is -1 to sodium's $+1$.

10. **(A)**   11. **(B)**   12. **(D)**   13. **(C)**

Alkanes have the general molecular formula C_nH_{2n+2}, such as butane, C_2H_6. Alkenes conform to C_nH_{2n}, for example butene, C_2H_4. Alkynes, CnH_{2n-2}, include butyne, C_2H_2. Alcohols, such as butyl alcohol, include an OH in the carbon chain. Amines are nitrogen derivatives, and are not represented.

14. **(C)**

$HC_2H_3O_2/C_2H_3O_2^-$ is the only conjugate acid/base pair, each of which is different from the other by only a proton. Cu/Cu^{++} are different from each other by two electrons. N_2/NH_3 are different from each other by hydrogen atoms—protons and electrons. $Al(OH)_3/[Al(OH)_4]^-$ are different by a hydroxide ion. PbI_2/Pb^{2+} are different by two iodine atoms.

15. **(C)**

Since nitrogen is in the second row, its highest energy electron is at $n = 2$, which is the first number. The second number signifies that its outer electron is in a p-orbital. The third number indicates the third p-orbital to receive an electron, since nitrogen is the third element in the p-block in the periodic table. The last number is the magnetic spin quantum number, which signifies that the highest energy electron is the only electron in the orbital.

16. **(D)**

The enthalpy of combustion for hydrogen, upon close inspection, is actually the same as the heat of formation for water.

$$\Delta H^\circ_{reaction} = \Sigma H^\circ_f(\text{products}) - \Sigma H^\circ_f(\text{reactants})$$

$$\Delta H^\circ_{reaction} = -285.85 \text{ kJ/mol}$$

17. **(C)**

Reaction rates of inorganic substances usually double with every 10°C increase in temperature. Therefore, if 35°C represents the new, doubled rate, then the original temperature must be 10° less: 35°C − 10°C = 25°C.

18. **(B)**

The order is not derived from the stoichiometric coefficients unless it is understood to be a single-step mechanism. The order is found from adding two exponents from the rate equation Rate = $k [A]^x[B]^y$ where order = $x + y$.

19. **(C)**

Other color indicator changes are: congo red 4, malachite green 12, phenophthalein 9, thymol blue 3.

20. **(D)**

Both pressures represent standard pressure while 25°C is considered the thermodynamic standard state; standard temperature for gases is 0°C, or 273K.

21. **(E)**

By temperature conversion, C = 5/9 (F − 32). C = 5/9 (122 − 32) = 50. A Centigrade value is converted to Kelvin by adding the constant 273: 50 + 273 = 323.

22. **(E)**

Two moles (4 grams) of hydrogen gas react with one mole (32 grams) of oxygen gas in this balanced reaction. Six grams of H_2 are 3 moles. By simple proportion, 1.5 moles of O_2 must react. One mole occupies 22.4 L at STP. 1.5 moles occupy 33.6 liters by simple proportion.

23. **(D)**

With atomic number 19 (19 electrons), the electrons will fill up n = 1 (2 electrons), n = 2 (8 electrons), and the s and p orbitals of n = 3. This array places potassium in group one of the periodic table.

24. **(C)**

Isotopes of an element have the same atomic number but their atomic mass varies due to a varying number of neutrons. This question compares two isotopes of oxygen.

25. **(A)**

Two electrons from calcium satisfy oxygen's requirement for eight valence electrons to obey the octet rule. They thus combine in a one-to-one ratio, CaO.

26. **(D)**

Beta rays consist of negatively charged particles moving close to the speed of light. Alpha rays are positive, and penetrating gamma rays are high frequency, near X-rays. All affect a photographic plate, a trait that led to their initial detection.

27. (B)

Cobalt is in group two of the periodic table and hence has two valence electrons. All elements of a given numbered family have that common valence electron number.

28. (E)

Iodine is at the bottom of the halogens in family seven of the periodic table. Elements that appear at the bottom of any family have more energy levels and are larger in size.

29. (B)

All of the choices are formed throughout the various steps of radioactive $^{238}_{92}U$ decay. $^{206}_{82}Pb$ is thus associated with $^{238}_{92}U$ in nature. The relative amounts of the two, along with knowledge of half-life periods, can be used to calculate the age of a geological structure harboring these two atoms.

30. (B)

The alkali metals are in family one of the period table. They are progressively more active as metals, losing their one valence electron as they descend through the vertical array.

31. (E)

Xe, xenon, is found in family eight of the periodic table, the noble gases. All other choices are active metals or nonmetals of other families.

32. (C)

Dalton's laws of partial pressures state that gases in a mixture exert their individual pressures independently.

33. (C)

By the balanced equation, two moles (244 grams) of $KClO_3$ yield 3 moles of O_2 (96 grams). By simple proportion:

$$\frac{2KClO_{3^-}}{3O_3} = \frac{244}{96} = \frac{x}{72} \text{ so } x = 183$$

34. **(A)**

    The equilibrium constant for the listed reaction is $1/K_b$, which, since $K_w = K_a \times K_b$, then equals K_a/K_w.

35. **(E)**

    With an atomic number of 21, the electron and proton numbers are each 21. For a mass of 45, 24 neutrons must exist with the 21 protons.

36. **(C)**

    An alpha particle consists of two protons and two neutrons as in a helium nucleus, ^4_2He . In the bombardment, boron incorporates the two protons for an atomic number increase from 5 to 7. These two protons plus one captured neutron yield an atomic mass increase from 11 to 14, thus $^{14}_7N$ as in nitrogen. The second neutron remains free.

37. **(A)**

    Carbon is neither a strong metal nor a strong nonmetal and has less electron-attracting power than the strong nonmetals bromine, chlorine, fluorine, and oxygen, in their covalent bond formation.

38. **(D)**

    Methane, CH_4, is a symmetrical molecule in terms of the direction of its four covalent bonds. Each C–H bond is at an approximate 109-degree bond angle, oriented toward the corner of an imaginary tetrahedron (a four-sided figure).

39. **(C)**

    Metals in family one and two of the periodic table have these characteristics. Note lithium's location in the periodic table.

40. **(B)**

    The respective cations, $H+$ and $Na+$, and anions, Cl^- and OH^-, swap places in the change from reactants to products.

41. **(A)**

    One mole of FeS, 88 grams (56 + 32) forms one mole of H_2S gas in the balanced equation. By simple proportion, one-quarter mole of the given 22 grams, thus yields one-quarter mole of H_2S. One mole of a gas fills 22.4 liters; thus .25 mole $\times$ 22.4 liters = 5.6 liters.

42. **(B)**

   One mole of sucrose is 342 grams:

   C 12 × 12 (atomic weight of carbon) = 144 g

   H 22 × 1 (atomic weight of hydrogen) = 22 g

   O 11 × 16 (atomic weight of oxygen) = 176 g

   These total 342 grams; 342 grams in one liter makes a 1M-strength solution. In one-half liter, 500 ml, this measured amount is also halved.

43. **(B)**

   Among reactants, uncombined potassium is 0. Hydrogen is +1 metallic behavior and chlorine is −1 (nonmetal) while combined in a compound. Among products, potassium is now combined, +1 (metal). Chlorine remains −1 as combined. Liberated hydrogen is uncombined as a liberated gas, 0.

44. **(D)**

   Enzymes are proteins which act as catalysts for biochemical reactions.

45. **(C)**

   Electronegativity is electron-attracting power. Fluorine, in the upper right-hand corner of the periodic table, is the most active nonmetal and has the highest electronegativity. Oxygen follows as very active. Aluminum is a metal, which means less electronegativity: it actually donates electrons. Sodium and cesium are metals, too, and cesium has the least electronegativity.

46. **(D)**

   For each gas, a temperature is reached where the kinetic energy of the molecules is so great that no pressure, however large, can liquefy the gas. Any pressure is insufficient to compress gas molecules back to the liquid state where molecules are closer together. This temperature is the critical temperature. The accompanying pressure is the critical pressure.

47. **(B)**

   For the general reaction

   $A \rightarrow B + C$

   The rate is written as

   rate $= [A]^n$

   where n is the experimentally determined order of the reaction. The only answer which conforms with the rate as written above is (B), i.e., rate $[PCl_5]$. In this case, $n = 1$.

48. **(D)**

   The molar mass is found by adding the atomic masses of each atom in the formula. $(2 \times 12.011) + (4 \times 1.008) + (16) = 44$ g/mol.

49. **(D)**

   The left-to-right reaction is exothermic, therefore, adding heat drives the reaction equilibrium to the left. From the equilibrium constant

   $$K_{eq} = \frac{[H_2S]}{[H_2][S]}$$

   it is clear that an increase in the concentration of H_2S increases the value of this ratio, *i.e.*, the equilibrium is disturbed. To return to the equilibrium constant value, H_2S decomposes, so that the reaction is shifted to the left. Blocking H_2 removes reactant, inhibiting formation to the right side. Removing S has the same effect. Removing H_2S, however, lowers the value of the equilibrium constant. To restore it, more H_2S is produced, *i.e.*, the reaction shifts to the right. The above analysis is the application of Le Chatelier's principle.

50. **(E)**

   $$32\,g = 2.0\,L\,solution \times \frac{04.0\,mol\,NaOH}{L\,NaOH\,solution} \times \frac{40\,g\,NaOH}{1\,mol\,NaOH}$$

51. **(D)**

   Hydrochloric acid, HCl, almost completely ionizes in solution, therefore allows passage of electricity; *i.e.*, it acts as a conductor. The other four choices do not ionize.

52. **(A)**

For a reaction $HA \leftrightarrow H^+ + A^-$, given initial concentrations:

$[x] \leftrightarrow 0 + 0$ and equilibrium concentrations: $[x - y] \leftrightarrow [y] + [y]$, then the ionization constant K_a is

$$K_a = \frac{[y][y]}{[x - y]}$$

$$K_a = \frac{[y]^2}{[x - y]}$$

If $x >> y$ (x is much greater than y), then

$$K_a \sim \frac{[y]^2}{x}$$

In our example, $x = 0.5$ moles/L and $y = 2.9 \times 10^{-3}$; therefore

$$K_a = \frac{(2.9 \times 10^{-3})^2}{0.5 - 0.0029} \quad \frac{8.41 \times 10^{-6}}{0.5}$$

$$K_a = 16.82 \times 10^{-6} \approx 1.7 \times 10^{-5}$$

53. **(C)**

pOH is negative the log of a solution's hydroxyl ion concentration. A .0001M KOH solution furnishes 10^{-4} hydroxyl ions in moles per liter. Molarity and normality are the same for KOH, as it yields one hydroxyl ion per KOH unit. $pOH = -\log [OH-]$; therefore $pOH = -\log 10^{-4} = 4$.

54. **(C)**

Carbon has four valence electrons. Two occupy the smaller s orbital and the two remaining fill the larger p orbital.

55. **(D)**

Percent composition is found by dividing the mass contributed by one element by the total molar mass of the compound, then multiplying by 100%.

$$\frac{16 \text{ g O}}{40.31 \text{ g MgO}} \times 100\% = 39.69 = 40\%$$

56. **(B)**

   The rate-determining step depends on the intermediate, I, which can be expressed in terms of A and B using the prior fast equilibrium step. Thus, in this mechanism, the rate is not proportional to just I and C, but A, B, and C.

57. **(B)**

   Three molecules of O_2 (6 atoms) supply 2 water molecules (2 oxygen atoms) and 2 sulfur dioxide molecules (4 atoms). Four hydrogen atoms from H_2S (2×2) also supply the four hydrogens in the water produced (2×2).

58. **(D)**

   The acid and base react by the equation:

   $$HCl + NaOH \rightarrow HCl + H_2O.$$

   Each compound donates single ions to form an NaCl unit. By this assumption: molarity of an acid x volume of an acid = (normality of a base) $\times$ (volume of a base).

   By substitution:

   $$0.01 \times 3 = 0.3 \times V_2$$

   $$V_2 = \frac{0.01 \times 3\,\text{liters}}{0.3} = 0.1\,\text{liter}$$

   $$0.1\,\text{liter} = 100\,\text{mL}$$

59. **(C)**

   Illustration A shows the molecular formula of glucose. (D) shows an amino acid's formula. (E) is cyclopropane. Both (B) and (C) are outlines of fatty acids. (B), however, is not saturated with hydrogen atoms, covalently bonded to its carbon chain. This is because of the double C–to–C bonds, limiting availability for hydrogen covalent bonding. Carbon's valence is four. The carbon atoms in illustration (C) are single bonded, leaving more bonding sites for hydrogen atoms. It is relatively saturated with these atoms. Fatty acids are the molecular sub-units of fat molecules.

60. **(B)**

   The ice cube will melt by gaining heat from the water. The temperature of the water drops below room temperature; therefore, heat flows from the surroundings into the water until room temperature is attained. The resultant effect is an increase in energy for the ice and the water system. When the ice melts, it changes from an ordered to a disordered system. Entropy is a measure of disorder (randomness). The higher the disorder, the higher the entropy. In this case, energy and entropy both increase.

61. **(B)**

The molar solubility can be found by equating the solubility product constant to the product of the molar concentrations of the dissolved ions. Therefore, in this case, the molar solubility is simply the square root of the solubility product constant of $PbCrO_4$.

$$x^2 = 1.0 \times 10^{-16}$$

$$x = 1.0 \times 10^{-8}$$

62. **(E)**

Zinc oxide's formula weight is 81 (65 + 16). Therefore, 162 grams is twice this weight or two moles. If one mole liberates 84 calories, two liberates twice that amount of energy. The minus sign indicates energy liberation.

63. **(A)**

The alcohol's molecular weight is 46: 24 (C_2) + 6 (6H) + 16 (O). Twenty-three grams is one-half mole. It, therefore, changes boiling and freezing points by one-half the stated increments.

64. **(C)**

The other statements are the opposite of what is correct due to substances' ability to ionize (soluble) or not ionize (insoluble) among the molecules of the solvent water. Silver salts form insoluble precipitates except for the ionizing silver nitrate, $AgNO_3$.

65. **(D)**

HCl is an acid. NaCl is formed from a strong acid and strong base. Na_2CO_3 is a product of a weak acid and strong base. NH_4CN is produced from two weak compounds. A strong acid, HCl, and weak base NH_4OH, react to produce NH_4Cl.

66. **(C)**

This is a law applied every time an equation is balanced.

67. (D)

Hematite is Fe_2O_3. Magnetite or lodestone is Fe_3O_4. Siderite is $FeCO_3$. All choices given are the most common iron ores in the Earth's crust.

68. (D)

The number of energy shells stays constant with the valence electrons tending to increase from left to right. Atomic numbers and mass change for each element.

69. (B)

Hydrogen's most common atomic form has one proton and one electron.

70. (C)

Boyle's law ($P_1V_1 = P_2V_2$) predicts an inverse pressure-volume relationship. A pressure increase means a volume decrease. The multiplied fraction is thus less than one:

$$500 \times \frac{760}{800} = 475$$

71. (D)

Atomic mass is the sum of protons and neutrons. In a neutral atom, the number of positive protons equals the number of electrons. Hence, 11 is added to 12.

72. (E)

The weakest acid, with the lowest K_a, would have the highest pH at any given concentration. HCN is by far the weakest acid on the list with the smallest ionization constant.

73. (B)

Graham's law of effusion can be used to calculate how much faster hydrogen gas moves than oxygen gas.

$$\frac{M_{oxygen}}{M_{hydrogen}} = \frac{r^2_{hydrogen}}{r^2_{oxygen}} = \frac{32}{2} = 16$$

$(16)^{\frac{1}{2}} = 4$; hydrogen is 4 times faster than oxygen.

74. (C)

   22.4 liters of a gas is occupied by one mole. This mole contains 6.02×10^{23} molecules, Avogadro's number. The given volume in this problem is twice that.

75. (E)

   This is a strict statement of the law, predicting that the universe is gradually approaching randomness. Chemical reactions are a part of this.

Detailed Explanations of Answers

Section II

1. (a) $HOCl\ (aq) \leftrightarrow H^+\ (aq) + OCl^-\ (aq)$

   Before equilibrium: 0.030 M   0   0

   After equilibrium: 0.030 − x   x   x

   $$K_a = \frac{(x^2)}{(0.030-x)} = 3.2 \times 10^{-8}$$

   $x^2 = 3.2 \times 10^{-8} \times 0.030$

   $x = [H^+] = 3.1 \times 10^{-5};\ pH = -\log [H^+]$

   $pH = 4.50$

   (b) Percent dissociation = $3.1 \times 10^{-5} / 0.030 \times 100\% = 0.1\%$ dissociated

   (c) $[H^+] = \dfrac{K_a}{[OCl^-]} = \dfrac{(3.2 \times 10^{-8})(.03\ M)}{(.02\ M)} = 4.8 \times 10^{-8}\ M$

   (d) $HOCl\ (aq) + OH- \leftrightarrow H_2O(aq) + OCl^-\ (aq)$

   Before reaction: $.03 \times .05 = .0015$ mol   0   0

   After reaction (mol):   0   0   0.0015 mol

   After equilibrium (M):   x   x   0.0015 mol/.1L − x

   $$K_b = \frac{(x^2)}{(0.015-x)} = 3.1 \times 10^{-7}$$

   $x^2 = 3.1 \times 10^{-7} \times 0.015$

   $x = [OH^-] = 6.8 \times 10^{-5}$

$[H^+] = 1.5 \times 10^{-10}$

$pH = 9.8$

(e) Additional sodium hypochlorite needs to be added so that the concentration of the weak acid equals the concentration of the weak base.

2.   (a) $25.0 \text{ g Fe} \times \dfrac{1 \text{ mol Fe}}{55.85 \text{ g Fe}} \times \dfrac{1 \text{ mol Fe}_2O_3}{2 \text{ mol Fe}} \times$

$\dfrac{159.7 \text{ g Fe}_2O_3}{1 \text{ mol Fe}_2O_3} = 35.74 \text{ g Fe}_2O_3$

$\dfrac{20.0 \, l \times 3.0 \text{ atm K mol oxygen}}{.082 \text{ L atm } 298 \text{ K}} \times \dfrac{1 \text{ mol Fe}_2O_3}{1.5 \text{ mol oxygen}} \times$

$\dfrac{159.7 \text{ g Fe}_2O_3}{1 \text{ mol Fe}_2O_3} = 261 \text{ g Fe}_2O_3$

Therefore, 35.74 g Fe_2O_3 is produced.

(b)   The calculations above demonstrate that iron (Fe) is the limiting reactant.

(c)
$\text{total moles oxygen} = \dfrac{20.0 \text{ L} \times 3.0 \text{ atm K mol O}_2}{.082 \text{ L atm } 298 \text{ K}}$

$= 2.46 \text{ mol oxygen}$

$35.74 \text{ g Fe}_2O_3 \times \dfrac{1 \text{ mol Fe}_2O_3}{159.9 \text{ g Fe}_2O_3} \times \dfrac{1.5 \text{ mol O}_2}{1 \text{ mol Fe}_2O_3}$

$= 0.34 \text{ moles oxygen used}$

moles oxygen to further react = total moles oxygen − moles used = 2.46 − .34 = 2.12 moles

$2.12 \text{ mol oxygen} \times \dfrac{2 \text{ mol Fe}}{1.5 \text{ mol O}_2} \times \dfrac{55.85 \text{ g Fe}}{1 \text{ mol Fe}} =$

158 g Fe needs to be added

(d) $\Delta G° = \Delta H° − T\Delta S°$

$0 = \Delta H° − T\Delta S°$

$\Delta H° = T\Delta S°$

$\Delta S° = \Delta H°/T = −824 \text{ kJ}/ 298 \text{ K} = −2.7 \text{ kJ/K}$

3.   (a) If the reaction is zero order, then the ratio of the change in concentration over time will be the same at any concentration. This can be tested by comparing any two concentration and time data points.

$$\frac{50.8 − 19.7}{900 − 0} = \frac{31.1}{900} = 0.0346$$

$$\frac{19.7 − 7.62}{1800 − 900} = \frac{12.08}{900} = 0.013$$

The two ratios do not match, so it is not a zero order.

If the reaction is first order, then the ratio of the change in the natural log of the concentration over time will be the same at any concentration.

$$\frac{\ln 50.8/19.7}{900} = \ln 2.58/900 = 0.001$$

$$\frac{\ln 19.7/7.62}{900} = \ln 2.58/900 = 0.001$$

The two ratios are identical, so the reaction is first order with respect to A.

(b) The slope of the ratio calculated in the previous problem is the specific rate constant for the reaction.

$k = \ln 2.58/900 = 0.001$

The rate constant would be used in the rate law, where rate $= k$ [A]. The units of rate are M/sec; the units of [A] are M. Therefore, the units of the rate constant are 1/sec.

(c) Half-life for first order reactions $= 0.693/k = 693$ sec

(d)   First find the specific rate constant at 35°C.

$$\frac{\ln 80/26.7}{900} = 0.0012 = k$$

Then use the following equation to find the activation energy.

$$\ln(k_2/k_1) = E_a/R \, (1/T_1 - 1/T_2)$$

$$E_a = 8.31 \text{ J/mol } (0.18)/0.00011 = 13600 \text{ J/mol} = 13.6 \text{ kJ/mol}$$

(e)   The integrated rate law may be used to find the concentration at some time in the future.

$$\ln[A] = -kt + \ln[A_{initial}] = -.001(2400) + \ln(50.8) = 1.53$$

$$[A] = e^{1.53} = 4.62 \text{ M}$$

4.   (a)

  i. $Zn + 2 H^+ \rightarrow Zn^{2+} + H_2$

  ii.   Zinc is oxidized; each atom of zinc increases in oxidation state by two.

(b)

  i. $BF_3 + NH_3 \rightarrow BF_3NH_3$

  ii.   Boron triflouride is the Lewis acid because it acts as an electron pair receptor during the reaction.

(c)

  i. $Mg + O_2 \rightarrow MgO$

  ii.   The magnesium would burn brilliantly and then leave a grey flaky powder once the combustion was complete.

5.   (a)   Magnesium is much softer than the other metals. Also, the magnesium will readily produce hydrogen gas in a 1.0 molar HCl solution. Aluminum will eventually react slowly, but drastically so; and silver will not react at all.

(b)   Silver will react with nitric acid, but aluminum will not because of the protective oxide coating around it.

(c) $Ag + HNO_3 + H^+ \rightarrow Ag^+ + NO_2 + H_2O$

The oxidation state of nitrogen decreases by one, and the oxidation state of silver increases by one.

(d) The hydrochloric acid will react with the soluble lead ions to produce a cloudy precipitate of lead (II) chloride. $Hcl + Pb \rightarrow PbCl_2$

6. (a)

$$
\begin{array}{cc}
CH_3 & CH_3 \\
\backslash & / \\
C = C & \quad \text{cis isomer} \\
/ & \backslash \\
Cl & Cl
\end{array}
$$

$$
\begin{array}{cc}
CH_3 & Cl \\
\backslash & / \\
C = C & \quad \text{trans isomer} \\
/ & \backslash \\
Cl & CH_3
\end{array}
$$

(b) The methyl group carbons are sp^3 hybridized, while the carbons attached to double bonds are sp^2 hybridized.

(c) There is only one pi bond in this molecule; it is between the second and third carbons.

(d) The trans isomer will tend to re-form upon heating, because the larger methyl groups will take up space and hinder the formation of the cis isomer.

(e) In the compound, 2,3-dichloro, 2-butene, we have two isomers, the cis- and trans-isomers. The cis- and trans-isomers are diastereoisomers (i.e., stereoisomers that are not mirror images of each other) or, in this case, more specifically, geometric isomers. This means that they have the same molecular formula, but the substituents (in this case the methyl groups and chlorine) are respectively positioned in the cis- and trans-positions.

Diastereoisomers have different physical properties such as melting point. The cis-isomer will have the lower melting point temperature, and the trans-isomer the higher melting point temperature, and therefore can be separated on the basis of the differences in melting points.

Answer Sheet

Section I

1. Ⓐ Ⓑ Ⓒ Ⓓ Ⓔ
2. Ⓐ Ⓑ Ⓒ Ⓓ Ⓔ
3. Ⓐ Ⓑ Ⓒ Ⓓ Ⓔ
4. Ⓐ Ⓑ Ⓒ Ⓓ Ⓔ
5. Ⓐ Ⓑ Ⓒ Ⓓ Ⓔ
6. Ⓐ Ⓑ Ⓒ Ⓓ Ⓔ
7. Ⓐ Ⓑ Ⓒ Ⓓ Ⓔ
8. Ⓐ Ⓑ Ⓒ Ⓓ Ⓔ
9. Ⓐ Ⓑ Ⓒ Ⓓ Ⓔ
10. Ⓐ Ⓑ Ⓒ Ⓓ Ⓔ
11. Ⓐ Ⓑ Ⓒ Ⓓ Ⓔ
12. Ⓐ Ⓑ Ⓒ Ⓓ Ⓔ
13. Ⓐ Ⓑ Ⓒ Ⓓ Ⓔ
14. Ⓐ Ⓑ Ⓒ Ⓓ Ⓔ
15. Ⓐ Ⓑ Ⓒ Ⓓ Ⓔ
16. Ⓐ Ⓑ Ⓒ Ⓓ Ⓔ
17. Ⓐ Ⓑ Ⓒ Ⓓ Ⓔ
18. Ⓐ Ⓑ Ⓒ Ⓓ Ⓔ
19. Ⓐ Ⓑ Ⓒ Ⓓ Ⓔ
20. Ⓐ Ⓑ Ⓒ Ⓓ Ⓔ
21. Ⓐ Ⓑ Ⓒ Ⓓ Ⓔ
22. Ⓐ Ⓑ Ⓒ Ⓓ Ⓔ
23. Ⓐ Ⓑ Ⓒ Ⓓ Ⓔ
24. Ⓐ Ⓑ Ⓒ Ⓓ Ⓔ
25. Ⓐ Ⓑ Ⓒ Ⓓ Ⓔ

26. Ⓐ Ⓑ Ⓒ Ⓓ Ⓔ
27. Ⓐ Ⓑ Ⓒ Ⓓ Ⓔ
28. Ⓐ Ⓑ Ⓒ Ⓓ Ⓔ
29. Ⓐ Ⓑ Ⓒ Ⓓ Ⓔ
30. Ⓐ Ⓑ Ⓒ Ⓓ Ⓔ
31. Ⓐ Ⓑ Ⓒ Ⓓ Ⓔ
32. Ⓐ Ⓑ Ⓒ Ⓓ Ⓔ
33. Ⓐ Ⓑ Ⓒ Ⓓ Ⓔ
34. Ⓐ Ⓑ Ⓒ Ⓓ Ⓔ
35. Ⓐ Ⓑ Ⓒ Ⓓ Ⓔ
36. Ⓐ Ⓑ Ⓒ Ⓓ Ⓔ
37. Ⓐ Ⓑ Ⓒ Ⓓ Ⓔ
38. Ⓐ Ⓑ Ⓒ Ⓓ Ⓔ
39. Ⓐ Ⓑ Ⓒ Ⓓ Ⓔ
40. Ⓐ Ⓑ Ⓒ Ⓓ Ⓔ
41. Ⓐ Ⓑ Ⓒ Ⓓ Ⓔ
42. Ⓐ Ⓑ Ⓒ Ⓓ Ⓔ
43. Ⓐ Ⓑ Ⓒ Ⓓ Ⓔ
44. Ⓐ Ⓑ Ⓒ Ⓓ Ⓔ
45. Ⓐ Ⓑ Ⓒ Ⓓ Ⓔ
46. Ⓐ Ⓑ Ⓒ Ⓓ Ⓔ
47. Ⓐ Ⓑ Ⓒ Ⓓ Ⓔ
48. Ⓐ Ⓑ Ⓒ Ⓓ Ⓔ
49. Ⓐ Ⓑ Ⓒ Ⓓ Ⓔ
50. Ⓐ Ⓑ Ⓒ Ⓓ Ⓔ

51. Ⓐ Ⓑ Ⓒ Ⓓ Ⓔ
52. Ⓐ Ⓑ Ⓒ Ⓓ Ⓔ
53. Ⓐ Ⓑ Ⓒ Ⓓ Ⓔ
54. Ⓐ Ⓑ Ⓒ Ⓓ Ⓔ
55. Ⓐ Ⓑ Ⓒ Ⓓ Ⓔ
56. Ⓐ Ⓑ Ⓒ Ⓓ Ⓔ
57. Ⓐ Ⓑ Ⓒ Ⓓ Ⓔ
58. Ⓐ Ⓑ Ⓒ Ⓓ Ⓔ
59. Ⓐ Ⓑ Ⓒ Ⓓ Ⓔ
60. Ⓐ Ⓑ Ⓒ Ⓓ Ⓔ
61. Ⓐ Ⓑ Ⓒ Ⓓ Ⓔ
62. Ⓐ Ⓑ Ⓒ Ⓓ Ⓔ
63. Ⓐ Ⓑ Ⓒ Ⓓ Ⓔ
64. Ⓐ Ⓑ Ⓒ Ⓓ Ⓔ
65. Ⓐ Ⓑ Ⓒ Ⓓ Ⓔ
66. Ⓐ Ⓑ Ⓒ Ⓓ Ⓔ
67. Ⓐ Ⓑ Ⓒ Ⓓ Ⓔ
68. Ⓐ Ⓑ Ⓒ Ⓓ Ⓔ
69. Ⓐ Ⓑ Ⓒ Ⓓ Ⓔ
70. Ⓐ Ⓑ Ⓒ Ⓓ Ⓔ
71. Ⓐ Ⓑ Ⓒ Ⓓ Ⓔ
72. Ⓐ Ⓑ Ⓒ Ⓓ Ⓔ
73. Ⓐ Ⓑ Ⓒ Ⓓ Ⓔ
74. Ⓐ Ⓑ Ⓒ Ⓓ Ⓔ
75. Ⓐ Ⓑ Ⓒ Ⓓ Ⓔ

Section II

Use the following pages to prepare your free-response answers.

Section II *(continued)*

Glossary

activated complex A short-lived, high-energy arrangement of atoms that is found in an energy diagram; often referred to as the *transition state* between reactants and products.

activation energy The minimum amount of energy required in order for a reaction to proceed from reactants to products.

alkali metals Elements that are located in Group IA of the periodic table.

alkaline earth metals Elements that are located in Group IIA of the periodic table.

alloy A homogeneous mixture of metals.

anion A negatively charged ion formed by the gain of electrons by an atom.

anode Electrode in an electrochemical cell where oxidation takes place.

atom Smallest building block of matter that still retains its properties; composed of subatomic particles called *protons*, *neutrons*, and *electrons*.

atomic mass The weighted average of the mass numbers of individual isotopes of an atom.

atomic number The number of protons found in an element; distinguishes one element from another.

Aufbau principle Electrons will fill atomic orbitals from lowest energy to highest energy.

boiling point Temperature at which the vapor pressure of a liquid equals the pressure of the atmosphere.

buffer A solution of a weak acid and its conjugate or a weak base and its conjugate whose pH will not change appreciably when additional acid or base is added to the solution.

calorimeter Device used to measure the energy change in a chemical reaction; based on the law of conservation of energy.

catalyst A substance added to a chemical reaction that speeds up the reaction by changing the mechanism and lowering the energy of activation; although it speeds up the reaction, it is never used up and is fully recovered.

cathode Electrode in an electrochemical cell where reduction takes place.

cation A positively charged ion formed by the loss of electrons by an atom.

chromatography Separation technique in which substances are separated based on their polarity.

colligative property Physical property of a solution that depends on the number of solute particles dissolved in solution (boiling point elevation, freezing point depression, osmotic pressure).

compound Chemical combination of two or more atoms.

conjugate acid Species produced after accepting a hydrogen ion from an acid.

conjugate base Species remaining after removing a hydrogen ion from an acid.

covalent bond Chemical bond in which atoms share electrons; caused by the overlap of orbitals.

Dalton's law of partial pressures If a container contains multiple gases, the total pressure inside the container is the sum of the pressures of the individual gases in the mixture.

dipole–dipole forces Intermolecular force between two polar molecules in close contact to one another.

distillation Separation technique for liquids based on boiling points.

electrolyte A solute that produces ions in aqueous solution and will conduct an electric current.

electrolytic cell Electrochemical cell in which energy must be added to the cell for oxidation and reduction to take place.

electron Negatively charged species located outside of the nucleus of an atom; has properties of both a wave and a particle.

electronegativity The ability of an atom to attract electrons in a chemical bond.

element Pure substance that cannot be broken down further by chemical means.

empirical formula Formula that represents the smallest whole number ratio of atoms in a compound; may or may not be the same as the molecular formula.

endothermic A chemical reaction in which the system absorbs energy from the surroundings (reaction feels cold).

enthalpy Heat content of a substance at constant pressure; energy released or absorbed during a chemical reaction.

entropy A measure of the amount of randomness or disorder in a system.

equilibrium Ongoing and dynamic process in which a reaction forms products to a certain point then reforms the reactants.

exothermic A chemical reaction in which the system releases energy to the surroundings (reaction feels hot).

filtration Technique for physical separation of a solid from a liquid by means of a filter.

formula unit Smallest whole-number ratio between cations and anions in an ionic compound.

freezing point Temperature at which a liquid undergoes a phase change to a solid.

Gibbs free energy Measure of the amount of useful work a chemical reaction can do; determines whether a reaction will be spontaneous or nonspontaneous.

Graham's law of effusion Rate of effusion of a gas is inversely proportional to the square root of its molar mass.

group Vertical columns on the periodic table; chemical properties are similar to one another due to similar electron configurations.

half-reaction One of the two parts of an oxidation–reduction reaction representing either the oxidation or reduction of a given element.

halogen Group of reactive nonmetal elements located in Group VIIA on the periodic table.

heat Total kinetic energy of all of the particles in a sample.

Hund's rule Electrons having the same spin will occupy orbitals at the same energy before a pairing with opposite spin electrons occurs.

hydrate An ionic compound that also contains water molecules trapped inside the crystal.

hydrogen bond Intermolecular force that occurs when a hydrogen atom is covalently bonded to either a fluorine, oxygen, or nitrogen (FON) atom and is simultaneously attracted to a neighboring nonmetal atom; strongest of all intermolecular forces.

indicator Compound that changes color based on the pH of the solution; used in acid–base titrations to determine the equivalence point.

insoluble Does not dissolve or dissociate in solution; precipitate.

ion Atom that has an overall charge due to the loss or gain of electrons.

ionic bond Bond that involves the transfer of electrons between atoms to form cations and anions that is held together by electrostatic attractions.

ionization energy Energy required to remove an electron in the ground state from an atom in the gas phase.

isotopes Atoms of the same element that have different numbers of neutrons resulting in different mass numbers.

law of conservation of energy Energy cannot be created or destroyed during chemical reactions, only changed from one form into another; nuclear reactions violate this principle.

law of conservation of mass Matter is not created or destroyed during a chemical reaction—atoms are merely rearranged to form new substances.

Le Chatelier's principle When stress is placed on a system at equilibrium (by changing the temperature, concentration, or pressure), the system will respond by shifting away from the stress.

mass number The sum of the protons and neutrons in an atom giving rise to the overall mass.

metal Element that is typically a solid at room temperature, has luster, conducts electricity and heat, and is malleable and ductile; on the left side of the periodic table; most elements are classified as metals.

miscible Two liquids that can be mixed to form a solution based on similar intermolecular forces between them.

molar mass The number of grams in 1 mole of substance; can be found by using the atomic masses on the periodic table.

mole A unit used to describe the amount of substance present in exactly 12 g of carbon-12; equivalent to 6.022×10^{23} particles.

molecular formula Formula that shows the exact number of atoms of each element present in a molecule or formula unit.

molecule Compound that contains two or more atoms covalently bonded to one another.

net ionic equation Chemical equation that showcases the particles involved in the production of a product such as a precipitate, gas, or liquid.

neutron Subatomic particle located in the nucleus of an atom that has no charge, but a mass that is essentially the same as a proton (but slightly heavier).

noble gas Elements located in Group VIIIA that have filled electron shells and are especially stable, unreactive elements.

nonmetals Elements that are dull, brittle, and typically gases at room temperature that are poor conductors of heat and electricity; generally located on the right side of the periodic table.

nucleus The massive center of an atom that contains protons and neutrons.

octet rule Atoms gain, lose, or share electrons in order to have 8 valence electrons (filled s and p-shells), thus acquiring a noble gas electron configuration.

orbital Three-dimensional region around the nucleus of an atom that describes the probable location of an electron.

oxidation Loss of electrons from a atom, thereby increasing the charge.

oxidation number Positive or negative charge on an atom.

Pauli exclusion principle There is a maximum of 2 electrons in any orbital and they must have opposite spins; no two electrons can have the same set of four quantum numbers.

period Horizontal rows on the periodic table.

pH Scale that describes the acidity of substances, where acidic substances have values between 0 and 7 and bases are between 7 and 14; negative logarithm of the hydrogen ion (hydronium) concentration.

photon Packet of electromagnetic radiation that contains a quantum of energy.

polar covalent Bond in which the electrons are unevenly shared between two atoms, creating separate centers of positive and negative partial charge; gives rise to dipole-dipole and hydrogen bonding intermolecular forces.

precipitate Insoluble solid that is formed during a chemical reaction.

proton Subatomic particle located in the nucleus of an atom that has a positive charge; the number of protons in the nucleus distinguishes atoms one from another.

radioactive decay Unstable nuclei break apart to form separate isotopes, releasing radiation such as alpha and beta particles or gamma rays during the process.

rate law Mathematical relationship that describes the relationship between concentration of reactants and the overall rate.

reduction Gain of electrons by an atom, thereby decreasing the charge.

salt Ionic compound formed as the result of an acid–base reaction containing the cation from the base and the anion from the acid.

saturated solution Solution in which no additional solute can dissolve at a given temperature and pressure; specific for a given solute.

solubility The maximum amount of solute that will dissolve at a given temperature and pressure.

solute The substance being dissolved in a solution; usually present in the smaller amount.

solution Homogeneous mixture of a solute dissolved in a solvent.

solvent The substance doing the dissolving in a solution; usually present in the larger amount.

spectator ion Charged species that does not participate in a chemical reaction but is present to balance the charge of other ions in solution; ions that are not included in the net ionic equation.

standard reduction potential Potential for a reduction half-reaction compared to the standard hydrogen electrode at 1 molar concentration, 298 K, and 1 atm of pressure; measure of the relative oxidizing or reducing ability of a substance.

supersaturated solution Solution that contains more than the maximum amount of solute dissolved at a given temperature and pressure; unstable solution that can be crystallized by adding a single crystal of undissolved solute.

temperature Measure of the average kinetic energy of particles.

titration Lab technique in which substances are added to one another until the endpoint, at which the reactants are in perfect stoichiometry with one another; makes use of an indicator.

transition elements Metallic elements that have varying oxidation states depending on the specific bonding interactions; found on the periodic table in the *d* and *f*-blocks.

unsaturated solution Solution in which more solute can dissolve at a given temperature and pressure.

valence electrons Electrons that are farthest from the nucleus and determine the properties of elements; electrons showcased by the noble gas (shorthand) electron configurations.

van der Waals forces Intermolecular force caused by the formation of an instantaneous dipole and whose strength is proportional to the number of electrons in the molecule; weakest of all intermolecular forces; also called *London dispersion* or simply *dispersion forces*.

vapor pressure Pressure exerted by a substance in the gas phase that is normally in a different state of matter at a given temperature and pressure (vapor).

voltaic cell Electrochemical cell that converts chemical energy into electrical energy via a redox reaction.

AP Chemistry Equations & Constants

ATOMIC STRUCTURE

$$E = h\nu \qquad c = \lambda\nu$$

$$\lambda = \frac{h}{m\upsilon} \qquad p = m\upsilon$$

$$E_n = \frac{-2.178 \times 10^{-18}}{n^2} \text{ joule}$$

EQUILIBRIUM

$$K_a = \frac{[H^+][A^-]}{[HA]}$$

$$K_b = \frac{[OH^-][HB^+]}{[B]}$$

$$K_w = [OH^-][H^+] = 1.0 \times 10^{-14} \text{ @ } 25°C$$
$$= K_a \times K_b$$

$$pH = -\log[H^+], \quad pOH = -\log[OH^-]$$
$$14 = pH + pOH$$

$$pH = pK_a + \log\frac{[A^-]}{[HA]}$$

$$pOH = pK_b + \log\frac{[HB^+]}{[B]}$$

$$pK_a = -\log K_a, \quad pK_b = -\log K_b$$

$$K_p = K_c(RT)^{\Delta n},$$

where Δn = moles product gas − moles reactant gas

THERMOCHEMISTRY/KINETICS

$$\Delta S° = \sum S° \text{ products} - \sum S° \text{ reactants}$$

$$\Delta H° = \sum \Delta H_f° \text{ products} - \sum \Delta H_f° \text{ reactants}$$

$$\Delta G° = \sum \Delta G_f° \text{ products} - \sum \Delta G_f° \text{ reactants}$$

$$\Delta G° = \Delta H° - T\Delta S°$$
$$= -RT \ln K = -2.303 \, RT \log K$$
$$= -n\mathscr{F}E°$$

$$\Delta G = \Delta G° + RT \ln Q = \Delta G° + 2.303 \, RT \log Q$$
$$q = mc\Delta T$$

$$C_p = \frac{\Delta H}{\Delta T}$$

$$\ln[A]_t - \ln[A]_0 = -kt$$

$$\frac{1}{[A]_t} - \frac{1}{[A]_0} = kt$$

$$\ln k = \frac{-E_a}{R}\left(\frac{1}{T}\right) + \ln A$$

E = energy υ = velocity
ν = frequency n = principal quantum number
λ = wavelength m = mass
p = momentum

Speed of light, $c = 3.0 \times 10^8 \text{ m s}^{-1}$

Planck's constant, $h = 6.63 \times 10^{-34} \text{ J s}$

Boltzmann's constant, $k = 1.38 \times 10^{-23} \text{ J K}^{-1}$

Avogadro's number $= 6.022 \times 10^{23} \text{ mol}^{-1}$

Electron charge, $e = -1.602 \times 10^{-19}$ coulomb

1 electron volt per atom $= 96.5 \text{ kJ mol}^{-1}$

Equilibrium Constants

K_a (weak acid)

K_b (weak base)

K_w (water)

K_p (gas pressure)

K_c (molar concentrations)

$S°$ = standard entropy

$H°$ = standard enthalpy

$G°$ = standard free energy

$E°$ = standard reduction potential

T = temperature

n = moles

m = mass

q = heat

c = specific heat capacity

C_p = molar heat capacity at constant pressure

E_a = activation energy

k = rate constant

A = frequency factor

Faraday's constant, $\mathscr{F}$ = 96,500 coulombs per mole of electrons

Gas constant, R = 8.31 J mol^{-1} K^{-1}
$= 0.0821$ L atm mol^{-1} K^{-1}
$= 8.31$ volt coulomb mol^{-1} K^{-1}

AP Chemistry Equations & Constants

GASES, LIQUIDS, AND SOLUTIONS

$$PV = nRT$$

$$\left(P + \frac{n^2 a}{V^2}\right)(V - nb) = nRT$$

$$P_A = P_{total} \times X_A, \text{ where } X_A = \frac{\text{moles A}}{\text{total moles}}$$

$$P_{total} = P_A + P_B + P_C + \dots$$

$$n = \frac{m}{M}$$

$$K = {}^{\circ}C + 273$$

$$\frac{P_1 V_1}{T_1} = \frac{P_2 V_2}{T_2}$$

$$D = \frac{m}{V}$$

$$u_{rms} = \sqrt{\frac{3kT}{m}} = \sqrt{\frac{3RT}{M}}$$

$$KE \text{ per molecule} = \frac{1}{2} m v^2$$

$$KE \text{ per mole} = \frac{3}{2} RT$$

$$\frac{r_1}{r_2} = \sqrt{\frac{M_2}{M_1}}$$

$$\text{molarity, } M = \text{moles solute per liter solution}$$

$$\text{molality} = \text{moles solute per kilogram solvent}$$

$$\Delta T_f = iK_f \times \text{molality}$$

$$\Delta T_b = iK_b \times \text{molality}$$

$$\pi = iMRT$$

$$A = abc$$

P = pressure
V = volume
T = temperature
n = number of moles
D = density
m = mass
v = velocity

u_{rms} = root-mean-square speed
KE = kinetic energy
r = rate of effusion
M = molar mass
π = osmotic pressure
i = van't Hoff factor
K_f = molal freezing-point depression constant
K_b = molal boiling-point elevation constant
A = absorbance
a = molar absorptivity
b = path length
c = concentration
Q = reaction quotient
I = current (amperes)
q = charge (coulombs)
t = time (seconds)
E° = standard reduction potential
K = equilibrium constant

OXIDATION-REDUCTION; ELECTROCHEMISTRY

$$Q = \frac{[C]^c [D]^d}{[A]^a [B]^b}, \text{ where } a\,A + b\,B \rightarrow c\,C + d\,D$$

$$I = \frac{q}{t}$$

$$E_{cell} = E_{cell}^{\circ} - \frac{RT}{n\mathscr{F}} \ln Q = E_{cell}^{\circ} - \frac{0.0592}{n} \log Q \ @ \ 25^{\circ}C$$

$$\log K = \frac{nE^{\circ}}{0.0592}$$

Gas constant, R = 8.31 J mol^{-1} K^{-1}

= 0.0821 L atm mol^{-1} K^{-1}

= 8.31 volt coulomb mol^{-1} K^{-1}

Boltzmann's constant, k = 1.38 × 10^{-23} J K^{-1}

K_f for H_2O = 1.86 K kg mol^{-1}

K_b for H_2O = 0.512 K kg mol^{-1}

1 atm = 760 mm Hg

= 760 torr

STP = 0.000°C and 1.000 atm

Faraday's constant, $\mathscr{F}$ = 96,500 coulombs per mole
of electrons

THE PERIODIC TABLE

KEY

Atomic Number →	22
	IVA / IVB (Group Classification)
Symbol →	Ti
Atomic Weight →	47.88

( ) indicates most stable or best known isotope

METALS — NONMETALS

1 IA IA	2 IIA IIA	3 IIIA IIIB	4 IVA IVB	5 VA VB	6 VIA VIB	7 VIIA VIIB	8 VIIIA VIII	9 VIIIA VIII	10 VIIIA VIII	11 IB IB	12 IIB IIB	13 IIIB IIIA	14 IVB IVA	15 VB VA	16 VIB VIA	17 VIIB VIIA	18 VIII 0
1 H 1.008																	2 He 4.003
3 Li 6.941	4 Be 9.012											5 B 10.811	6 C 12.011	7 N 14.007	8 O 15.999	9 F 18.998	10 Ne 20.180
11 Na 22.990	12 Mg 24.305											13 Al 26.982	14 Si 28.086	15 P 30.974	16 S 32.066	17 Cl 35.453	18 Ar 39.948
19 K 39.098	20 Ca 40.078	21 Sc 44.956	22 Ti 47.88	23 V 50.942	24 Cr 51.996	25 Mn 54.938	26 Fe 55.847	27 Co 58.933	28 Ni 58.693	29 Cu 63.546	30 Zn 65.39	31 Ga 69.723	32 Ge 72.61	33 As 74.922	34 Se 78.96	35 Br 79.904	36 Kr 83.8
37 Rb 85.468	38 Sr 87.62	39 Y 88.906	40 Zr 91.224	41 Nb 92.906	42 Mo 95.94	43 Tc (97.907)	44 Ru 101.07	45 Rh 102.906	46 Pd 106.4	47 Ag 107.868	48 Cd 112.411	49 In 114.818	50 Sn 118.710	51 Sb 121.757	52 Te 127.60	53 I 126.905	54 Xe 131.29
55 Cs 132.905	56 Ba 137.327	57 La 138.906	72 Hf 178.49	73 Ta 180.948	74 W 183.84	75 Re 186.207	76 Os 190.23	77 Ir 192.22	78 Pt 195.08	79 Au 196.967	80 Hg 200.59	81 Tl 204.383	82 Pb 207.2	83 Bi 208.980	84 Po (208.982)	85 At (209.982)	86 Rn (222.018)
87 Fr (223.020)	88 Ra (226.025)	89 Ac (227.028)	104 Unq (261.11)	105 Unp (262.114)	106 Unh (263.118)	107 Uns (262.12)	108 Uno (265)	109 Une (266)	110 Uun (269)	111 Uuu (272.153)	112 Uub (277)						

Group 1: Alkali Metals — Group 2: Alkaline Earth Metals — Groups 3–12: TRANSITIONAL METALS — Group 17: Halogens — Group 18: Noble Gases

LANTHANIDE SERIES

58 Ce 140.115	59 Pr 140.908	60 Nd 144.24	61 Pm (144.913)	62 Sm 150.36	63 Eu 151.965	64 Gd 157.25	65 Tb 158.925	66 Dy 162.50	67 Ho 164.930	68 Er 167.26	69 Tm 168.934	70 Yb 173.04	71 Lu 174.967

ACTINIDE SERIES

90 Th 232.038	91 Pa 231.036	92 U 238.029	93 Np 237.048	94 Pu (244.064)	95 Am (243.061)	96 Cm (247.070)	97 Bk (247.070)	98 Cf (251.080)	99 Es (252.083)	100 Fm (257.095)	101 Md (258.1)	102 No (259.101)	103 Lr (262.11)

Standard Reduction Potentials in Aqueous Solution at 25°C

Half-reaction			$E°(V)$
$F_{2(g)} + 2\,e^-$	$\rightarrow$	$2\,F^-$	2.87
$Co^{3+} + e^-$	$\rightarrow$	Co^{2+}	1.82
$Au^{3+} + 3\,e^-$	$\rightarrow$	$Au_{(s)}$	1.50
$Cl_{2(g)} + 2\,e^-$	$\rightarrow$	$2\,Cl^-$	1.36
$O_{2(g)} + 4\,H^+ + 4\,e^-$	$\rightarrow$	$2\,H_2O_{(l)}$	1.23
$Br_{2(l)} + 2\,e^-$	$\rightarrow$	$2\,Br^-$	1.07
$2\,Hg^{2+} + 2\,e^-$	$\rightarrow$	Hg_2^{2+}	0.92
$Hg^{2+} + 2\,e^-$	$\rightarrow$	$Hg_{(l)}$	0.85
$Ag^+ + e^-$	$\rightarrow$	$Ag_{(s)}$	0.80
$Hg_2^{2+} + 2\,e^-$	$\rightarrow$	$2\,Hg_{(l)}$	0.79
$Fe^{3+} + e^-$	$\rightarrow$	Fe^{2+}	0.77
$I_{2(s)} + 2\,e^-$	$\rightarrow$	$2\,I^-$	0.53
$Cu^+ + e^-$	$\rightarrow$	$Cu_{(s)}$	0.52
$Cu^{2+} + 2\,e^-$	$\rightarrow$	$Cu_{(s)}$	0.34
$Cu^{2+} + e^-$	$\rightarrow$	Cu^+	0.15
$Sn^{4+} + 2\,e^-$	$\rightarrow$	Sn^{2+}	0.15
$S_{(s)} + 2\,H^+ + 2\,e^-$	$\rightarrow$	$H_2S_{(g)}$	0.14
$2\,H^+ + 2\,e^-$	$\rightarrow$	$H_{2(g)}$	0.00
$Pb^{2+} + 2\,e^-$	$\rightarrow$	$Pb_{(s)}$	−0.13
$Sn^{2+} + 2\,e^-$	$\rightarrow$	$Sn_{(s)}$	−0.14
$Ni^{2+} + 2\,e^-$	$\rightarrow$	$Ni_{(s)}$	−0.25
$Co^{2+} + 2\,e^-$	$\rightarrow$	$Co_{(s)}$	−0.28
$Tl^+ + e^-$	$\rightarrow$	$Tl(s)$	−0.34
$Cd^{2+} + 2\,e^-$	$\rightarrow$	$Cd_{(s)}$	−0.40
$Cr^{3+} + e^-$	$\rightarrow$	Cr^{2+}	−0.41
$Fe^{2+} + 2\,e^-$	$\rightarrow$	$Fe_{(s)}$	−0.44
$Cr^{3+} + 3\,e^-$	$\rightarrow$	$Cr_{(s)}$	−0.74
$Zn^{2+} + 2\,e^-$	$\rightarrow$	$Zn_{(s)}$	−0.76
$Mn^{2+} + 2\,e^-$	$\rightarrow$	$Mn_{(s)}$	−1.18
$Al^{3+} + 3\,e^-$	$\rightarrow$	$Al_{(s)}$	−1.66
$Be^{2+} + 2\,e^-$	$\rightarrow$	$Be_{(s)}$	−1.70
$Mg^{2+} + 2\,e^-$	$\rightarrow$	$Mg_{(s)}$	−2.37
$Na^+ + e^-$	$\rightarrow$	$Na_{(s)}$	−2.71
$Ca^{2+} + 2\,e^-$	$\rightarrow$	$Ca_{(s)}$	−2.87
$Sr^{2+} + 2\,e^-$	$\rightarrow$	$Sr_{(s)}$	−2.89
$Ba^{2+} + 2\,e^-$	$\rightarrow$	$Ba_{(s)}$	−2.90
$Rb^+ + e^-$	$\rightarrow$	$Rb_{(s)}$	−2.92
$K^+ + e^-$	$\rightarrow$	$K_{(s)}$	−2.92
$Cs^+ + e^-$	$\rightarrow$	$Cs_{(s)}$	−2.92
$Li^+ + e^-$	$\rightarrow$	$Li_{(s)}$	−3.05

Index

NOTES

NOTES